Especially for

....

From

....

Date

....

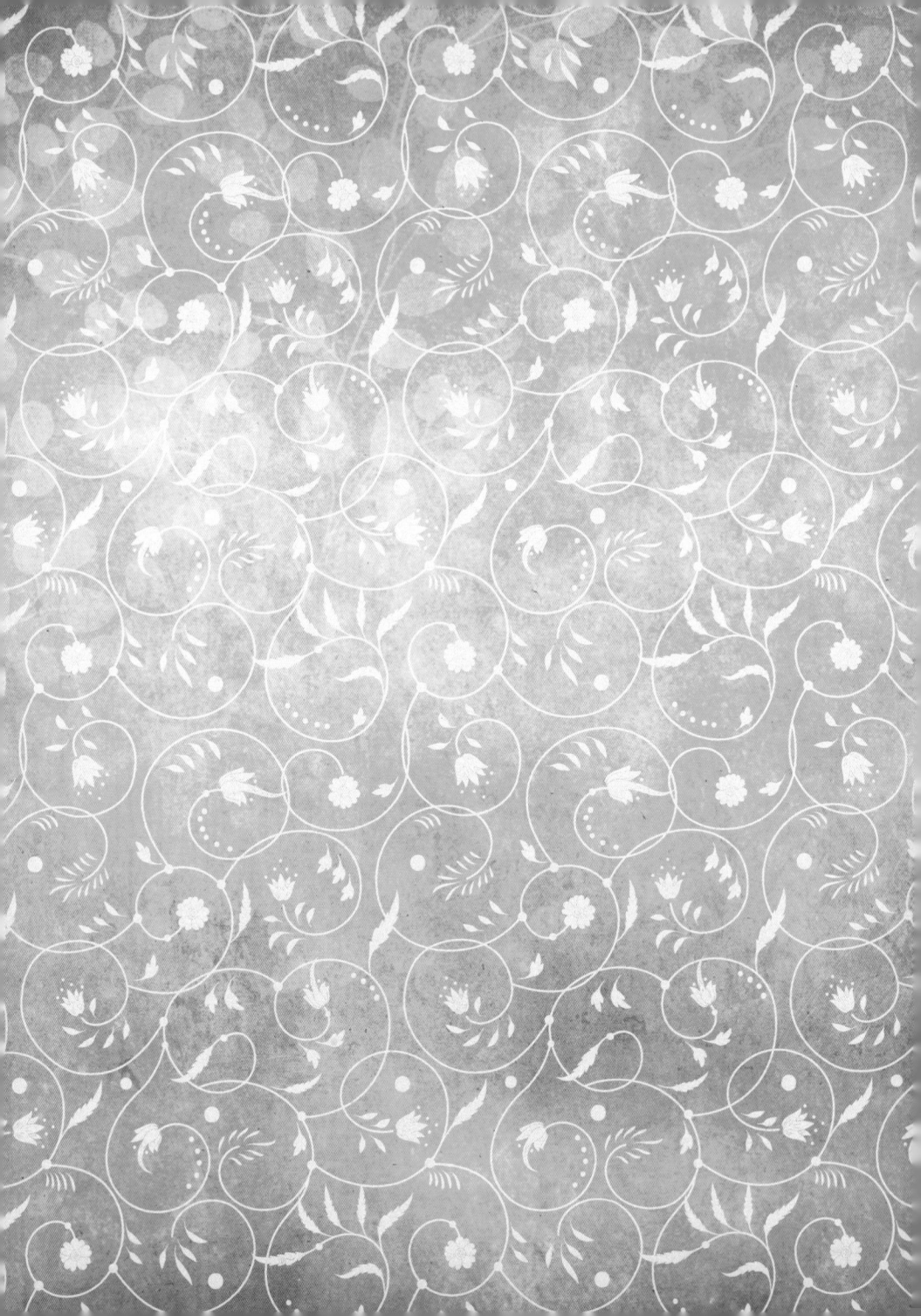

The
Woman's
Secret
of a Happy Life

for Morning & Evening

Donna K.
Maltese

BARBOUR BOOKS
An Imprint of Barbour Publishing, Inc.

The Woman's Secret *of a* Happy Life

And these things write we unto you,
that your joy may be full.
1 JOHN 1:4 KJV

This prayer-full book, *The Woman's Secret of a Happy Life: Morning and Evening*, will help you realize the deep, inner happiness you can have 24-7 as you connect to God with a devotional thought, prayer, and scriptures—two times a day for every day of the year.

As a believer, a deep, inner happiness is available to you. Such happiness is based on a calm assurance that, in spite of what's happening around you, you're trusting in Jesus, certain that the Holy Spirit is with you and that God will work all things out to your good. It's about allowing your *happiness* in the Lord, which is strong and eternal, to overrule the *happenings* in the world.

While you're traveling down this pathway, it's vital to daily remind yourself who you are in Christ. To, each day, put on your new nature as you become more like your Creator (see Colossians 3:10). To help you in this quest, twenty Joy-Filled Woman's Pathmarkers sections are included throughout these readings. Each points out one of God's *promises* to you, *provisions* for you, and *proofs* of His work relating to that particular *portrait* of the "new you."

May you open your heart and mind as you claim and journey to a joyful life in the Lord.

Pathmarker's Index
by Portrait Statement

In Christ. . .

I am able to have joy in any situation (see Days 14–17).

I am being transformed into a new person (see Days 29–32).

I know God will provide me with everything I need (see Days 49–52).

I am standing firm (see Days 69–72).

I am holy, pure in God's sight, and empowered by the Holy Spirit (see Days 85–88).

I live by faith, not sight (see Days 105–108).

I have access to God's will (see Days 129–132).

I have access to God's wisdom and direction (see Days 152–155).

I have inherited God's promises (see Days 167–170).

I am more than a conqueror (see Days 188–191).

I am not only redeemed but forgiven (see Days 204–207).

I am assured of God's presence in any and all situations (see Days 222–225).

I am a free woman, a daughter of God, and an heir of His promises (see Days 240–243).

I am growing in the grace and knowledge of the Lord (see Days 263–266).

I am strong enough to do whatever God calls me to do (see Days 279–282).

I am spiritually transformed with energy, strength, and purpose every day (see Days 299–302).

I am loved by God and delight to do His will (see Days 316–319).

I am spiritually blessed because He lives in me (see Days 332–335).

I am raised to new life, setting my eyes on the realities of heaven (see Days 347–350).

I am raised up and sitting in heaven (see Days 362–365).

DAY 1

MORNING - *A Woman of the Way*

You did it: you changed wild lament into whirling dance;
You ripped off my black mourning band and decked me with
wildflowers. I'm about to burst with song; I can't keep quiet
about you. GOD, my God, I can't thank you enough.

PSALM 30:11 MSG

Let's settle down to the fact that you are a woman of the Way. As such, you are weary of being ruled by the world and are ready to embark upon a joyful journey. This does not mean you will ignore the world's myriad of woes, but you will no longer allow them to rule your state of mind or influence your sense of peace. You will expectantly seek and find joy.

EVENING - *Finding Joy*

We wait for the LORD. He is our help and our shield.
In him our hearts find joy. In his holy name we trust.

PSALM 33:20–21 GW

Lord, I am a woman of the Way and know that I am not to be caught up in the cares of this world but instead be filled with Your joy. Open my eyes and heart to Your Word. Help me to discover Your beauty in the people and things surrounding me. Enlighten my mind and allow the joy I find to feed my spirit. Amen.

DAY 2

MORNING - *A Daring Woman*

*In Christ Jesus our Lord. . .we dare to have the boldness
(courage and confidence) of free access (an unreserved
approach to God with freedom and without fear).*
EPHESIANS 3:11–12 AMPC

When you are filled with shame and discouragement, you may distance yourself from the very source of light, love, peace, power, and joy that has rescued you. Like Eve in the garden, you may find yourself hiding from the very One who could—and already did—save you.

But although weary, sorrow laden, and worn, you know that hiding from God is not the answer. You must and *can* meet God face-to-face. And because you have faith, you dare to do so!

EVENING - *Tapping In*

*On the day I called, You answered me;
You made me bold with strength in my soul.*
PSALM 138:3 NASB

Lord, I know You will answer when I call. So I refuse to hide anymore. No longer will I allow the burdens of my life to bury me. With boldness I come to You, tapping into Christ's power. Because of my faith in You, I can uproot trees and plant them in the sea. You give me strength in my soul. You transform me from a weak woman into a fearless female. You are the source of staying power.

DAY 3

MORNING - *A Free Woman*

The Lord came to help Sarah and did for her what he had promised.
So she became pregnant, and at the exact time God had promised, she gave
birth to a son for Abraham in his old age. . . . Sarah said, "God has brought
me laughter, and everyone who hears about this will laugh with me."
GENESIS 21:1–2, 6 GW

Your life in Christ is to be lived to the fullest, not in partial victories and agonizing defeats. You are not to live as a Hagar, a slave to sin, but as a free woman like Sarah. For once she trusted God to deliver as promised, He brought her laughter.

EVENING - *Filled with Laughter*

Let go of your concerns! Then you will know that I am God.
I rule the nations. I rule the earth. The Lord of Armies is
with us. The God of Jacob is our stronghold. Selah.
PSALM 46:10–11 GW

Right here, right now, God, I banish all my fear and doubt. I give up trying to fix things myself. I am going to let go of my concerns, leave them at Your feet, and let You take control—because You are God—not me! In this place, Your promises become my reality. I am overjoyed. I am filled with laughter! What freedom I have in You!

DAY 4

MORNING - *A Saved Woman*

*"After her baby is born, name him Jesus, because
he will save his people from their sins."*
MATTHEW 1:21 CEV

❧

So, you are to "let go and let God." But how do you know He will deliver you? Where's the proof that Jesus came to save you? That He is all-powerful? That you are more than a conqueror through Him? That because of all He has done for you, you are to be filled with joy? To find the answers, bring your thirsty heart, mind, and soul to the source, the well of God's Word. Here you will find proof that Jesus did come to save you.

EVENING - *Watered with the Word*

*"I am bringing you good news that will be a great joy
to all the people. Today your Savior was born in the
town of David. He is Christ, the Lord."*
LUKE 2:10–11 NCV

❧

Lord, I love Your Word. For in it I find the strength and joy that I thirst for. Thank You for saving me—even before I knew You! Thank You for giving me the power to live in victory. Continue to water me with Your Word. And for the peace that it brings me—heart, mind, and soul.

DAY 5

MORNING · *A Debt-Free Woman*

You were dead because of your sins and because your sinful nature was not yet cut away. Then God made you alive with Christ, for he forgave all our sins. He canceled the record of the charges against us and took it away by nailing it to the cross.

COLOSSIANS 2:13–14 NLT

As a believer in Christ, you can be joyful because you are *saved*—not because you don't *sin*. You still miss the mark. But you can find your joy in believing that your debt for sin has been paid in full—through the death of Jesus on the cross.

EVENING · *Showing Gratitude*

God showed his great love for us by sending Christ to die for us while we were still sinners. . . . So now we can rejoice in our wonderful new relationship with God because our Lord Jesus Christ has made us friends of God.

ROMANS 5:8, 11 NLT

Dear Jesus, sometimes I find it hard to fathom that even though I was missing the mark, You gave Your life for me. And because of Your sacrifice, that sin, that huge obstacle standing between me and God, has been expunged from my record. That is a debt that I can in no way repay. But to show my gratitude, I aim to live my life rejoicing in You.

DAY 6

MORNING - *The Empowered Woman*

I want you to know about the great and mighty power that God has for us followers. It is the same wonderful power he used when he raised Christ from death and let him sit at his right side in heaven.
EPHESIANS 1:19–20 CEV

Are you living as if you are saved and guilt-free? Or are you exhausted from trying to live the holy life in your own power? Are you hiding, hoping that no one picks up on the fact that your Christian life isn't "working"? Here is where you need to *believe you have the power* of the One who calmed the sea and stopped the wind. All you need to do to access that mighty power is to let Christ live through you, to trust Him with your life, to honor Him with your mouth.

EVENING - *Forever Saved*

He is forever able to save the people he leads to God, because he always lives to speak to God for them.
HEBREWS 7:25 CEV

Dear Christ, I want to stop cowering and understand that in every way, shape, and form, I have won more than a victory because of You who loves me. I know through thick and thin, because of You, God is on my side, not just once in a while but over and over again. So I needn't have any fear at any time! That alone brings joy and peace into my heart!

DAY 7

MORNING · *A Kingdom Woman*

*God's kingdom . . . . It's what God does with your life as he sets it right,
puts it together, and completes it with joy. Your task is to single-mindedly
serve Christ. Do that and you'll kill two birds with one stone: pleasing the
God above you and proving your worth to the people around you.*
ROMANS 14:17–18 MSG

You know that in Jesus you're saved (see Hebrews 7:25), you've access to
power (see Romans 8:31), and you're more than a conqueror (see Romans
8:37). Where then does an expectation or promise of joy come in? It comes
in Christ! It comes in trusting Him, applying His Word to your life, living
out your faith. Being right with God, inner peace, and joy in the Spirit are
the prerequisites if you deem to live in a God's-kingdom palace instead of a
spiritual pauper's house.

EVENING · *Rejoicing*

*"If you keep my commands, you will remain in my love, just as I have
kept my Father's commands and remain in his love. I have told you
this so that my joy may be in you and that your joy may be complete."*
JOHN 15:10–11 NIV

Lord, as Your good, trusting, and faithful servant, I know You want me to have
the same joy Jesus does so that my joy will be as full as it can be. All I need to
do is ask for it and I will receive it! I rejoice in that promise!

DAY 8

MORNING · *A Daughter of God*

We have been set free to experience our rightful heritage. You can tell for sure that you are now fully adopted as his own children because God sent the Spirit of his Son into our lives crying out, "Papa! Father!"
GALATIANS 4:5–6 MSG

Living in Christ does not promise a trial-free life. You may suffer a loss, have sickness, dashed hopes, and unmet expectations. Jesus Himself was disappointed and angry with people, including His own disciples at times. He, too, suffered His share of loss. But He also had the joy of a deep relationship with His Father God. Because You, too, are a child of God, you have the same freedom and privilege to cry out to Him. And by following in Jesus' steps, walking as He walked, you can have the same joyous relationship with Papa God.

EVENING · *Abounding in Hope*

Now may the God of hope fill you with all joy and peace in believing, so that you will abound in hope by the power of the Holy Spirit.
ROMANS 15:13 NASB

You alone are my hope in this world, Lord. When I rely on things, myself, or others, I am often disappointed. So I'm fixing my focus on You and You alone. As I form a smile, I feel Your joy springing up from deep within. I experience an overwhelming peace in my heart. The power of Your Holy Spirit fills me with hope. Because of You, I can do anything You've called me to do!

DAY 9

MORNING - *A New Woman*

*Just as Christ was raised from the dead by the
glorious power of the Father, now we also may live new lives.*
ROMANS 6:4 NLT

You can have joy even when you suffer, because you know "these troubles produce patience" (Romans 5:3 NCV). So you *can* and *should expect* joy in this life. If you don't have joy, you're not maturing in your faith. Paul wrote to the Philippians, "I am convinced that I will remain alive so I can continue to help all of you grow and experience the joy of your faith" (Philippians 1:25 NLT). He exhorted his readers to "always be full of joy in the Lord" (Philippians 4:4 NLT). You can trust God to deliver you no matter what your circumstances because you are a new woman in Christ whether or not you feel like it.

EVENING - *Transformed*

Now we look inside, and what we see is that anyone united with the Messiah gets a fresh start, is created new. The old life is gone; a new life burgeons!
2 CORINTHIANS 5:17 MSG

Jesus, I need a fresh start every day, every moment! I long to be transformed but know I can only change with You working through me. If I try this in my own power, I will remain the same. So I continue to be encouraged, Lord, knowing that You understand my difficulties and are walking with me, hand in hand, from this day, this moment, forward! Thank You for being so patient!

DAY 10

MORNING · *A Returned Woman*

Return to the LORD your God, for he is gracious and compassionate, slow to anger and abounding in love.
JOEL 2:13 NIV

So, you are a new woman in Christ, whether you feel like one or not. And as such, available to you are love, forgiveness, peace, and joy in Christ—*if* you stop sweeping your sins under the rug and, mired by guilt, shrinking from His presence. For there's no need to be afraid of Father God. Because of Jesus' sacrifice for you, you can call on *Abba*! And be assured of the Holy Spirit's comfort and guidance into all truth—about you, how much you may be falling short, the saving grace of Jesus, and the fruit that is found by abiding in and focusing on Him.

EVENING · *Walking in the Spirit*

The fruit of the Spirit is love, joy, peace, longsuffering, gentleness, goodness, faith, meekness, temperance.
GALATIANS 5:22–23 KJV

I want to walk in the Spirit, Jesus. I want to bear good fruit in this world. Help me to look at others with love; to feel Your deep, abundant joy; to radiate peace to all; to suffer patiently, knowing You'll work everything out in my life; to be gentle with others; to focus on Your goodness; to keep my eyes on You; to be humble in spirit; and to gain self-control.

DAY 11

MORNING - *A Sister in Christ*

There is a friend who sticks closer than a brother.
PROVERBS 18:24 NKJV

You have a "Big Brother" who can and will defend you against all enemies, look out for you, size up your situations, and advise you. He loves you like no other, shielding you from evil, taking on all challengers, gladly bearing your burdens. When others disappoint, discourage, depress, or desert you, He stands by your side. He watches over you as you sleep, guarding the gates. What joy His constant presence gives! But you must be *aware* of His presence—within and without, above and below, to the right and the left.

EVENING - *Dancing in Celebration*

Weeping may last for the night, but there is a song of joy in the morning. . . . You have changed my sobbing into dancing. You have removed my sackcloth and clothed me with joy so that my soul may praise you with music and not be silent.
PSALM 30:5, 11–12 GW

Brother Jesus, I have come to tell You all of my troubles, including my sins. I want to do better. I call on Your death-defying power. I am counting on our Father's protection. I will follow the Holy Spirit's guidance. Wholly aware of Your presence, I sing a new song of joy unto the Lord who sees me as His dear daughter. I dance in celebration of Your saving grace and power.

DAY 12

MORNING · *An Open-Eyed Woman*

I will see you again, and [then] your hearts will rejoice,
and no one can take away from you your joy.
JOHN 16:22 AMPC

❧

Remember that no one can take your joy away from you. Refuse to be like Hagar, sitting down in the midst of your troubles, sobbing, allowing the weight of the world's woes to oppress you. Just like He called Hagar, God is calling you: " 'Don't be afraid!' . . . God opened her eyes. Then she saw a well. She filled the container with water" (Genesis 21:17, 19 GW). God is and always will be with you. Don't let your faith dry up. Run to His well and tap into His life-giving water.

EVENING · *Energized by God's Goodness*

I would have lost heart, unless I had believed that I
would see the goodness of the LORD in the land of the living.
PSALM 27:13 NKJV

❧

Discouragement is keeping me from looking on the bright side of life. Give me courage, Lord; give me hope. Help me to realize that this temporal world is not all there is, that there is a silver lining—and it is You. Energize me for the work I have before me today. Help me not to lose heart but to know, to believe, to have a vision for Your goodness in this land of the living.

DAY 13

MORNING - *An Enlightened Woman*

I pray that your hearts will be flooded with light so that you can understand the confident hope he has given to those he called—his holy people who are his rich and glorious inheritance. I also pray that you will understand the incredible greatness of God's power for us who believe him. This is the same mighty power that raised Christ from the dead and seated him in the place of honor at God's right hand in the heavenly realms.

EPHESIANS 1:18–20 NLT

Hannah Whitall Smith wrote, "When you have begun to have some faint glimpses of this power, learn to look away utterly from your own weakness, and, putting your case into His hands, trust Him to deliver you."

EVENING - *Becoming His Vision*

I urge you. . .by the mercies of God, to present your bodies a living and holy sacrifice, acceptable to God, which is your spiritual service of worship.

ROMANS 12:1 NASB

My Lord Jesus, I bring myself to You today, straining to hear a whisper from Your mouth, to feel the touch of Your hand, to taste the goodness of Your Word, to see the light of Your presence in my life. I am Yours to mold and shape. Help me to become what You've called me to be, to become the vision You have had of me since the beginning.

DAY 14

MORNING - *The Joy-Filled Woman's Path Marker: Promise No. 1*

Up to this time you have not asked a [single] thing in My Name [as presenting all that I AM]; but now ask and keep on asking and you will receive, so that your joy (gladness, delight) may be full and complete.
JOHN 16:24 AMPC

Jesus has promised you a life of joy. He wants you to ask for anything and everything—in His name! He wants you to ask and *keep on asking*. Don't give up. Believe in this promise. When you do, you will receive whatever you need. And your joy will be not only full, but complete.

EVENING - *Blessed in Believing*

The Lord has blessed you because you believed that he will keep his promise.
LUKE 1:45 CEV

Lord, I'm amazed at the way You keep blessing me. Your promises are solid. What a comfort, what a burst of confidence I gain when I believe in You. I bow to You today, knowing that all good things come from You—and they are many! And I vow that I will keep on asking and believing. I won't give up!

DAY 15

MORNING - *The Joy-Filled Woman's Path Marker: Proof No. 1*

While Peter was in prison, the church prayed very earnestly for him. . . . Suddenly. . .an angel of the Lord stood before Peter. . . . So Peter left the cell, following the angel. . . . He went to the home of Mary, the mother of John Mark, where many were gathered for prayer. He knocked at the door in the gate, and a servant girl named Rhoda came to open it. When she recognized Peter's voice, she was so overjoyed that, instead of opening the door, she ran back inside and told everyone, "Peter is standing at the door!"

ACTS 12:5, 7, 9, 12–14 NLT

The Word gives you proof that God does indeed reward you when you continue to come to Him in prayer and faith. Claim that proof and, like the servant girl Rhoda, you will be overjoyed at the results!

EVENING - *The Reward of Persevering*

"As for you, be strong and do not give up, for your work will be rewarded."

2 CHRONICLES 15:7 NIV

Lord, sometimes I feel as if I'm ready to give up. But You are the light of this world. You lighten my burdens. You give me the power to keep on keeping on. So help me to be strong, to preserve, to keep on asking You. For one day, I know all my work will be rewarded with the joy You offer. In this I hope and pray.

DAY 16

MORNING · *The Joy-Filled Woman's Path Marker: Provision No. 1*

I have told you these things, that My joy and delight may be in you, and that your joy and gladness may be of full measure and complete and overflowing.
JOHN 15:11 AMPC

Jesus has provided all you need to have a joy-filled life by telling you "these things," that is how to abide in Him and His love, just like a branch (that's you) that is empowered, nurtured, fed by the vine (Jesus). When you continually live in Him, you will not only have complete joy—it will be overflowing, spilling over onto everything and everyone around you! So claim this provision and watch your joy become unmeasurable!

EVENING · *Overflowing*

You revive my drooping head; my cup brims with blessing.
PSALM 23:5 MSG

I am awed, Jesus, by the joy and delight that You make available to me—if I would only claim it! So I stake my claim for it here and now, Lord! And in so doing, You not only lift my head but fill my cup to overflowing with blessings. I praise and thank You, Lord, for all You offer and provide.

DAY 17

MORNING - *The Joy-Filled Woman's Path Marker: Portrait No. 1*

Celebrate God all day, every day. I mean, revel in him! . . . I've found the recipe for being happy whether full or hungry, hands full or hands empty.
PHILIPPIANS 4:4, 12 MSG

Jesus has not only *promised* you joy by saying, "Ask, using my name, and you will receive, and you will have abundant joy" (John 16:24 NLT) and presented living *proof* in His Word that it has been, is, and will be possible (see Acts 2:5, 7–9, 11–14), He has also made *provision* for it (see John 15:11). In the days ahead, impress these things in your mind. And claim this first *portrait* statement (based on Philippians 4:4, 12) as your very own!

In Christ, I am able to have joy in any situation.

EVENING - *Joyful in Any Situation*

I've learned by now to be quite content whatever my circumstances. I'm just as happy with little as with much, with much as with little. I've found the recipe for being happy whether full or hungry, hands full or hands empty. Whatever I have, wherever I am, I can make it through anything in the One who makes me who I am.
PHILIPPIANS 4:12–13 MSG

With You, Jesus, I can have joy in any situation, no matter what my circumstances. That's because I can do all things through You, the one who gives me strength—and the ultimate joy!

DAY 18

MORNING · *A Trusting Woman*

O Lord, You are our Father; we are the clay, and
You our potter; and all we are the work of Your hand.
ISAIAH 64:8 NKJV

In regard to the subject of God transforming you into the image of His Son, Jesus Christ, there are two sides—God's side and your side. Simply put, God's role is to work and yours is to trust that He's doing it. You have already been delivered from the danger of sin. Now God works to transform you into a vessel He can use.

EVENING · *Refocusing*

And do not be conformed to this world, but be transformed by the
renewing of your mind, so that you may prove what the will
of God is, that which is good and acceptable and perfect.
ROMANS 12:2 NASB

There are so many worldly woes tumbling around in my mind, steering my behavior, driving me out of Your path for me, God. Fill my mind with Your light. Help me to focus on the good things of this world—on the rose, not its thorns. For I want to know and to do Your will. I want to see Your beauty working its way out through me. I want to be a vessel You can use!

DAY 19

MORNING - *A Shapened Woman*

*If you keep yourself pure, you will be a special utensil
for honorable use. Your life will be clean, and you will
be ready for the Master to use you for every good work.*
2 TIMOTHY 2:21 NLT

God has given you the Word to live by, the power of prayer, and love. Now you're to be further shaped—by His transforming power—from a lump of clay into a vessel of honor. He begins to shift your shape, knead you, and mold you. Your role is to remain still, patient, and pliable. Then like all potters, He puts His clay upon the wheel, continually turning you until, satisfied with your new shape, He smoothes you down. You're put into the furnace and baked until you're exactly what He envisioned you to be. As clay, you're not expected to do the Potter's work but simply to yield yourself up to His working. But in order to trust the Potter to do with you what He will, you must firmly believe in Him and the process.

EVENING - *In Progress*

Create in me a clean heart, O God, and renew a steadfast spirit within me.
PSALM 51:10 NKJV

Sometimes my ego wants to take over, Lord. I want to take myself out of Your hands and attempt my transformation in my own power. But it's exhausting! I feel weak and spent. Renew my patience, Lord. Help me to persevere. Lead me to see myself through Your eyes—a work in progress—with the end goal of glorifying You.

DAY 20

MORNING - *A Woman Water-Walker*

Peter left the boat and walked on the water to Jesus. But when Peter saw the wind and the waves, he became afraid and began to sink. He shouted, "Lord, save me!" Immediately Jesus reached out his hand and caught Peter. Jesus said, "Your faith is small. Why did you doubt?"
MATTHEW 14:29–31 NCV

When you step out of the boat and head to Jesus' side, you're putting yourself in His hands. But when you look away from Him and stare at the wind and waves, you're no longer trusting in or focusing on Jesus. Then, like Peter, you begin to sink. It's as if you've taken yourself out of the Potter's hands and retreated into your clay pit. No longer surrendering yourself to the Potter's skill, you obstruct the Master Creator's work and so remain a lump of clay instead of transforming into a beautiful vessel. So yield today!

EVENING - *Buoyed by Faith*

He did not many mighty works there because of their unbelief.
MATTHEW 13:58 KJV

Jesus, I know that where there's no faith, there's no trust and no transforming work can be done—just like what happened in Your own hometown! God forbid that I should be found wanting and remain a lump of clay. Or that I miss out on the grand plans You have in store for me! Keep me from sinking down into the dark and deep blue sea! Lift me and my faith up into Your presence and transforming power.

DAY 21

MORNING - *A Listening Woman*

"To those who listen to my teaching, more understanding will be given, and they will have an abundance of knowledge. But for those who are not listening, even what little understanding they have will be taken away from them."
MATTHEW 13:12 NLT

Elisabeth Elliot wrote, "God is God. Because He is God, He is worthy of my trust and obedience. I will find rest nowhere but in His holy will, a will that is unspeakably beyond my largest notions of what He is up to." Can you say the same thing? Are you resting in His will—even though it may make no sense? Or are you allowing your limited knowledge and experience to override His unfathomable wisdom and eternal dealings with His creatures? Are you listening? Today, lean on His understanding—not yours.

EVENING - *Ready to Receive*

"If you believe, you will receive whatever you ask for in prayer."
MATTHEW 21:22 NIV

Matthew Henry's commentary says that a lack of belief does, "in effect, tie [Jesus'] hands. . . . Unbelief is the great obstruction to Christ's favours. So that if mighty works be not wrought in us, it is not for want of power or grace in Christ, but for want of faith in us." May this prompt you to pray, *Lord, I believe. Do a mighty work in me! In Jesus' name. Amen.*

DAY 22

MORNING - *A Believing Woman*

One of the rulers of the synagogue came, Jairus by name. And when he saw Him, he fell at His feet and begged Him earnestly, saying, "My little daughter lies at the point of death. Come and lay Your hands on her, that she may be healed, and she will live."

MARK 5:22–23 NKJV

As Jesus walked with Jairus toward his home, some people came from the house, saying, "Your daughter is dead. Why trouble the Teacher any further?" (Mark 5:35 NKJV). But Jesus reassured Jairus, telling him not to be afraid but just believe. When Jesus got to Jairus's house, He had the mourners, the mockers, the faithless driven out of the house. He went to the little girl's bedside and ordered her to rise. That instant, she got up and began walking around.

Be a believer—and you will witness miracles in your house.

EVENING - *Willing in Jesus' Hands*

"Do not be afraid; only believe."
MARK 5:36 NKJV

Jesus, it's so awesome how You work when I believe! I don't want to miss the miracles You can perform, the amazing way You can transform me—and can then, in turn, transform the world around me! I dare not but trust and surrender my life to Your power. Today, in this moment, I willingly put myself into Your capable hands, expecting to become a beautiful vessel, inside and out. I will not be afraid. I will only believe!

DAY 23

MORNING - *A Stayed Woman*

As the clay is in the potter's hand, so are ye in mine hand.
JEREMIAH 18:6 KJV

Hannah Whitall Smith wrote:

> *All that we claim, then, in this life of sanctification is that by an act of faith we put ourselves into the hands of the Lord, for Him to work in us all the good pleasure of His will, and then, by a continuous exercise of faith, keep ourselves there. . . . Although it may require years of training and discipline to mature us into a vessel that shall be in all respects to His honor and fitted to every good work.*
>
> *A lump of clay won't be transformed into a vessel overnight. It'll take many spins of the Potter's wheel. But you can rest assured you're safer in His hands than in a deep, dark pit. That although you may experience growing pains, you'll someday be a mature Christian, energized and transformed by the Holy Spirit.*

EVENING - *Confident in the Master Designer*

Jesus answered and said to him, "Truly, truly, I say to you,
unless one is born again he cannot see the kingdom of God."
JOHN 3:3 NASB

Lord, I seek Your kingdom, Your face, Your presence, Your Word. Each day I rise to new challenges, knowing You're walking with me every step of the way. I have confidence that You're designing me for something special. May who I am glorify You!

MORNING · *A Patient Woman*

Sarah laughed within herself, saying, after I am waxed old shall I have pleasure, my lord being old also? And the LORD said unto Abraham, Wherefore did Sarah laugh?

GENESIS 18:12–13 KJV

Sarah laughed—then denied doing so—when God said she'd be a mother in her old age. Wracked with doubt, she became impatient while waiting to see His promise come to pass. She believed God needed her to provide the solution. Edith Deen wrote in *All the Women of the Bible* that "not understanding the divine delay" of Abraham's promised son, an impatient Sarah "concluded she was the obstacle." Sarah ended up giving her servant Hagar to Abraham. In doing so, she created a volatile situation between Hagar's son, Ishmael, and Sarah's son, Isaac, a decision that to this day has repercussions in the Middle East. Are you patient enough to wait for God?

EVENING · *Joyfully Confident in God*

Is any thing too hard for the LORD?

GENESIS 18:14 KJV

Lord, I don't want to be bold and impatient like Sarah but humble myself and allow You time to work me into a shapely vessel for You. While You do the work of transformation as I yield myself to You, I'll have the faith and belief that You are indeed doing so, knowing that nothing is too hard for You. I turn to Your Word and embed it in my heart, remaining steady in prayer and Your presence.

MORNING - *A Trusting Woman*

People won't receive God's approval because of their own efforts. . . .
Christ came so that we could receive God's approval by faith.
GALATIANS 2:16; 3:24 GW

You need not stress yourself out with trying to help God transform you. That's like the batter attempting to help the baker make it into a cake. It just doesn't happen. All the batter can do is keep on trusting and surrendering to the baker. You also need not try to tell your Creator what you think you should be and do. In effect, it's out of your hands and in God's. And thank God for that! It takes all the pressure off because the stress to perform is removed.

EVENING - *Re-surrendering*

Whenever the pot the potter was working on turned out badly,
as sometimes happens when you are working with clay, the potter
would simply start over and use the same clay to make another pot.
JEREMIAH 18:4 MSG

I feel like I fell out of Your hands, Lord. And it's not that You let me fall but that my ego has taken over. I'm trying to reshape myself, and of course it's not working out at all! Forgive me if I have fallen short. Help me not to give in to feelings, the opinions of others, or my own skewed reasoning. I once again surrender myself to You and Your work. And it's a relief to do so!

DAY 26

MORNING - *A Mary-Like Woman*

"There is only one thing worth being concerned about.
Mary has discovered it, and it will not be taken away from her."
LUKE 10:42 NLT

⁓

Madame Jeanne Guyon wrote, "It is a great truth, wonderful as it is undeniable, that all our happiness—temporal, spiritual, and eternal—consists in one thing; namely, in resigning ourselves to God, and in leaving ourselves with Him, to do with us and in us just as He pleases." Thus, instead of being like Martha, who was worried, troubled, and distracted, be like Mary. Set yourself down at Jesus' feet, leave yourself with Him, listening to His every word—"the one thing" needed (Luke 10:42 NKJV). When you do, Jesus will commend you because you have "chosen that good part, which will not be taken away" (Luke 10:42 NKJV).

EVENING - *Choosing One Thing*

"Grow up. You're kingdom subjects. Now live like it.
Live out your God-created identity. Live generously and
graciously toward others, the way God lives toward you."
MATTHEW 5:48 MSG

⁓

Lord, only by Your working in and through me can I handle the challenges and distractions of this world. Only because of the unconditional love You give me can I love others—even those who are hard to like. Each day, as I sit at Your feet, I feel Your presence, love, and guiding hand. Thank You for helping me become the woman You want me to be, choosing that one thing.

DAY 27

MORNING - *A Reflecting Woman*

*We all, with unveiled face, beholding as in a mirror the glory of
the Lord, are being transformed into the same image from
glory to glory, just as by the Spirit of the Lord.*
2 CORINTHIANS 3:18 NKJV

Your transformation is all part of God's process. But can you be patient in
this I-want-it-now society? John Ortberg wrote that "biblically, waiting is not
just something we have to do until we get what we want. Waiting is part of
the process of becoming what God wants us to be." Have you drifted out of
the Potter's hands? Has impatience driven you to work in your own power?
If so, surrender yourself on the altar. Put yourself back into God's hands
and await His working in your life. He will transform you into the image of
Christ "from glory to glory."

EVENING - *Becoming More Like Christ*

*Each of you is now a new person. You are becoming more
and more like your Creator, and you will understand him better.*
COLOSSIANS 3:10 CEV

God, although I don't understand everything now, I will—as days pass—know
more and more about You. For now, I praise You for being so patient with
me when I try to work in my own power. I thank You for the kindnesses You
have shown. I am grateful that You stick with me in my best and worst of
times. Thank You for growing me up to be more like You.

DAY 28

MORNING - *A Truly Believing Woman*

With God's help we will do mighty things.
PSALM 60:12 NLT

With the Lord as your eternal master designer, with your ongoing surrender, with your power of belief, with your patient awaiting of His working, you can be assured that God is shaping you into an amazing, confident, expectant, joy-filled woman. There's no telling what feats He is designing you to perform! And your part is merely to trust, to surrender, and to follow Christ's injunction: "Do not be seized with alarm and struck with fear; only keep on believing" (Mark 5:36 AMPC). For when you truly believe, you can accomplish the seemingly impossible!

EVENING - *Re-created by the Master*

*For I am not ashamed of the Gospel (good news) of Christ,
for it is God's power working unto salvation [for deliverance
from eternal death] to everyone who believes with a personal
trust and a confident surrender and firm reliance.*
ROMANS 1:16 AMPC

Lord, I surrender myself to You—not only in this moment but in each moment of every day. I trust You to take care of me, to re-create me, to fashion me on Your potter's wheel. I am excited about living out Your dream for me. So give me the fortitude to keep myself in Your hands, to allow myself to be re-formed for every good work.

DAY 29

MORNING - *The Joy-Filled Woman's Path Marker: Promise No. 2*

There has never been the slightest doubt in my mind that the God who started this great work in you would keep at it and bring it to a flourishing finish on the very day Christ Jesus appears.
PHILIPPIANS 1:6 MSG

God has made you a promise. That the good work He began doing in you He'll continue to do until it's finished! Your job is to *claim that promise*! Since you accepted Him into your life, He's been transforming you into the woman He has already envisioned you to be. Believe it! It's a certain thing that He's going to keep going! Just rest easy and let Him do it, assured you're in good hands.

EVENING - *Blessed with Peace*

The peace of God, which passeth all understanding, shall keep your hearts and minds through Christ Jesus.
PHILIPPIANS 4:7 KJV

Dear Jesus, sometimes I doubt my ability, my vision, and my talent. At times, I'm worn and weary, feeling as if I'm spinning my wheels. But then I give up myself to You again. And I become not only re-energized to do Your will, to work *Your* way, but am blessed with Your amazing peace as well. Thank You, Lord!

DAY 30

MORNING - *The Joy-Filled Woman's Path Marker: Proof No. 2*

As he went along, he saw a man blind from birth. His disciples asked him, "Rabbi, who sinned, this man or his parents, that he was born blind?" "Neither this man nor his parents sinned," said Jesus, "but this happened so that the works of God might be displayed in him. As long as it is day, we must do the works of him who sent me. Night is coming, when no one can work. While I am in the world, I am the light of the world." After saying this, he spit on the ground, made some mud with the saliva, and put it on the man's eyes. "Go," he told him, "wash in the Pool of Siloam" (this word means "Sent"). So the man went and washed, and came home seeing.

JOHN 9:1–7 NIV

The Word gives you proof that God does indeed transform those who surrender to His work—and all for God's glory! So claim that proof and, like the blind man who washed in the Pool of Siloam, you will see the results!

EVENING - *Uncovered*

There is a covering over their minds. But when a person changes and follows the Lord, that covering is taken away.

2 CORINTHIANS 3:15–16 NCV

Help me to claim the proof that when I surrender myself to You, Jesus, You will transform me. As I wash myself in Your love, may I see more clearly each day the amazing work You are doing in my life.

DAY 31

MORNING - *The Joy-Filled Woman's Path Marker: Provision No. 2*

God's divine power has given us everything we need for life and for godliness. This power was given to us through knowledge of the one who called us by his own glory and integrity. Through his glory and integrity he has given us his promises that are of the highest value.

2 PETER 1:3–4 GW

Jesus has not only promised He'll keep up the good work He's started in you and given you proof that He has the ability to do amazing things with you, but He has also provided all you need for a godly and transformed life. So take courage! God has given you all the power and motivation to become everything He has called you to be!

EVENING - *Sharing in the Divine Nature*

Through these promises you will share in the divine nature because you have escaped the corruption that sinful desires cause in the world.

2 PETER 1:4 GW

God, I love the fact that I have a way to share in the divine nature. And it's all because of the promises of Your Word and the provisions that You have made for me. I am a willing piece of clay in Your hands. Make me over, Lord! Transform my life!

DAY 32

MORNING - *The Joy-Filled Woman's Path Marker: Portrait No. 2*

Anyone who belongs to Christ has become a new person. The old life is gone; a new life has begun!

2 Corinthians 5:17 NLT

⌒—✦—⌒

Know that Jesus has begun and will continue to re-create you (see Philippians 1:6). It's a *promise*! And there is living *proof* in His Word that it has been, is, and will be possible for Him to make anyone—including you—into a new woman (see John 9:1–7). For He has the power in His hands! In fact, He has *provided* all that is needed to accomplish such a feat (see 2 Peter 1:3–4) when you surrender yourself to His work. Keep all these things firmly in mind as you make this second *portrait* statement (based on 2 Corinthians 5:17) your very own!

In Christ, I am being transformed into a new person.

EVENING - *In Transformation*

Hosea put it well: I'll call nobodies and make them somebodies; I'll call the unloved and make them beloved. In the place where they yelled out, "You're nobody!" they're calling you "God's living children."

Romans 9:25–26 MSG

⌒—✦—⌒

I'm amazed, Lord, that You'd take notice of me. I'm thrilled that in Your eyes I'm a somebody who is loved. I rejoice in the fact that I'm Your living daughter. I have faith in Your process and vision for me. May I bring You the glory You deserve, in this life and beyond.

DAY 33

MORNING - *A Hidden Woman*

*[As far as this world is concerned] you have died,
and your [new, real] life is hidden with Christ in God.*
COLOSSIANS 3:3 AMPC

The true Christian life is best described as the life "hidden with Christ in God" (Colossians 3:3 NASB). Unlike the usual Christian experience, in which a woman believes and has been saved but does not exhibit Christ-likeness, the so-called higher Christian life is described in the Bible as one of continual rest in Jesus, of peace that surpasses all understanding. It's about having calm assurance and abundant joy in the midst of trials and chaos. But how do you live out this higher life? The key is obtaining childlike trust and faith in God.

EVENING - *Hands Free!*

*"I removed the burden from his shoulder. His hands were freed
from the basket. When you were in trouble, you called out to me,
and I rescued you. I was hidden in thunder, but I answered you."*
PSALM 81:6–7 GW

I know, Lord, that through thick and thin, You are with me and want to carry my burdens. After all, Jesus has already taken on the burden of my sins. So why should I think I have to carry the load of my worries, woes, and cares about the present—and sometimes future—upon my own inadequate shoulders? Take them from me now, Lord. Free my hands of worry so that I can receive more of You!

DAY 34

MORNING - *The Woman-Child*

The foolish things of God are wiser than human wisdom.
The weakness of God is stronger than human strength.

1 CORINTHIANS 1:25 NIrV

You may, at times, hesitate to give God your burdens because you're not sure He can handle them. It's as though you're telling God that you know better. It's as if *He* is the child and *you* are the father, always knowing what's best. That is a ludicrously fantastic role reversal when the fact of the matter is that *you* are the child and *God* is the Father—the Father who *always* knows best.

EVENING - *With Childlike Faith and Trust*

"I tell you the truth, you must accept the kingdom of
God as if you were a little child, or you will never enter it."

MARK 10:15 NCV

In Your eyes, Lord, I am Your daughter. With childlike faith and trust in You, I need not worry about yesterday, today, or tomorrow. With You holding on to me and loving me, I feel special. You wake me with a kiss in the morning and securely tuck me in at night. With Your love and protection, nothing can harm me. It's wonderful being a daughter of the King!

DAY 35

MORNING - *An Open Woman*

He put his fingers into the man's ears. Then, spitting on his own fingers, he touched the man's tongue. Looking up to heaven, he sighed and said, "Ephphatha," which means, "Be opened!" Instantly the man could hear perfectly, and his tongue was freed so he could speak plainly!
MARK 7:33–35 NLT

Consider the story of Jesus healing a man who was deaf and also had trouble speaking. When the people brought him to Jesus, your Lord took him aside, away from the crowd. Then Jesus put His fingers in the man's ears, spit on them, touched his tongue, and looking up to Father God, commanded the man's ears to open! And immediately, the man could clearly hear and speak! This Jesus is a God who can *clearly* handle your problems!

EVENING - *Amazed Again and Again*

Jesus told the crowd not to tell anyone, but the more he told them not to, the more they spread the news. They were completely amazed and said again and again, "Everything he does is wonderful. He even makes the deaf to hear and gives speech to those who cannot speak."
MARK 7:36–37 NLT

Lord, everything You do *is* amazing. You work Your wonders over and over again in my life. Help me to remember that fact when I hesitate to give You the load I can't carry.

DAY 36

MORNING · *The Woman in Training*

*Jesus of Nazareth, a man approved of God among you by miracles and
wonders and signs, which God did by him in the midst of you.*
ACTS 2:22 KJV

How ridiculous for you to think that Jesus—who stilled the wind and waves,
healed the deaf, mute, blind, and lame, and rose from the dead—is unable
to handle your problems. You must train your mind and heart to believe
what the hymn writer Fanny Crosby, who was blind, understood: "For I
know that whate'er befall me, Jesus doeth all things well!" Notice her use
of the present tense—"doeth." Jesus is with you now, waiting to carry your
load. To turn your trial into triumph! Will you let Him?

EVENING · *Confident in Christ*

*If you are tired from carrying heavy burdens,
come to me and I will give you rest.*
MATTHEW 11:28 CEV

Lord, I am weary of worrying about everything. My emotions are as volatile
as the stock market. So I come to You today, ready to unburden myself. I lay
my plans, my loved ones, and my life at Your feet. In exchange, I pick up
Your peace, love, kindness, and strength, confident that You do *all* things well.

DAY 37

MORNING - *A Watched Woman*

The eyes of the Lord are in every place,
keeping watch upon the evil and the good.
PROVERBS 15:3 AMPC

Perhaps you think your prayers are going nowhere, that God—too busy with bigger world problems—will not respond. That seems to be a small view of a God whose eyes are everywhere. With His panoramic vision, He can see the solutions you cannot even begin to imagine. Not only that, but as soon as you cry out to Him, He hears you and responds with His all-encompassing love and affection.

EVENING - *Always Heard*

Is anyone crying for help? God is listening, ready to rescue you.
PSALM 34:17 MSG

It's so good to know, Lord, that You see everything that's going on in my life. That You have the answer to my problem before I even bring it to You! Knowing that You hear as soon as I cry out to You—and respond immediately, showering on me all Your love and affection—fills me with such peace. Thank You, Lord, for being my all in all.

DAY 38

MORNING - *A Suckled Woman*

Zion said, "I don't get it. God has left me. My Master has forgotten I even exist." "Can a mother forget the infant at her breast, walk away from the baby she bore? But even if mothers forget, I'd never forget you—never."
ISAIAH 49:14–15 MSG

God created an amazing process called breastfeeding that, at times, can prove embarrassing. Sometimes, while minding her own business, the mother of a helpless infant can have her letdown reflex respond to an infant that is not her own! And just as a woman immediately responds to her infant's cries (and sometimes another's), God immediately responds to *your* cries–*His* baby girl's cries—for help.

EVENING - *Receiving Promised Blessings*

You are God's child, and God will give you the blessing he promised, because you are his child.
GALATIANS 4:7 NCV

Your Word, Lord, is filled with Your promises. Because I believe in and look to You for everything, I will receive every blessing You have for me. I am awed at Your love for me. I am overwhelmed with joy that You will not withhold any good thing from me. Just knowing that, I feel very blessed.

DAY 39

MORNING · *An Unattached Woman*

*All believers, come here and listen, let me tell you what
God did for me. I called out to him with my mouth.*
PSALM 66:17 MSG

Madame Jeanne Guyon, in *Experiencing the Depths of Jesus Christ*, wrote:
*You must come to the Lord and there engage in giving up all your
concerns. All your concerns go into the hand of God. You forget yourself,
and from that moment on you think only of Him.*
*By continuing to do this over a long period of time, your heart will
remain unattached; your heart will be free and at peace!*

EVENING · *Giving Over Self*

*He most surely did listen, he came on the double when he
heard my prayer. Blessed be God: he didn't turn a
deaf ear, he stayed with me, loyal in his love.*
PSALM 66:19–20 MSG

God, Your Word says You will never forget me. You are always listening,
waiting for me to share and let go of all my burdens—the greatest of which
is self. Often I am so focused on my feelings, my unique temperament, my
own peccadilloes and temptations, my expectations, fears, and plans that I
cannot see clearly. I allow these things to take over my thoughts, to hold me
in bondage. So I give my "self" over to You, God, knowing I am totally safe
in Your love.

DAY 40

MORNING · *A Rescued Woman*

"Then call on me when you are in trouble,
and I will rescue you, and you will give me glory."
PSALM 50:15 NLT

You are to give God all your burdens—of health, Christian service, careers, husbands, children, households, friends—everything that produces those horrible worry lines. Don't be so consumed with the worries of this world that you lose your focus on God. In this information age, one hears bad news from every corner of the world! It's enough to stoop your shoulders. But God reminds you over and over again that you are not to carry these burdens. You were not made for it. And when all you can focus on is trouble, you'll miss God's miracles! Allow God to rescue you!

EVENING · *Resting in Assurance*

"Give your entire attention to what God is doing right now, and don't
get worked up about what may or may not happen tomorrow. God will
help you deal with whatever hard things come up when the time comes."
MATTHEW 6:34 MSG

I have decided that I'm going to stop thinking about what may or may not happen today and tomorrow, God. Instead I am going to rest assured that no matter what difficulties may arise, all is well. You will help me through the conflict as I pray my way through. I rejoice at the challenges before me, knowing that with You on my side, I need not fear anything!

DAY 41

MORNING - *The Miracle-Minded Woman*

"The Lord is my strength and song, and He has become
my salvation; this is my God, and I will praise Him."
EXODUS 15:2 NASB

By focusing on misfortunes, you may miss miracles. So take a step back, close your mouth, and watch for God working. When you see where and how He is moving, you will be driven to praise instead of petitions!

In June 2012 in Ohio, high school track champion Meghan Vogel saw that a fellow runner had collapsed during the 3,200-meter race. Not only did she pick the girl up and help her finish the race, but she pushed her across the finish line ahead of herself. That is where God is working! This is cause for praise!

EVENING - *Peppering Petitions with Praise*

O Lord of hosts, blessed (happy, fortunate, to be envied) is the man
who trusts in You [leaning and believing on You, committing all
and confidently looking to You, and that without fear or misgiving]!
PSALM 84:12 AMPC

Lord, no matter what is happening in my life, I can't help but praise You! For I know that when I pepper my petitions with praise, You are pleased. For I am focusing on Your miracle-working power instead of allowing my problems to pester me. In You alone, I have confidence. To You alone, do I look.

DAY 42

MORNING - *A Myopic Woman*

"For as the heavens are higher than the earth, so are My ways higher than your ways, and My thoughts than your thoughts."
ISAIAH 55:9 NKJV

Your vision is limited. You cannot see the future and are at times uncertain of the present. If you're not focused on or looking for God's working, your imagination can run away with you. Soon you are thinking of the worst-case scenario, reasoning that you should, after all, be prepared just in case. Before you know it, your thoughts careen out of control. Next your emotions respond, and you sink in despair over an imagined outcome that may never be realized! Go to prayer before your thoughts run away with you. Go to God with your troubles and leave them at His feet.

EVENING - *Getting a New Outlook*

Be constantly renewed in the spirit of your mind
[having a fresh mental and spiritual attitude].
EPHESIANS 4:23 AMPC

I don't have Your vision, Lord. So help me not to let my imagination run away with me. Instead, renew the spirit of my mind. Give me fresh thoughts and a new outlook as I come to You in prayer and leave my troubles at Your feet.

DAY 43

MORNING - *A Refocused Woman*

*For You are my hope; O Lord God, You are my trust
from my youth and the source of my confidence.*
PSALM 71:5 AMPC

In regard to your cares, it is not your circumstances that need altering. It is you yourself. It is your mind-set that must first be shifted. Then the conditions will naturally be changed. With a simple, childlike faith in God who sees all and knows all, your whole world—indeed your entire outlook—changes.

EVENING - *Praising*

*Upon You have I leaned and relied from birth; You are He
Who took me from my mother's womb and You have been my
benefactor from that day. My praise is continually of You.*
PSALM 71:6 AMPC

I know, Lord, that it is not my current situation that needs to be changed. It's me and me alone. Help me to shift my mind-set. For in so doing, I know that everything—and everyone—around me will change as well. You've been with me since the very beginning. You have been my helper since day one. So help me now. Change my petitions into nothing but praise!

DAY 44

MORNING · *A Once-Restive Woman*

He gives [blessings] to His beloved in sleep.
PSALM 127:2 AMPC

Hannah Whitall Smith gives a wonderful analogy about how to trust in God with simple faith:

> *Do you recollect the delicious sense of rest with which you have sometimes gone to bed at night. . . ? How delightful was the sensation of relaxing every muscle and letting your body go in a perfect abandonment of ease and comfort! . . .*
>
> *But suppose you had doubted the strength or the stability of your bed and had dreaded each moment to find it giving way beneath you and landing you on the floor; could you have rested then? . . .*
> Let this analogy teach you what it means to rest in the Lord.

EVENING · *Resting Securely*

"Then you would trust, because there is hope; and you would look around and rest securely. You would lie down and none would disturb you."
JOB 11:18–19 NASB

Smith writes:

> *Let your souls lie down upon the couch of His sweet will, as your bodies lie down in their beds at night. Relax every strain, and lay off every burden. Let yourself go in a perfect abandonment of ease and comfort, sure that, since He holds you up, you are perfectly safe.*
> Pray: *Lord, trusting You, I lie my soul down in You.*

DAY 45

MORNING - *A Well-Fed Woman*

"Truly I tell you, unless you change and become like little children, you will never enter the kingdom of heaven."
MATTHEW 18:3 NIV

Remember your years as a little child? You did not worry about your dinner. You knew that in some magical way when your playtime was over, a meal would be waiting for you. You trusted those who cared for you—your parents, teachers, and at times even those not worthy of your trust. As a child, you provided nothing for yourself, yet whatever you needed was provided. You didn't worry about tomorrow but lived in the now. That's how God wants you to live today!

EVENING - *Full in Faith*

You will have plenty to eat, until you are full, and you will praise the name of the LORD your God, who has worked wonders for you.
JOEL 2:26 NIV

You have always worked wonders for me, Lord. So I am resting in You, knowing and trusting You will always provide whatever I need. Help me to keep this attitude not only today—but every day, as I live and breathe in You!

DAY 46

MORNING - *A Woman Immediately Provided For*

And Jesus, immediately knowing in himself that virtue had gone out of him. . .said, Who touched my clothes?
MARK 5:30 KJV

A woman had an "issue of blood" (Mark 5:25 KJV) for twelve years. She'd spent all her money on doctors but could not be healed. When she heard of Jesus, she made her way through the crowd and came up behind Him. As she touched His robe, she said to herself, "If I may touch but his clothes, I shall be whole" (Mark 5:28 KJV). Immediately, she was healed! In the same moment, Jesus knew someone had drawn on His healing power. He asked who had touched His garment. When the woman admitted her boldness, Jesus said, "Daughter, thy faith hath made thee whole; go in peace" (Mark 5:34 KJV). You are God's daughter, and He lovingly provides everything you need—*in the moment*!

EVENING - *Made Whole*

If I may touch but his clothes, I shall be whole.
MARK 5:28 KJV

Jesus, You are my security blanket. I'm bringing to You the issue on my mind—myself, my plans, my partner, my children, my work, the world's woes, my misgivings, apprehensions, or anxiety. I am reaching out for Your garment. By faith, I allow You to take my burden up and leave me whole.

DAY 47

MORNING - *An Assured Daughter*

Behold, I have indelibly imprinted (tattooed a picture of) you on the palm of each of My hands; [O Zion] your walls are continually before Me.
ISAIAH 49:16 AMPC

Be calm. Be carefree. Become an assured daughter of God, knowing that He will never leave you. He will never forget you. He has "written *your* name on the palms" of His hands (Isaiah 49:16 NIrV, emphasis added) in indelible ink. Rest in this promise.

EVENING - *With Peace in Hand*

Jesus heard what they said, and he said to Jairus, "Don't worry. Just have faith!"
MARK 5:36 CEV

Sometimes, Lord, people say things that are just not true. They are driven by the ways and worries of this world. But I am Your daughter, and I have faith in You. I know that oftentimes things are not what they appear to be. So I am not going to allow others to alarm me, but instead I am putting my hand in Yours and resting in Your presence. Thank You, Lord, for always being here.

DAY 48

MORNING - *A Fretless Woman*

*Give all your worries and cares to God,
for he cares about you.*
1 PETER 5:7 NLT

You are to give all your fears, frets, and frustrations to God. Let go of the past, present, and future. God has promised to take care of you. It's not a theory, but fact! Look to the lilies and the birds. If God is taking care of them, He is more than attentive to what those created in His image need, desire, and deal with, every moment of every day.

EVENING - *Finding Power*

Do not let your hearts be troubled, neither let them be afraid. [Stop allowing yourselves to be agitated and disturbed; and do not permit yourselves to be fearful and intimidated and cowardly and unsettled.]
JOHN 14:27 AMPC

Jesus, only You can put my worries to rest, for You are the only One I can truly count on. In Your presence I find true peace. With You by my side, I can face any and all situations. With Your Word as my firm foundation, I find the power to move mountains. How wonderful to hide myself in You!

DAY 49

MORNING - *The Joy-Filled Woman's Path Marker: Promise No. 3*

Be careful for nothing; but in every thing by prayer and supplication with thanksgiving let your requests be made known unto God. And the peace of God, which passeth all understanding, shall keep your hearts and minds through Christ Jesus.
PHILIPPIANS 4:6–7 KJV

What a wonderful blessing this promise is. That you need not worry about anything! Just pray, bringing all your needs—big and small—before God. Leave them at His feet. And then you will be overwhelmed with His unfathomable peace, for Christ Himself will take the place of all the worries at the center of both your heart and mind. Because He is all you need.

EVENING - *Finding Perfect Peace and Rest*

You will keep in perfect peace all who trust in you, all whose thoughts are fixed on you!
ISAIAH 26:3 NLT

Jesus, just like a nursing mother, You hear my every sigh, whine, and cry, and respond immediately. I am Your precious baby girl. I trust You as I trust the earth to support me. I know I am in Your hands, heart, and thoughts. And that it is through You—who does all things well and takes such good care of me—that I will find my peace and rest.

DAY 50

MORNING - *The Joy-Filled Woman's Path Marker: Proof No. 3*

We don't want you in the dark, friends, about how hard it was when all this came down on us in Asia province. It was so bad we didn't think we were going to make it. We felt like we'd been sent to death row, that it was all over for us. As it turned out, it was the best thing that could have happened. Instead of trusting in our own strength or wits to get out of it, we were forced to trust God totally—not a bad idea since he's the God who raises the dead! And he did it, rescued us from certain doom. And he'll do it again, rescuing us as many times as we need rescuing.

2 CORINTHIANS 1:8–10 MSG

What a great proof that in the direst of situations, God will come through for you, providing what you need, exactly when you need it, again and again! Claim this proof and, like Paul and Timothy, you'll experience that amazing power of the one who raises the dead!

EVENING - *Provided For*

I am the LORD thy God, which brought thee out of the land of Egypt: open thy mouth wide, and I will fill it.

PSALM 81:10 KJV

God, I'm relying on Your power, not mine, to provide for me. For when I do, You not only fill me up every day but continually rescue me from dire circumstances! What a wonderful caretaker You are!

DAY 51

MORNING - *The Joy-Filled Woman's Path Marker: Provision No. 3*

But seek (aim at and strive after) first of all His kingdom and His righteousness (His way of doing and being right), and then all these things taken together will be given you besides.
MATTHEW 6:33 AMPC

Jesus has promised that you will be provided with everything you could possibly need if you seek Him—what He stands for and His way of doing things—above everything else in this life. Begin doing so today, claiming the provision of a seeker's life and attitude, and you will be rewarded beyond belief!

EVENING - *Never Left Lacking*

GOD was on Jehoshaphat's side because he stuck to the ways of his father Asa's early years. He didn't fool around with the popular Baal religion— he was a seeker and follower of the God of his father and was obedient to him. . . . And GOD secured the kingdom under his rule, gave him a firm grip on it. . . . Jehoshaphat ended up very rich and much honored.
2 CHRONICLES 17:3–5 MSG

I want to be stuck on You, seeking You, and doing things Your way, Lord. For whenever I do that, come looking for You above all else, I *gain* everything else—including the peace and joy of knowing You will never leave me lacking! So it's Your way, Lord, not mine!

DAY 52

MORNING - *The Joy-Filled Woman's Path Marker: Portrait No. 3*

And my God will liberally supply (fill to the full) your every need according to His riches in glory in Christ Jesus.
PHILIPPIANS 4:19 AMPC

Jesus has not only *promised* He will provide all that you need if you just come to Him in prayer (see Philippians 4:6–7) and presented living *proof* in His Word that it has been, is, and will be done in even the direst of circumstances (see 2 Corinthians 1:8–10), He has made *provision* for it when you seek Him above all things (see Matthew 6:33). Keep all these things in the forefront of your mind and heart by claiming this third *portrait* statement as your very own!

In Christ, I know God will provide me with everything I need.

EVENING - *Provision of Peace*

Now may the Lord of peace Himself continually grant you peace in every circumstance.
2 THESSALONIANS 3:16 NASB

Every day, Lord, I need a new parcel of Your peace to help me through. Knowing You continually give me confidence and assurance in every situation is incredible and quite calming. I am going to seek after You throughout the day, visualizing You with me, holding my hand through every circumstance I encounter. For my peace comes from knowing *You will provide* for me!

DAY 53

MORNING - *A Woman Entering In*

*Whatever is good and perfect is a gift
coming down to us from God our Father.*
JAMES 1:17 NLT

Now that you know what the true Christian life is, how do you enter in? How do you spend your days confidently cool in the midst of worldly turmoil? The true Christian experience is not something you can achieve by any sort of directed effort on your part. Rather, it is something you gain possession of by receiving it. A child does not earn affection from its mother. Instead, it receives something the mother can't help but give. So does your Father God give you this life, as a gift He can't help but express to you. Your only role is to receive the good and perfect gift of Christ Jesus in God with a thankful heart.

EVENING - *With Open Eyes*

*Open my eyes so I can see what you
show me of your miracle-wonders.*
PSALM 119:18 MSG

Open my eyes, mind, heart, and spirit, Jesus, so I can see how wonderful my life is hidden in You. I want to know You, feel Your presence. I want to do what You would have me do. I want to love others as I love myself. Teach me, show me, give me Your vision. Enlighten me so that I may not be afraid but give myself to You willingly—moment by moment.

MORNING - *The Set-Apart Woman*

And you shall be to Me a kingdom of priests,
a holy nation [consecrated, set apart to the worship of God].
EXODUS 19:6 AMPC

To understand how to enter in, you must comprehend what it means to set yourself apart to be totally dedicated or committed to God. Like a patient who must absolutely obey her doctor or remain stricken by her disease, you must consecrate or commit your life to God. You must put yourself entirely in His hands and allow Him to have His way with you—no matter how you feel or what you judge to be right! This will inevitably lead to a life of blessings and peace in Christ, for God the Father only wants what is best for you.

EVENING - *Under God's Care*

" 'Now if you will obey me and keep my covenant,
you will be my own special treasure from among all
the peoples on earth; for all the earth belongs to me.' "
EXODUS 19:5 NLT

Lord, I am committing myself to You. I'm going to tell You everything that's going on in my life, all my "symptoms." And I will take all the "remedies" You prescribe me, all the advice You give me—whether or not it makes sense to me. I leave myself entirely in Your care and will follow Your instructions precisely, without objections or second thoughts!

DAY 55

MORNING - *A Surrendered Woman*

*"But I am afraid to surrender," the king said, "for the Babylonians
may hand me over to the Judeans who have defected to them.
And who knows what they will do to me!" Jeremiah replied,
"You won't be handed over to them if you choose to obey the LORD.
Your life will be spared, and all will go well for you."*
JEREMIAH 38:19–20 NLT

You may be afraid of giving yourself totally to God. You may believe He will
endeavor to make your life miserable, that He will take away all the things you
love and enjoy, that all your perceived blessings will fall by the wayside. But the
exact opposite is true! If you totally give yourself over to God, all will be well!

EVENING - *Wholly Committed to Christ*

*Roll your works upon the Lord [commit and trust them wholly to Him;
He will cause your thoughts to become agreeable to His will, and]
so shall your plans be established and succeed.*
PROVERBS 16:3 AMPC

I want to roll everything upon You, Lord, including myself. I want to trust
You entirely. I want my thoughts to be Your thoughts. In doing so, I fully
believe that everything You have in mind for me is good. I know that in You
I will succeed—perhaps not as the world defines success but how You define
it. And that's all I need or want.

DAY 56

MORNING - *A Loving Daughter*

*How happy I was to meet some of your children
and find them living according to the truth.*
2 JOHN 1:4 NLT

Let's say you had a child whom you dearly loved, and this child came to you and said, "From now on, I am going to do everything you tell me to without crying, pouting, objecting, or throwing a tantrum. In fact, I will trust you because you love me, and you can do to me whatever you want from this time forward." What would your response be? To make this child miserable for the rest of its life? No! Of course not! Instead, you would be overjoyed! Just like God is overjoyed when you trust and obey Him!

EVENING - *Peppered with Kisses*

The Father himself loves you dearly.
JOHN 16:27 NLT

I come to You, Lord, ready to be Your obedient child. I know You delight in my living Your way, trusting You in all things. I feel You hugging me to Yourself, peppering kisses on my brow in response to my allowing You to be in charge of me and my life. For I know that, because of my obedience, You are going to fill my life with the best and loveliest things on heaven and earth. What a loving Father—in whom love begets love!

DAY 57

MORNING - *A Redeemed Woman*

"There is salvation in no one else! God has given no other name under heaven by which we must be saved."
ACTS 4:12 NLT

ꕥ

Is it not true that God Himself is so much more loving to you than you could ever be to one cherished individual? Isn't He the One who gave you His one and only Son to save you from your sins? To save you from yourself? In fact, He is just aching for you to enter not only the kingdom of God but the kingdom of heaven. Bill Gillham, author of *What God Wishes Christians Knew about Christianity*, wrote, "Christ's death saved you from hell *below* the earth; Christ's life saves you from hell *upon* the earth." So allow God to redeem you. Enter into His kingdom!

EVENING - *Loved by Her Savior*

[God] did not spare his own Son but gave him for us all. So with Jesus, God will surely give us all things.
ROMANS 8:32 NCV

ꕥ

Jesus, I can't imagine how broken God's heart was when He sacrificed You, His one and only Son, for me. Such love is unfathomable, yet such love is mine. And surely as I remain hidden in You, Jesus, God will withhold nothing else. Everything that is good and right will be met in my life. Thank You for saving me. Make my life something special for You.

DAY 58

MORNING - *An Enthusiastic Woman*

I saw a door standing open in heaven. I heard the first voice like a trumpet speaking to me. It said, "Come up here, and I will show you what must happen after this." Instantly, I came under the Spirit's power. I saw a throne in heaven.

REVELATION 4:1–2 GW

Hannah Whitall Smith wrote:

Heaven is a place of infinite bliss because His will is perfectly done there, and our lives share in this bliss just in proportion as His will is perfectly done in them. He loves us—loves us, I say—and the will of love is always blessings for its loved one. Could we but for one moment get a glimpse into the mighty depths of His love, and our hearts would spring out to meet His will and embrace it as our richest treasure; and we would abandon ourselves to it with an enthusiasm of gratitude and joy that such a wondrous privilege could be ours.

EVENING - *Claiming the Gift*

"You know the way to the place where I am going."

JOHN 14:4 GW

Loving God, "Thy will be done." I have faith in You. I wholeheartedly believe that through my faith and obedience, I can—and hereby do—claim as mine the gift that Your sacrifice has given to me—the bliss of living in Your will and presence, here on earth and in heaven to come.

DAY 59

MORNING - *A Believing Woman*

*O give thanks to the Lord of lords, for His mercy and loving-kindness
endure forever. . . . To Him Who [earnestly] remembered us in our
low estate and imprinted us [on His heart], for His mercy
and loving-kindness endure forever.*
PSALM 136:3, 23 AMPC

Remember how much Christ loves you and how you cannot be separated from
that love? Remember how much He has forgiven you? Remember how He
has you imprinted on His heart? Until you believe in this love and forgiveness
and claim both as your own, they will not really be yours. Claim them today!

EVENING - *Awed by Love*

*Nothing now, nothing in the future, no powers, nothing above us,
nothing below us, nor anything else in the whole world will ever be
able to separate us from the love of God that is in Christ Jesus our Lord.*
ROMANS 8:38–39 NCV

Lord, I am awed by the fact that nothing can separate me from Your love.
Nothing from my past or future. Nothing in the day that stands before me.
Nothing from above or below. No power on heaven or earth can keep me from
Your love for me. I feel Your warmth bubbling up inside of me. Suddenly, I
am not afraid of anything!

MORNING - *The "Now" Woman in Motion: The First & Second Movements*

Once, you Gentiles were rebels against God, but when the people of Israel rebelled against him, God was merciful to you instead.
ROMANS 11:30 NLT

When it comes to living your life for Christ, you may think that once you're saved and forgiven, you need to live by works and effort. Instead of *receiving* all that He has to offer, you begin to *do*, trying to work your way into the kingdom when in actuality you have already arrived! It's a matter of moving from "then" into "now."

Then you were "disobedient to God"; but *now* you have "obtained mercy" (Romans 11:30 NKJV). *Then* you received Christ in faith, but *now* you walk in Him (see Colossians 2:6).

EVENING - *Walking the Walk*

As you therefore have received Christ Jesus the Lord, so walk in Him.
COLOSSIANS 2:6 NKJV

I remember when I first received You, Christ Jesus. What a wonderful day that was! But that was then. And now, I am to walk in You, walk the way You walked, in Your footsteps. That includes loving and forgiving others, including myself—and so much more. Continue to lead me, Lord. Show me the way, as I walk the walk!

DAY 61

MORNING - *The "Now" Woman in Motion:*
The Third, Fourth & Fifth Movements

For the law of the Spirit of life [which is] in Christ Jesus [the law
of our new being] has freed me from the law of sin and of death.
ROMANS 8:2 AMPC

Continuing to move from "then" into "now". . . *Then* Christ set you free from the law of sin and death, so *now* don't walk according to the flesh but according to the Spirit (see Romans 8:2, 4). *Then* Christ made you free—*now* "be free indeed"! (John 8:36 NASB). *Then* you were "striving to please men," but *now* you are to seek to please "God who examines our hearts" (Galatians 1:10 NASB; 1 Thessalonians 2:4 NASB).

EVENING - *Living the New Life*

For am I now seeking the favor of men, or of God?
Or am I striving to please men? If I were still trying
to please men, I would not be a bond-servant of Christ.
GALATIANS 1:10 NASB

Lord, I don't want to live in the past anymore. I want to live the life You gave me when I accepted You. So help me to live in line with the Spirit. Help me to live as a free woman. Remind me that I am not to be a people pleaser—but above all, a God pleaser. Help me to glorify You in this new life You have given me when You set me free!

DAY 62

MORNING - *The "Now" Woman in Motion: The Sixth, Seventh & Eighth Movements*

Once you were separated from God. The evil things you did showed your hostile attitude.

COLOSSIANS 1:21 GW

And the walk from "then" into "now" continues. . . Now that You are Christ's, God reminds you to move from the *then* of alienation from Him to the *now* of reconciliation to Him (see Colossians 1:21–22); from the *then* of godliness as "a means of gain" to *now* knowing "godliness with *contentment* is great gain" (1 Timothy 6:5–6 NKJV, emphasis added). *Then* Christ lifted you "up also out of an horrible pit" but *now* you are "set. . .down in the highest heaven in company with Jesus" (Psalm 40:2 KJV; Ephesians 2:6 MSG)! Are you living the life of the *new you*?

EVENING - *Up Close and Personal with God*

But now Christ has brought you back to God by dying in his physical body. He did this so that you could come into God's presence without sin, fault, or blame.

COLOSSIANS 1:22 GW

Lord, I can't believe how much of the "old life" I've been living. As if nothing ever even changed. Help me to remember that I am no longer separated from, but actually able to come into Your presence. And that where once I was as far down as I could go, now I am set high up in heaven with the Savior I love and cherish!

DAY 63

MORNING - *The "Now" Woman in Motion: The Ninth and Tenth Movements*

Once you lived in the dark, but now the Lord has filled you with light. Live as children who have light.
EPHESIANS 5:8 GW

And last of all, *then* by grace you were saved by faith, as a gift from God but *now* "according to your faith let it be to you" (see Ephesians 2:8; Matthew 9:29 NKJV). Finally, *then* "you were once darkness" but *now* "you are light in the Lord. Walk as children of light" (Ephesians 5:8 NKJV). So endeth the lesson in moving from your *then* (prior) life—*before* being saved and forgiven—to your *now* (new) life in Christ! Wait no longer! Live in the *now*!

EVENING - *Living in the New Light*

God saved you through faith as an act of kindness. You had nothing to do with it. Being saved is a gift from God.
EPHESIANS 2:8 GW

I cannot believe all the gifts I was given when I received You into my life and heart, Jesus. Continue to remind me of the joy this new light gives me. And it all comes to me in accordance with my faith in You. You have made a believer out of me! Thank You, Lord, the one who is the ultimate Giver of gifts beyond imagining!

DAY 64

MORNING · *A Sister in Christ*

*Believe in the Lord Jesus Christ [give yourself up to Him,
take yourself out of your own keeping and entrust yourself
into His keeping] and you will be saved.*
ACTS 16:31 AMPC

Sister in Christ, how you will live in Christ is according to your faith. That has always been the limit and the rule. And this faith must be a present—now—faith.

Smith wrote, "No faith that looks for a future deliverance from the power of sin will ever lead a soul into the life we are describing. Perhaps no four words in the language have more meaning in them than the following. . . . *Jesus saves me now.*"

EVENING · *Continually Saved*

" 'Whoever calls on the name of the Lord will be saved.' "
ACTS 2:21 GW

Repeat these words over and over again—not only with your voice, but with your heart, with your soul, and with your spirit. Each time you are to emphasize a different word:

Jesus saves me now. (It is *He* who continually saves you.)

Jesus *saves* me now. (It is His *work*, not yours, *to save you continually*.)

Jesus saves *me* now. (*You are the one* He is continually saving.)

Jesus saves me *now*. (He is saving you *every moment of every day*—right now!)

Pray: *Jesus, thank You for saving me now!*

DAY 65

MORNING - *The Restored Woman*

*"Those who drink the water I give will never be thirsty again.
It becomes a fresh, bubbling spring within them, giving them eternal life."*
JOHN 4:14 NLT

In Christ, you taste the joy of the kingdom of heaven. He is that "pearl of great price" (Matthew 13:46 KJV), your hidden treasure (see Matthew 13:44). He is the well of living water you so desperately thirst for and to which you may continually come.

Hidden in Christ, you are led through Psalm 23. You arrive, protected and guided by your Good Shepherd. You are fed in green pastures. Immersed in still, calm waters. You need not fear anything but simply lie down in His luscious field, your soul restored as God originally planned in the Garden of Eden. What a life of rest and triumph in Christ!

EVENING - *Immersed and Hidden*

*I will not be afraid, because the LORD is with me.
People can't do anything to me.*
PSALM 118:6 NCV

Hidden in You, Jesus, I have nothing to fear. No one can touch me. Your love and presence, Your strength and truth shield me from whatever weapons this world can use against me. How wonderful to have such protection! How glorious to have such courage in You. I can face anything within the One who will never leave me.

DAY 66

MORNING - *The Divine Woman*

By his divine power, God has given us everything we need for living a godly life. We have received all of this by coming to know him, the one who called us to himself by means of his marvelous glory and excellence. And because of his glory and excellence, he has given us great and precious promises. These are the promises that enable you to share his divine nature and escape the world's corruption caused by human desires.

2 Peter 1:3–4 NLT

The more time you spend in Christ, the more you become like Him and the closer you grow to God. It's a win-win-win!

EVENING - *With Wonderful Taste*

How sweet your words taste to me; they are sweeter than honey.

Psalm 119:103 NLT

How wonderful is that taste of heaven, Your divine nature that becomes part of me, Christ, as I remain hidden in You. To enter into this blessed new life of rest and triumph within, I know I am to take two steps—entire abandonment and absolute faith. As I focus on those two things, I know I will reach that higher life far sooner than I ever imagined possible! And I praise You for this privilege!

DAY 67

MORNING - *An Unwavering Woman*

Behold, I am laying in Zion a stone, a tested stone,
a costly cornerstone for the foundation, firmly placed.
ISAIAH 28:16 NASB

John Greenleaf Whittier wrote, "The steps of faith fall on the seeming void, but find the rock beneath." Christ is a mighty Rock on which you stand in this life and the next. So don't be afraid to take these steps of faith. With Him beneath you, you will not sink in the sand but stand triumphant upon your Lord and Master.

EVENING - *On the Rock*

Then you will go safely on your way, and you will not hurt your foot.
When you lie down, you will not be afraid. As you lie there,
your sleep will be sweet. Do not be afraid. . . . The LORD will
be your confidence. He will keep your foot from getting caught.
PROVERBS 3:23–26 GW

I sometimes feel so weak, Lord. I have trouble believing myself worthy of anyone or anything. But when I hide in You, I suddenly have confidence. I know that I am safe and secure on the Rock of Your presence—which is always with me. Even if I stumble, I will come to no harm. And when I lie down to sleep at the end of the day, I rest secure in Your strong arms. Help me, Jesus, to keep my footing on You.

DAY 68

MORNING - *The Courageous Woman*

I will be with thee: I will not fail thee, nor forsake thee. Be strong and of a good courage. . . . Only be thou strong and very courageous. . . . Have not I commanded thee? Be strong and of a good courage; be not afraid, neither be thou dismayed: for the LORD thy God is with thee whithersoever thou goest. . . . Only be strong and of a good courage.
JOSHUA 1:5–7, 9, 18 KJV

If you are still hesitant to hide yourself in Christ, check out the verses above, spoken by the God who calls you to enter His Promised Land. It contains a total of four "be strongs" and "of a good courage" or "courageous," along with three assurances that God will be with you and never leave you. Wow!

EVENING - *Filled with Assurance*

God can do anything, you know—far more than you could ever imagine or guess or request in your wildest dreams! He does it not by pushing us around but by working within us, his Spirit deeply and gently within us.
EPHESIANS 3:20 MSG

With You in my corner, Lord, Your courage and strength in my heart, and myself hidden in Christ, I have all the assurance I need to cross the river and make it into the Promised Land of Your love and light. I know You can do more than I can ask and imagine with Your Spirit within me!

DAY 69

MORNING - *The Joy-Filled Woman's Path Marker: Promise No. 4*

Then He touched their eyes, saying, According to your faith and trust and reliance [on the power invested in Me] be it done to you.
MATTHEW 9:29 AMPC

When you have entire abandonment to God and absolute faith, amazing things will happen. That's the promise Jesus gave all His believers. And His Word proves it over and over again. Keep this in mind as you walk throughout your day. Claim this promise and watch what happens in your life. You'll become a witness to the wondrous.

EVENING - *In This Time of Becoming*

"Become what you believe."
MATTHEW 9:29 MSG

Jesus, Your Word tells me that I become what I believe. I base my faith on that idea—that promise. I truly believe You can work miracles—within and without! And, oh my Lord, I so need them. So help me hang on to Your Word as I stand firm in You in this time of becoming the joy-filled believing woman You created me to be since the beginning of time.

MORNING - *The Joy-Filled Woman's Path Marker: Proof No. 4*

As Jesus passed on from there, two blind men followed Him, shouting loudly, Have pity and mercy on us, Son of David! When He reached the house and went in, the blind men came to Him, and Jesus said to them, Do you believe that I am able to do this? They said to Him, Yes, Lord. Then He touched their eyes, saying, According to your faith and trust and reliance [on the power invested in Me] be it done to you; and their eyes were opened.

MATTHEW 9:27–30 AMPC

In His Word, Jesus proves over and over again that when you believe He is able to do anything, in accordance with that faith, that absolute trust, that complete reliance on His power, your eyes will be opened. Claim that proof and, like the two blind men who followed Jesus, He will touch you, opening up your awareness to the miracles He is doing in your very midst.

EVENING - *Flourishing Faith*

Dear brothers and sisters, we can't help but thank God for you, because your faith is flourishing and your love for one another is growing.

2 THESSALONIANS 1:3 NLT

Being reminded of how many others witness miracles because of their faith only increases my own. Thank You, Lord, for all You do and have done as my faith continues to grow and feed my joy in You all the more!

DAY 71

MORNING - *The Joy-Filled Woman's Path Marker: Provision No. 4*

For God, who said, "Light shall shine out of darkness,"
is the One who has shone in our hearts to give the Light
of the knowledge of the glory of God in the face of Christ.
2 CORINTHIANS 4:6 NASB

In *Intimate Friendship with God*, Joy Dawson wrote, "To have a nodding acquaintance with the Creator of the universe is no small thought. But to be on intimate terms with Him is enough to give us heart flutters for the rest of our lives." When you claim the idea that God provides the light that shines into your heart to give you the knowledge of His Son, you'll find yourself so comfortable in His presence, so intimate with Him, that you can't wait to hide in Him.

EVENING - *No More Groping*

You groped your way through that murk once, but no longer.
You're out in the open now. The bright light of Christ makes your
way plain. So no more stumbling around. Get on with it!
EPHESIANS 5:8 MSG

Thank You, God, for giving me the gospel light, which reveals Jesus to me. No more groping around for me. I am finding my way in faith as the truth, the light, and the way is made plain.

MORNING - *The Joy-Filled Woman's Path Marker: Portrait No. 4*

We have been filled with comfort and cheer about you [because of] your faith (the leaning of your whole personality on God in complete trust and confidence). Because now we [really] live, if you stand [firm] in the Lord.
1 THESSALONIANS 3:7–8 AMPC

Jesus *promises* "it shall be done to you according to your faith" (see Matthew 9:29 NASB). The Word has *proven* that all that you see and are has been given you according to your faith (see Matthew 9:27–30). And God has *provided* the heart-light to help you see Him through Christ (see 2 Corinthians 4:6). Lean on God all the way, allowing Him to help you stand. Claim this fourth *portrait* statement (based on 1 Thessalonians 3:8) as your very own and watch your faith stature rise!

In Christ, I am standing firm.

EVENING - *Standing Firm*

The Lord is good, a Strength and Stronghold in the day of trouble; He knows (recognizes, has knowledge of, and understands) those who take refuge and trust in Him.
NAHUM 1:7 AMPC

Lord, You are my Strength and my Stronghold. I need not fear, for You are the mightiest of fortresses. I hide in Your strength. And I trust You with everything I am, everything I have, and everything I hope to be. I stand firm in You.

DAY 73

MORNING - *A Holy Empowered Woman*

God is greater than our feelings, and he knows everything.
1 JOHN 3:20 NLT

Just as your soul awakens and begins its upward journey of a higher life in Christ, just when you begin to hunger and thirst for Jesus, to do right and to *be* right with God, a myriad of challenges wait to face you. The initial challenge is your feelings. When you base the truth of God and your commitment on what you feel—or don't feel— you are misdirected, thinking that perhaps you have not given yourself over to God at all. Don't be fooled. Because you're saved, you are a holy, empowered woman.

EVENING - *Ready to Learn*

*Lead me by your truth and teach me, for you are the
God who saves me. All day long I put my hope in you.*
PSALM 25:5 NLT

Lord, I want to be led by Your truth, not by my feelings. I am ready to learn. So teach me the way to get there from here. Help me to remember You are the God that saves me. I am putting my hope in You, every minute of this day. Override my feelings with a faith based on Your truths.

DAY 74

MORNING - *The Gotten Woman*

The life of every living creature and the
spirit in every human body are in his hands.
JOB 12:10 GW

Since your feelings belie the truth—that you've indeed committed heart, body, mind, and soul to God—you cannot believe that He has you in His hands. "As usual, we put feeling first and faith second, and fact last of all," wrote Hannah Whitall Smith. "Now, God's invariable rule in everything is, fact first, faith second, and feelings last of all." So go with the fact—or truth of the matter—that God indeed has got you!

EVENING - *In God's Order*

God made the two bright lights: the larger light to rule the day and the
smaller light to rule the night. He also made the stars. God put them
in the sky to give light to the earth, to dominate the day and the night,
and to separate the light from the darkness. God saw that it was good.
GENESIS 1:16–18 GW

God, You created all that is, has been, and will be. You've ordered it all. You created the sun to rule the day, the moon and stars to rule the night. You've separated the light from the darkness so I can find my way. And it's all good. So help me to keep the right order of things. Remind me that in all ways and through all days, I'm in Your capable hands. Help me to keep Your order right—fact first, faith second, and feelings last.

DAY 75

MORNING - *The Fact's-First Woman*

She came up in the crowd behind Him and touched His cloak.
For she thought, "If I just touch His garments, I will get well."
MARK 5:27–28 NASB

This rule of God—fact, faith, then feelings—is confirmed by the woman who had been hemorrhaging blood for twelve years. Instead of allowing feelings of discouragement and hopelessness to override the fact that Jesus was a worker of miracles, she resolutely and boldly sought Him out. Her facts about the situation were followed by her faith—and she reached out and touched Him! The result? Her blood dried up and she was immediately healed. What joy must have filled her heart!

EVENING - *Made Well by Faith*

"Daughter, your faith has made you well; go in peace."
MARK 5:34 NASB

Oh my Lord, the woman with an issue of blood, what a marvelous example of how Father God's order is fact first, faith second, and feelings last. What a woman of daring, to make her way through a crowd and reach out for Your healing power! And then to admit that she'd done so had to take even more courage! May I be so bold with such faith so that I, too, can receive from You, not only healing, but the experience of You seeing me and speaking the words, "Daughter, your faith has made you well; go in peace"!

DAY 76

MORNING - *A Willing Woman*

"Now, who is willing to consecrate themselves to the LORD today?"
1 CHRONICLES 29:5 NIV

The way to meet the challenge of consecration, to give yourself entirely to God, is to get in line with God's order of things—fact, faith, and only then feeling. Are you afraid to turn yourself over completely to God's will? Afraid of losing your personality? You need not be!

In C. S. Lewis's delightful book *The Screwtape Letters*, a senior devil writes to his minion: "When He [Jesus, their 'Enemy'] talks of their [believers] losing their selves, He means only abandoning the clamour of self-will; once they have done that, He really gives them back all their personality, and boasts (I am afraid, sincerely) that when they are wholly His they will be more themselves than ever!"

EVENING - *With the Re-Maker*

Give me your heart and let your eyes observe and delight in my ways.
PROVERBS 23:26 AMPC

I come to You now, Lord, unafraid of losing myself in You. So here is my heart, my self-will, my ego. I put all that I am and ever hoped to be into Your hands. My eyes are ready to observe the pleasure of living *Your* way. As You make me wholly Yours, I become more than ever who I truly am. How exciting! How wonderful are You, the Re-maker!

MORNING - *A Settled Woman*

The good, the wise, and all that they do are in God's hands.
ECCLESIASTES 9:1 MSG

Be courageous. Take the step. Turn yourself over to God. Then consider it a fact that you are His. He has accepted you—lock, stock, and barrel. Allow your faith to kick in. Know that you are in His hands, that He will work through You to do His will. As the days go by, don't give in to the idea that nothing has really changed after all just because you don't *feel* it. This kind of wrestling will go on and on unless you cut it short by faith. Smith wrote, "Come to the point of considering that matter an accomplished and settled thing, and leave it there before you can possibly expect any change of feeling whatever."

EVENING - *Living a God-Shaped Life*

*Doing whatever you feel like whenever you feel like it,
and grabbing whatever attracts your fancy. That's a life
shaped by things and feelings instead of by God.*
COLOSSIANS 3:5 MSG

Lord, I find it so easy to give in to my feelings. The next thing I know, I've distanced myself from You. Yet I long to be close to You in every way in every moment of the day. Help me to obey You, not give in to whatever mood overtakes me. Give me Your peace in this process, reminding me that I am a work in progress but headed in the right direction—to Your side.

DAY 78

MORNING - *A Holy Woman*

"Anything specially set apart for the LORD. . .must never be sold or bought back. Anything devoted in this way has been set apart as holy, and it belongs to the LORD."
LEVITICUS 27:28 NLT

Under Levitical law, everything given to God, because it had been given, became something holy, or consecrated, set apart. And although you are no longer under Levitical law, there is a parallel. Romans 12:1 implores believers as Christians "to give your bodies to God because of all he has done for you. Let them be a living and holy sacrifice—the kind he will find acceptable. This is truly the way to worship him" (NLT). So, having given yourself to Christ, whose one sacrifice perfected you, you are acceptable to God (see 1 Corinthians 1:30), you are holy—whether you feel like it or not!

EVENING - *Standing Firmly in Truth*

You are holy. . . . But you must continue to believe this truth and stand firmly in it. Don't drift away from the assurance you received when you heard the Good News.
COLOSSIANS 1:22–23 NLT

Dearest Jesus, I feel treasured that You have chosen me, set me apart to be holy. Increase my faith, Lord. Remind me every day that I am Your saint. Assure me with Your Gospel truths. Plant them in my heart so that I will not waver from the path You have chosen for me. Help me be the woman You have called me to be.

DAY 79

MORNING - *The Saintly Woman*

To the saints and faithful brethren in Christ which are at Colosse: Grace be unto you, and peace, from God our Father and the Lord Jesus Christ.
COLOSSIANS 1:2 KJV

Another challenge linked to your feelings is your behavior. Remember, your thoughts fuel your feelings, and your feelings orchestrate your actions. So if you don't feel consecrated to God, you will certainly not act like it. This will force you to try to *act* holy on the surface, trying in your own power to do all the things a saint should do: attend church on Sunday, read the Bible every day, pray unceasingly, love others, etc. In the process, you're wearing yourself out, doing things that at times you really don't feel like doing. Or worse yet, doing nothing at all and feeling guilty about it. Remember that in spite of what you *do*, you *are* still holy to God.

EVENING - *In the Light*

Be filled with the knowledge of His will in all wisdom and spiritual understanding. . .giving thanks to the Father who has qualified us to be partakers of the inheritance of the saints in the light.
COLOSSIANS 1:9, 12 NKJV

Although I sometimes misbehave, Lord, in Your eyes, I'm still a saint—pure, holy, unblemished—in Your light. Help me constantly remember I *am* holy—not because of what I've done but because of what Your Son has done for me.

DAY 80

MORNING - *The Elected Woman*

*You died, which means that your life is hidden with Christ,
who sits beside God. Christ gives meaning to your life,
and when he appears, you will also appear with him in glory.*
COLOSSIANS 3:3–4 CEV

Although the Colossians have been behaving badly, Paul still calls them "the elect of God, holy and beloved," and instructs them to "put on tender mercies, kindness, humility, meekness, longsuffering; bearing with one another, and forgiving one another" (Colossians 3:12–13 NKJV).

Because God has done it all and made you holy, His work is what is going to change your behavior. So why, if you are misbehaving, are you acting as if He hasn't done anything at all?

EVENING - *Set Apart by God*

*You were consecrated (set apart, hallowed), and you were
justified [pronounced righteous, by trusting] in the name of
the Lord Jesus Christ and in the [Holy] Spirit of our God.*
1 CORINTHIANS 6:11 AMPC

It's all about trust, isn't it, Lord? I must look to You as my source, as my haven, as my refuge and not allow my feelings, circumstances, or behavior to decrease my confidence in what You are doing in my life. I reaffirm the fact that I am Your holy servant and that You will give me the power to live as You did, to walk as You walked.

MORNING - *A Designing Woman*

*We always pray that God will show you everything he wants you to
do and that you may have all the wisdom and understanding that
his Spirit gives. Then you will live a life that honors the Lord. . . .
His glorious power will make you patient and strong enough
to endure anything, and you will be truly happy.*
COLOSSIANS 1:9–11 CEV

God's given you all you need to be everything He wants you to be. It is up
to you to use what He's given you to make you holy. Not using the power
and strength God has given you is like a woman who decides to redecorate
her living room. She buys new furniture, repaints, and recarpets. When all is
arranged, she stands back, sighs, and smiles. Yet she refuses to sit in the room
and enjoy it because, "It's just for show. I don't want to wear it out." Yet that's
what the room is designed for—to occupy, sit down in, relax in, and enjoy!

EVENING - *A New Person*

*Each of you is now a new person. You are becoming more and
more like your Creator, and you will understand him better.*
COLOSSIANS 3:10 CEV

God, help me to understand You've made me a new woman in Christ! I'm
designed to be what You want me to be! And through the power of the Holy
Spirit, I have the same power and strength as Christ, to be that new woman.

DAY 82

MORNING - *The Believing Woman*

Now faith is the substance of things hoped for, the evidence of things not seen.
HEBREWS 11:1 KJV

⁂

Being a saint, being *consecrated*, isn't based on your feelings or behavior. It's based on the power God has given you as you have fully committed yourself to Him. He will work through you, to help you walk as Christ did, if you just believe. For that you need faith and prayer. To make your prayers more effective, you need to believe God is real—even though He is not visible to your human eyes. You must believe the fact that His presence is a certain thing and that He sees everything you do and hears everything you say. This takes the faith described in Hebrews 11:1.

EVENING - *Given an Amazing, Mighty Power*

I also pray that you will understand the incredible greatness of God's power for us who believe him. This is the same mighty power that raised Christ from the dead and seated him in the place of honor at God's right hand in the heavenly realms.
EPHESIANS 1:19–20 NLT

⁂

I want to understand the power that You have given us who believe in You. It's an amazing and mighty power, one that I have trouble comprehending. Help me understand what You have made available to me. Help me use that power to keep myself apart from the world. I want to be with You—my heaven here on earth.

DAY 83

MORNING - *The Committed Woman*

*Let your kingdom come. Let your will
be done on earth as it is done in heaven.*
MATTHEW 6:10 GW

If you are not sure you've committed yourself wholeheartedly to God, do so now. Imagine God beside you. Pray, "Dear Lord, in this moment, and for all the moments to come, I turn myself—mind, body, heart, and soul—over to You. May Your will be done in my life." Hannah Whitall Smith wrote, "Your emotions may clamor against the surrender, but your will must hold firm. It is your purpose God looks at, not your feelings about that purpose."

EVENING - *Flooded with Light*

*I pray that your hearts will be flooded with light so that you can
understand the confident hope he has given to those he called—
his holy people who are his rich and glorious inheritance.*
EPHESIANS 1:18 NLT

Flood my heart with Your light, Jesus. Help me tap into Your power. Lead me to understand and be confident in the hope You have given me. As a daughter of the King, I am rich in everything. And I thank You for allowing me to be a part of God's family, for calling me into Your kingdom—all to Your glory!

DAY 84

MORNING · *The Word-Wise Woman*

*"The words that come out of my mouth [will] not come back
empty-handed. They'll do the work I sent them to do,
they'll complete the assignment I gave them."*
ISAIAH 55:11 MSG

You are now in God's hands, ready to receive and *use* the power and strength to do what He wills you to do, to be who He wants you to be. If you begin to doubt your surrender, your wavering faith will cause both you and your experience to be wave-and-wind tossed. So take the remedy of repeating over and over the prayer below. Through the power and guidance of the Holy Spirit, may this be your moment-by-moment prayer as a daughter of God. Make it a continual practice to abide in Christ. Consider it a fact that, according to God's Word, you are a saint indeed, holy and pleasing in His sight.

EVENING · *Wholly Joy-Filled*

"So you'll go out in joy, you'll be led into a whole and complete life."
ISAIAH 55:12 MSG

Lord, I am Your daughter—heart, mind, body, and soul. I give myself entirely to You. I believe You have accepted me, and I put myself entirely in Your hands. Work through me to be the complete and whole joy-filled woman You have called me to be. I trust You now and forevermore.

MORNING - *The Joy-Filled Woman's Path Marker: Promise No. 5*

"Nothing that a man irrevocably devotes to GOD from what belongs to him. . .may be either sold or bought back. Everything devoted is holy to the highest degree; it's GOD's inalienable property."
LEVITICUS 27:28 MSG

God has promised, now that you have committed and dedicated yourself to Him, you will always be His—for keeps (see Leviticus 27:28)! That's something that can never be taken away from You. And no one can ever take you out of God's hand! That's a promise you can count on! Claim it and your confidence will soar—right up to God!

EVENING - *Exclusively God's*

The grace (blessing and favor) of the Lord Jesus Christ (the Messiah) be with all the saints (God's holy people, those set apart for God, to be, as it were, exclusively His). Amen (so let it be)!
REVELATION 22:21 AMPC

I am exclusively Yours, Lord. Not just today but every moment of every day to come. No one and nothing can separate me from You. You have blessed my life, and I am sincerely thankful. Because of Your light, my future is bright. That's a big AMEN!

MORNING · *The Joy-Filled Woman's Path Marker: Proof No. 5*

The Holy Spirit said, Separate now for Me Barnabas and Saul for the work to which I have called them. . . . So then, being sent out by the Holy Spirit, they went down to Seleucia, and from [that port] they sailed away to Cyprus. . . . And when the congregation of the synagogue dispersed, many of the Jews and the devout converts to Judaism followed Paul and Barnabas, who talked to them and urged them to continue [to trust themselves to and to stand fast] in the grace (the unmerited favor and blessing) of God.

ACTS 13:2, 4, 43 AMPC

Not only has God set you apart for a particular purpose, He has given you the power of the Holy Spirit and His grace to live it out! Walk in that proof and begin living your purpose in the confidence of Christ!

EVENING · *Set Apart in Christ*

"And now I entrust you to God and the message of his grace that is able to build you up and give you an inheritance with all those he has set apart for himself."

ACTS 20:32 NLT

If it weren't for Your grace, Lord, I would be in the dark, giving in to every feeling, being discouraged by my own behavior and that of others who call themselves Your followers. But because of Your grace, You see me and others as Your special people. Now, Lord, send me to where You would have me go!

DAY 87

MORNING - *The Joy-Filled Woman's Path Marker: Provision No. 5*

[God] has reconciled you to himself through the death of Christ in his physical body. As a result, he has brought you into his own presence, and you are holy and blameless as you stand before him without a single fault.
COLOSSIANS 1:22 NLT

Jesus has provided your reconciliation with God through His death on the cross. Thus, you are now holy and blameless in God's sight! Believe in this and walk hand in hand with Christ, in His presence from morning till night!

EVENING - *Back in Harmony with God*

All the broken and dislocated pieces of the universe—people and things, animals and atoms—get properly fixed and fit together in vibrant harmonies, all because of his death, his blood that poured down from the cross.
COLOSSIANS 1:20 MSG

Jesus, I can't begin to repay You for what You have done for me. You have put me—and all of creation—back in harmony with God. Living in You, I can walk in the Garden of Eden once again. So I thank You, Lord, for making me whole once more. Your love is overwhelming!

MORNING - *The Joy-Filled Woman's Path Marker: Portrait No. 5*

Blessed be the God and Father of our Lord Jesus Christ, who has blessed us with every spiritual blessing in the heavenly places in Christ, just as He chose us in Him before the foundation of the world, that we would be holy and blameless before Him.

EPHESIANS 1:3–4 NASB

You have been *promised* that having committed yourself to God, you are His holy possession (see Leviticus 27:28). The Word gives you *proof* that the Holy Spirit has set apart and energized believers like you for God's work (see Acts 13:2, 4, 43), and your holiness has been *provided* for you by Christ (see Colossians 1:22). What a life for a believing, joy-filled woman! Now claim this fifth *portrait* statement (based on Ephesians 1:4) as your very own! In Christ, I am holy, pure in God's sight, and empowered by the Holy Spirit.

EVENING - *Pure and Empowered*

I am filled with power—with the Spirit of the LORD—and with justice and courage.

MICAH 3:8 NASB

Thank You, Jesus, for bringing me back into the good graces of God. Without You, I would still be lost, in hiding, unable to get close to God. Help me to live out the idea that I am pure and holy in His sight. And remind me that I can have courage and do what You have called me to do through the power and might of the Holy Spirit, my Helper, Counselor, and Friend!

DAY 89

MORNING - *A Woman Living by Faith, Not Sight*

Some trust in and boast of chariots and some of horses,
but we will trust in and boast of the name of the Lord our God.

PSALM 20:7 AMPC

❧

In your first baby steps in this Christian life, you may have imagined that faith would be something you could feel, such as a heart overwhelmed with belief in God when you've received an answer to prayer or an unexpected blessing. You might say to yourself, *Now that is faith that I feel deep within.* Or you might have just had surface faith—the faith you think you can use to purchase God's blessings: *I have faith, so I will get what I want.*

Yet most times, faith is something that keeps you looking to the Lord during times of trial, knowing you can trust the One who knows so much better than you do. Faith is what you rely on when your pre-Christian friends jeer at your naiveté.

EVENING - *Surrounded by Love*

The LORD's unfailing love surrounds the one who trusts in him.

PSALM 32:10 NIV

❧

I don't want to look at anything other than You, Lord, when things get rough. Because You are the only one I can really trust. And You have so much more wisdom than any human being. So help me to rely on You, and only You, in all things. Then surround me with Your awesome love.

DAY 90

MORNING - *A Believing Woman*

"Don't let your hearts be troubled. Trust in God, and trust also in me."
JOHN 14:1 NLT

Faith is nothing you can see, touch, taste, hear, or smell. Hannah Whitall Smith wrote:

> *[Faith] is simply believing God. You see something and thus know that you have sight; you believe something and thus know that you have faith. For as sight is only seeing, so faith is only believing. If you believe the truth, you are saved; if you believe a lie, you are lost. Your salvation comes, not because your faith saves you, but because it links you to the Savior who saves.*

EVENING - *By Faith Obeying*

And though you have not seen Him, you love Him,
and though you do not see Him now, but believe in Him,
you greatly rejoice with joy inexpressible and full of glory.
1 PETER 1:8 NASB

Lord, I long to be like Abraham, who "by faith. . .obeyed when God called him" and "went without knowing where he was going" (Hebrews 11:8 NLT). Although I have never seen You in Your physical form, I love You and believe in You with all my heart, mind, body, and soul. Lead me on to the place You have for me. I trust You with my life—today, tomorrow, and forever.

DAY 91

MORNING - *An Eyes-of-Faith Woman*

Jesus was in the stern, sleeping on a cushion. The disciples woke him and said to him, "Teacher, don't you care if we drown?" He got up, rebuked the wind and said to the waves, "Quiet! Be still!" Then the wind died down and it was completely calm.

MARK 4:38–39 NIV

Do you think Jesus is sleeping just when you need Him the most? Do you think He is not watching you, that He will not keep you from perishing, that you cannot awaken Him with your prayers? Does your faith disappear the moment you are in danger and panic sets in?

As Kay Arthur wrote in *Beloved*, "You must see with the eyes of faith, beyond the moments, beyond the situation, to your God."

EVENING - *Knowing Christ*

He said to his disciples, "Why are you so afraid? Do you still have no faith?" They were terrified and asked each other, "Who is this? Even the wind and the waves obey him!"

MARK 4:40–41 NIV

Jesus, help me grow my faith. I want the kind of faith where I simply believe You when You say You have done or will do something and then trust You to totally come through for me. For then I will not be afraid. And I will know You are the Christ, the one whom even the wind and waves obey!

MORNING - *A Seeking Woman*

*Woe to those who go down to Egypt for help, who rely on horses, who trust in
the multitude of their chariots and in the great strength of their horsemen,
but do not look to the Holy One of Israel, or seek help from the LORD.*

ISAIAH 31:1 NIV

It's amazing how much people trust their fellow humans and how little they
trust God. When you fly in planes, you trust the pilot to deliver you safely
to your destination. When you pull out of the driveway, you have faith that
other drivers will stay on the right side of the road and obey all the traffic
laws. So how can you have faith in these strangers who are only human yet
not have faith in God—the One who has power over all creation? Seek to
trust God above all else!

EVENING - *Looking to the Master of Everything*

*He caused the storm to be still,
so that the waves of the sea were hushed.*

PSALM 107:29 NASB

You, God, have the power over all creation. Impress that idea on my mind.
Write it on my heart. For I want to look to no one other than You for all
things. For there is no wind You cannot still. No wave You cannot hush. No
thing You cannot do. You are the Master of everything!

DAY 93

MORNING · *A Believing-without-Seeing Woman*

Jesus said to him, because you have seen Me,
Thomas, do you now believe (trust, have faith)?
JOHN 20:29 AMPC

Can you imagine not going to London to see the Queen because, having never seen the former nor met the latter, you don't believe they exist? Can you imagine not believing that messages you received on your voice mail were actually sent by the person who claims to have sent them?

How can you have faith that other places on this planet exist without your ever having seen them or that the disembodied voice you hear is actually that of the person who left the message on your phone (without even seeing him or her!) yet not have faith that God actually exists? Do *you* believe He is real without seeing Him? Do you have a believing-without-seeing faith in God?

EVENING · *Blessed and Happy*

Blessed and happy and to be envied are those who have never seen
Me and yet have believed and adhered to and trusted and relied on Me.
JOHN 20:29 AMPC

Lord, I am not a doubting Thomasina! Never having even seen You, I *do* believe You are real. I trust and rely on You! And because I do, I am happy to say I feel so blessed, and am being continually led to a higher life in You! What joy in believing!

MORNING - *A Thought-Filled Woman*

For as he thinks within himself, so he is.
PROVERBS 23:7 NASB

This Savior of yours is the One who stilled the wind and the waves, who brought dead people back to life, who changed water into wine, and who healed the blind, deaf, and dumb. He is the One who God raised from the dead—just to save you! So why do you let your thoughts lead you astray the moment you are in peril? It is a fact that your thoughts are very powerful. What you believe within will appear without.

EVENING - *Back in Focus*

Things that are seen don't last forever, but things that are not seen are eternal. That's why we keep our minds on the things that cannot be seen.
2 CORINTHIANS 4:18 CEV

My negative, doubting thoughts are whirling up within me, Jesus. I'm focusing on what I can feel—the wind. My eyes are on what I can see—the waves. And I feel I am sinking. Lift me up, Lord. Help me keep my mind and eyes on You and You alone. By faith, I know I will rise ever closer to what You have in store for me—all that is good, all that is love, all that is You.

DAY 95

MORNING - *A Visible Woman*

Now faith is the assurance (the confirmation, the title deed) of the things [we] hope for, being the proof of things [we] do not see and the conviction of their reality [faith perceiving as real fact what is not revealed to the senses].
HEBREWS 11:1 AMPC

Because your thoughts lead you off course, you must continually look to God's Word, write it upon your hearts, and believe that He will do as He has promised. You must imprint the words of Hebrews 11:1 upon your mind: "Now faith is the substance of things hoped for, the evidence of things not seen" (KJV). Memorize this verse—in a Bible version that speaks directly to your heart—so that it will be there for you when your thoughts lead you astray. So that you believe regardless of what your senses, your mind—or the world—is telling you.

EVENING - *Trusting in the Invisible Creator*

By faith, we see the world called into existence by God's word, what we see created by what we don't see.
HEBREWS 11:3 MSG

Lord, You are the Master Creator, the only one that can make something out of nothing. So instead of trusting my physical senses—or those of others—I'm putting all of my faith in and thoughts on You *and* Your Words!

DAY 96

MORNING - *A Discerning Woman*

*Our gospel did not come to you in word only, but also
in power and in the Holy Spirit and with full conviction*

<small>1 THESSALONIANS 1:5 NASB</small>

Perhaps you think you lack faith because you don't feel the working of the Holy Spirit in your life. In believing this you have, in effect, not only made God out to be a liar and called false the "record that God gave of his Son" (1 John 5:10 KJV), but also lost any confidence in the Holy Spirit. In this regard, the fault lies in your lack of faith in God and His Word, *not* in the power of the Holy Spirit. Boost up your faith and realize the joy of believing in the Spirit's power, whether you feel it or not!

EVENING - *Abounding in Hope*

*Now the God of hope fill you with all joy and peace in believing,
that ye may abound in hope, through the power of the Holy Ghost.*

<small>ROMANS 15:13 KJV</small>

When I trust in You and Your Word, God, I am filled with joy and peace. Your message fills me with hope for today and tomorrow and gives me confidence in the Holy Spirit! Empowered by that Spirit, I rise up over the temporal, seeking the good things You have in store for me, the things above this earthly world. Because I seek You first in all things, because my eyes are on You, I will triumph!

DAY 97

MORNING · *A Sometimes-Faltering Woman*

They were broken off for their unbelief, but you stand by your faith.
ROMANS 11:20 NASB

Put your thoughts, then, over onto the side of faith. Say to yourself, *Lord, I will believe; I do believe.* Do so over and over again until it's a part of your very being. Replace every suggestion of doubt—from within yourself or out of the mouths of others—with a statement of faith until, whether facing triumph or trial, you stand firm in your faith, unbending.

EVENING · *Standing Firm in Faith*

The father cried, "Then I believe. Help me with my doubts!"
MARK 9:24 MSG

Lord, there are so many times my mind just goes crazy with thoughts that do not serve either me or You. And as soon as those doubts come in, I can feel myself—and my faith—beginning to falter. Help me to stand firm, Lord. *I will believe—I do believe! I will believe—I do believe.* That's my new mantra. My go-to statement when things get shaky. No matter what others say or my mind suggests, I will chase all doubts with that statement of faith! *I believe!*

DAY 98

MORNING - *A Trusting Woman*

God made great and marvelous promises, so that his nature would become part of us. Then we could escape our evil desires and the corrupt influences of this world.
2 PETER 1:4 CEV

Hannah Whitall Smith wrote:

> *Out of your very unbelief, throw yourself unreservedly on the Word and promises of God, and dare to abandon yourself to the keeping and the saving power of the Lord Jesus. If you have ever trusted a precious interest in the hands of an earthly friend, I entreat you, trust yourself and all your spiritual interest now in the hands of your heavenly Friend, and never, never, never allow yourself to doubt again.*

EVENING - *Believing in God's Promises*

It was by faith that even Sarah was able to have a child, though she was barren and was too old. She believed that God would keep his promise.
HEBREWS 11:11 NLT

What a miracle—that an old woman could give birth! But those who believe in You, Lord, should expect nothing less! You can do the impossible! And You always keep Your promises. I know You are working miracles in my life—right now! I trust You to work everything out for the good. Humbled that You would love me so much, I thank You, God, for being in my life.

DAY 99

MORNING - *A Persevering Woman*

They had hardly arrived when a Canaanite woman came down from the hills and pleaded, "Mercy, Master, Son of David! My daughter is cruelly afflicted by an evil spirit." Jesus ignored her. The disciples came and complained, "Now she's bothering us. Would you please take care of her? She's driving us crazy." Jesus refused, telling them, "I've got my hands full dealing with the lost sheep of Israel." Then the woman came back to Jesus, went to her knees, and begged. "Master, help me."
MATTHEW 15:22–25 MSG

Make it your aim to be as persevering in your faith, as strong in your belief, as the Canaanite woman who encountered Jesus. What joy, what blessings such perseverance will bring into your life!

EVENING - *Dog Jesus' Steps*

He said, "It's not right to take bread out of children's mouths and throw it to dogs." She was quick: "You're right, Master, but beggar dogs do get scraps from the master's table."
MATTHEW 15:26–27 MSG

I want to be as persevering in my faith as the woman who kept following after You, shouting out her requests. Even when You kept silent, ignoring her. She continued pleading, following after You, even got down on her knees! Here I am, Lord, on *my* knees. Help me have that kind of faith!

DAY 100

MORNING - *A Knowing Woman*

Jesus gave in. "Oh, woman, your faith is something else. What you want is what you get!" Right then her daughter became well.
MATTHEW 15:28 MSG

May Jesus and others around you be as amazed with your faith as He was with this woman's! Isn't it amazing that the moment she exhibited her absolute and persistent faith, her daughter was healed? Replace your doubting with knowing. Be as this woman—substituting fretting and fearing with firm faith. Don't give up—until Jesus gives in!

EVENING - *Persistent in Prayer*

[Jesus] told them a parable to the effect that they ought always to pray and not to turn coward (faint, lose heart, and give up).
LUKE 18:1 AMP

Jesus, You not only told a parable about how I should never give up in prayer. You gave us a living example of what it means to have great faith. May I be so steadfast in prayer and so determined to speak into Your ear that I, too, develop such an awesome faith! Help me in that endeavor, Lord. Give me the courage and persistence to replace my fretting with faith!

MORNING - *A Woman of Active Faith*

Jesus spoke to them: "Good morning! Did you catch anything for breakfast?" They answered, "No." He said, "Throw the net off the right side of the boat and see what happens." They did what he said. All of a sudden there were so many fish in it, they weren't strong enough to pull it in.
JOHN 21:5–6 MSG

Hannah Whitall Smith wrote:

> It is a law of spiritual life that every act of trust makes the next act less difficult, until at length, if these acts are persisted in, trusting becomes, like breathing, the natural unconscious action of the redeemed soul. Therefore put your will into your believing. Your faith must not be a passive imbecility but an active energy. You may have to believe against every appearance, but no matter.

EVENING - *Directed to Abundance*

Now unto him that is able to do exceeding abundantly above all that we ask or think, according to the power that worketh in us.
EPHESIANS 3:20 KJV

Lord, I feel like I have been fishing forever yet haven't caught anything because I've been trying to do it in my own power and wisdom. So as Your disciples did, I turn to You, believing You will direct me to the right spot. I know when I trust in You, my net will wind up so full of fish that I will not be able to pull it into shore. What a miracle of faith!

DAY 102

MORNING - *A Totally Trusting Woman*

We don't yet see things clearly. We're squinting in a fog, peering through a mist. But it won't be long before the weather clears and the sun shines bright!
1 CORINTHIANS 13:12 MSG

When panic knocks on your door, answer it with unswerving trust in the Lord. Speak to it with God's words of faith. Reach for His calm, for His peace. Don't allow fear and the panicked thumping of your heart to drown out the words God is speaking into your life. Banish discouragement—lack of courage—for it is a major impediment to your union with God.

EVENING - *Resting in the Comfort of God's Arms*

We'll see it all then, see it all as clearly as God sees us, knowing him directly just as he knows us!
1 CORINTHIANS 13:12 MSG

Lord, I can't see the forest for the trees. My mind is tempted to focus on a myriad of what-ifs. I can't imagine how You will straighten out this mess. But I refuse to worry. Instead, I will trust in You. I will not fret but stand firm in faith, no matter how circumstances seem. I refuse to go by feelings. Instead, I will rest in the strength of Your wisdom and the comfort of Your loving arms.

DAY 103

MORNING - *A Calm Woman*

You, LORD, are my shepherd. I will never be in need.
You let me rest in fields of green grass. You lead me
to streams of peaceful water, and you refresh my life.
PSALM 23:1–3 CEV

Nothing can discourage or panic you—unless you let it. So calm your racing heart. Get rid of that troubled frown. Stop your frenzied activity. Take a few deep breaths. Look into God's Word. Allow it to penetrate your spirit, soul, and mind. Write it upon your heart. As you build up your faith, peace will pervade.

EVENING - *In Perfect Peace*

You will keep in perfect peace all who trust in you,
all whose thoughts are fixed on you!
ISAIAH 26:3 NLT

This verse is one I'm going to memorize, Lord. Then whenever I feel caught in the storm, whenever fear and doubt start to rock my boat, I can call on these words to calm the sea. I don't want to live in turmoil. That is not of You. You are my peace and love—my still water. As I fix my thoughts on You, I am filled with calm confidence—and I am saved by Your Word.

DAY 104

MORNING - *A Woman Growing in Belief*

The apostles said to the Lord, increase our faith (that trust and confidence that spring from our belief in God).
LUKE 17:5 AMPC

⁓

Augustine said, "Faith is to believe what you do not yet see; the reward for this faith is to see what you believe." So, build up your faith. Begin with as much faith as the mustard seed. Determinedly repeat to yourself, "I believe and trust in my Lord and His power." If you are patient and persistent in this, your worries will fade, your fears will wane, your faith will blossom, and you will share in the Lord's joy to the glory of God, who will say to you, "O woman, great is thy faith" (Matthew 15:28 KJV).

EVENING - *Blossoms in Faith*

And the Lord answered, If you had faith (trust and confidence in God) even [so small] like a grain of mustard seed, you could say to this mulberry tree, be pulled up by the roots, and be planted in the sea, and it would obey you.
LUKE 17:6 AMPC

⁓

I believe and trust in You, Lord, and Your power. Persistent and patient with myself, I watch my faith grow. And in this new space, my worries begin to fade, my fears to diminish. My faith is blooming, allowing me to rejoice as You turn to me and say, "O woman, great is thy faith"!

DAY 105

MORNING - *The Joy-Filled Woman's Path Marker: Promise No. 6*

I assure you, most solemnly I tell you, if anyone steadfastly believes in Me, he will himself be able to do the things that I do; and he will do even greater things than these, because I go to the Father.
JOHN 14:12 AMPC

If you have faith in Jesus, the kind that never doubts, you will be able to do even more amazing things than He did—to God's glory! Just continue to trust in God, never wavering, and you will begin, day by day, to even amaze yourself! That's a promise you can count on!

EVENING - *Aware and Able*

Be alert and on your guard; stand firm in your faith (your conviction respecting man's relationship to God and divine things, keeping the trust and holy fervor born of faith and a part of it). . . . Be courageous; grow in strength!
1 CORINTHIANS 16:13 AMPC

Help me be aware of my thoughts, Lord, as well as what I'm saying to myself and others. I want to be alert for words of doubt so that I can replace them with statements of belief in You. I refuse to waver in worry or falter in fear. For I want to have the promised power and strength of saving faith—to Your glory and my joy!

DAY 106

MORNING - *The Joy-Filled Woman's Path Marker: Proof No. 6*

In Lystra there was a man who had been born with crippled feet and had never been able to walk. The man was listening to Paul speak, when Paul saw that he had faith in Jesus and could be healed. So he looked straight at the man and shouted, "Stand up!" The man jumped up and started walking around.
ACTS 14:8–10 CEV

The Word proves the promise that if you live by faith in God, rather than what you see in the world, you will have not only joy but the power to move mountains! Claim that proof, and like the apostle Paul, you will be able to bring God's light and healing into the world.

EVENING - *Moving Mountains*

And the prayer [that is] of faith will save him who is sick, and the Lord will restore him; and if he has committed sins, he will be forgiven.
JAMES 5:15 AMPC

It is amazing to me, Lord, how my faith in You can move mountains. But even more amazing (and perhaps useful) is the fact that our faith-filled prayers can restore those who are sick of body and soul. Build up my faith, Jesus, so I can be that kind of pray-er, one who puts not just her mind to it, but her heart, soul, spirit, and strength as well.

DAY 107

MORNING - *The Joy-Filled Woman's Path Marker: Provision No. 6*

The apostles said to the Lord, "Increase our faith!" And the Lord said,
"If you had faith like a mustard seed, you would say to this mulberry tree,
'Be uprooted and be planted in the sea'; and it would obey you."
LUKE 17:5–6 NASB

Jesus has shown you the way, provided all you need to live a life of never-ending possibilities. There is no limit to what you can do when you have a deep, unshakable faith in the Son of God who continues to change the world by believers like you. Take joy in that fact!

EVENING - *Doing the Impossible*

"Nothing will be impossible to you."
MATTHEW 17:20 NASB

Increase my faith, Lord! Help me to let go of my fears, panic, and negative thoughts. Replace them with faith, calm, and Your Word. Help me not to be discouraged but encouraged that You will help me, build up my belief, and speak to me. Show me the Bible verses that would most benefit me in the endeavor. Lead me, love me. Remind me every day that with You in my life, the impossible is more than possible.

DAY 108

MORNING - *The Joy-Filled Woman's Path Marker: Portrait No. 6*

That's why we live with such good cheer. You won't see us drooping our heads or dragging our feet! Cramped conditions here don't get us down. They only remind us of the spacious living conditions ahead. It's what we trust in but don't yet see that keeps us going.
2 Corinthians 5:6–7 MSG

Jesus has not only *promised* that with faith, you can do anything (see John 14:12). He's presented the *proof* that His disciples did just that (see Acts 14:8–10). And He has *provided* the power—simply by saying if you have faith as small as a mustard seed, you cannot just uproot a tree but replant it in the turbulent, wave-crashing sea (see Luke 17:5–6). It's all up to you now to make this sixth *portrait* statement (based on 2 Corinthians 5:7) part of who you are!

In Christ, I live by faith, not sight.

EVENING - *Unstoppable Faith*

Do you suppose a few ruts in the road or rocks in the path are going to stop us?
2 Corinthians 5:8 MSG

Lord, I am filled with energy and faith. I have an active belief in You. My faith makes me unstoppable. I am ready to move mountains, uproot trees—and then plant them deep in the sea. With You in my life, there is nothing but joy. For I no longer live by what the world shows me, but by what You are doing in the unseen realm.

DAY 109

MORNING - *A Woman Accessing God's Will*

You are partners with Christ Jesus because of God. Jesus has become our
wisdom sent from God, our approval, our holiness, and our ransom from sin.
1 CORINTHIANS 1:30 GW

Once you've stepped out in faith, trusting God as you live hidden in Christ and beginning to perceive the blessings of such a union, another challenge meets you. Although you've tasted Christ's peace and rest, both may begin to wane as you wonder if you're truly walking in God's will.

If you think you're not walking in God's will, you begin to perceive yourself as a hypocrite, merely acting the role of God's chosen child, with only a surface faith. You begin to think you have not dug deep enough, you're not wholly God's—thus, you're not holy; you're nothing more than a pretender. At this point, you've once again begun to rely upon your emotions instead of the truth of God. It's time once again to get back to God's truth, to facts not feelings.

EVENING - *Into Truth*

You have died, and your life is hidden with Christ in God.
COLOSSIANS 3:3 GW

Lord, here I go again. I seem to be relying on my emotions instead of Your wisdom and truth. Impress upon my heart the fact that, in spite of what my feelings say, I *am* holy—because of Jesus! Help me not to shy away from that truth but live it—in Your power!

DAY 110

MORNING - *A Hidden Woman*

Keep your eyes on Jesus, who both began and finished this race we're in.
HEBREWS 12:2 MSG

❧

If you consider your life hidden in Christ is lived in the things you feel, all your attention is focused on your emotions rather than where it belongs—on Christ.

Your emotions are as volatile as the stock market. When you are riding high, your faith life seems real. But when you are at your lowest point, you feel you may not have surrendered yourself to God's will at all. At this juncture, you must fall back upon the truth that the life in Christ is not lived in the emotions but in the will.

EVENING - *Standing Firm*

For we have no might to stand against this great company that is coming against us. We do not know what to do, but our eyes are upon You.
2 CHRONICLES 20:12 AMPC

❧

Sometimes, Lord, I feel as if my emotions are this huge army coming against me. And I don't know what to do to fight them off. But I don't have to know, do I? All I need to do is come to You, seek Your face, and focus on You. You are my continual Savior!

DAY 111

MORNING · *A Recentered Woman*

Guard your heart above all else,
for it determines the course of your life.
PROVERBS 4:23 NLT

❧

If you keep your will consistently abiding in its center—which is God's will, the true reality—your emotional ups and downs will not disturb you. But how do you get there from here? First, you must realize that when you are not walking in God's will, there is dissonance. For only when your will is tied to His, and His will obeyed, will harmony reign within you. That is when the Holy Spirit truly begins to gently guide you into right living.

EVENING · *Getting a Heart Check*

God, see what is in my heart. Know what is there. Test me.
Know what I'm thinking. See if there's anything in my life
you don't like. Help me live in the way that is always right.
PSALM 139:23–24 NIrV

❧

Abba, my spirit seems in dissonance with Yours. I'm feeling stress and anxiety in my heart, which makes me think I'm listening to the enemy's lies. But that's not what You want for me, so please, Father God, give me a heart check this evening. Make me aware of anything I am doing that is not of Your will. Bring me back in line with You. I long for the peace of living in Your will.

DAY 112

MORNING - *A Woman under the Influence*

As he thinks within himself, so he is.
PROVERBS 23:7 NASB

❧

Although your emotions belong to you and are tolerated and enjoyed by you, they are not your true self. They are not who you actually are. Thus, if your God is to take hold of you, it must be into this central will or personality that He enters in. Then if He is reigning within that central will by the power of His Spirit, all the rest of that personality must come under His influence. And as the will is, so is the woman.

EVENING - *Leaving No Room for Doubt!*

[We] refute arguments and theories and reasonings and every proud and lofty thing that sets itself up against the [true] knowledge of God; and we lead every thought and purpose away captive into the obedience of Christ (the Messiah, the Anointed One).
2 CORINTHIANS 10:5 AMPC

❧

Father God, everybody is talking at me. But I don't hear a word they're saying; I hear only Your voice of wisdom. I am filling my heart and mind with Your wonderfully wise Word—so there's no room for doubt or confusion, panic or fear. I bring every thought to Christ, knowing He will replace it with Your truths. In Him I have freedom to be what You would have me be!

DAY 113

MORNING - *A Shifting Woman*

God's way of putting people right shows up in the acts of faith, confirming what Scripture has said all along: "The person in right standing before God by trusting him really lives."
ROMANS 1:17 MSG

The first step to keeping your will consistently abiding in God's will—the true reality—so that your emotional ups and downs will not disturb you, is to realize that when you're not walking in God's will there's dissonance. The second step is to shift your will to the believing side. For when you choose to *believe*, you need not worry about how you *feel*. Your emotions will eventually be compelled to come into the harmony of the real you, the woman hidden in Christ, in the secret place of the Father!

EVENING - *Realigned*

In Christ we were chosen to be God's people, because from the very beginning God had decided this in keeping with his plan. And he is the One who makes everything agree with what he decides and wants.
EPHESIANS 1:11 NCV

I may not understand all You are doing, Lord, or why, but I rest secure in the knowledge that You have a plan for all of us. I am in harmony with You, Lord, ready and willing to do what You would have me do. Your wisdom trumps my erratic emotions, God. So I am realigning myself with Your will and Your wonderful ways!

DAY 114

MORNING - *A Delighted Woman*

*Then I said, "I have come! (It is written about me in the scroll of the book.)
I am happy to do your will, O my God." Your teachings are deep within me.*
PSALM 40:7–8 GW

At times, you find great difficulty in controlling your emotions, a well-known fact to the majority of females. But you *can* control your will. So you may say firmly and continually, "I give my will to God. I give my will to God. I give my will to God." For deep inside, you know He *always* knows best.

EVENING - *Putting Her Will in God's Hands*

*If any of you is deficient in wisdom, let him ask of the giving God
[Who gives] to everyone liberally and ungrudgingly, without
reproaching or faultfinding, and it will be given him.*
JAMES 1:5 AMPC

Lord, I come seeking You first—today and every day. Show me what You want me to do. Reveal Your Word to me. Whisper in my ear the way You want me to walk. My will is in Your hands. Do with it what You will. I remain Your instrument here on earth, longing for the day when I will see You face-to-face!

DAY 115

MORNING - *A Delivered Woman*

"Do I bring a mother to the moment of birth
and not let her deliver?" asks the LORD.
ISAIAH 66:9 GW

Hannah Whitall Smith provides a wonderful analogy in regard to the will, likening it to a wise mother in a nursery:

> *The feelings are like a set of clamoring, crying children. The mother, knowing that she is the authority figure, pursues her course lovingly and calmly in spite of all their clamors. The result is that the children are sooner or later won over to the mother's course of action and fall in with her decisions, and all is harmonious and happy. But if that mother should for a moment let in the thought that the children were the masters instead of herself, confusion would reign unchecked.*

Pray that God would help you make your will the loving, yet authoritative mother over your clamoring, childlike feelings.

EVENING - *Comforted by and in Harmony with God*

As a mother comforts her child, so will I comfort you.
ISAIAH 66:13 GW

Lord, I know You always know best. So regardless of what my clamoring, childlike emotions are telling me, I'm making my will the loving, yet authoritative mother over them. You are the God of all comfort. You are the God of all wisdom. Help me take charge of my life and my emotions. Make me the woman You designed me to be since the beginning of time.

DAY 116

MORNING - *A Once-Confused Woman*

*But this is the man to whom I will look and have regard:
he who is humble and of a broken or wounded spirit,
and who trembles at My word and reveres My commands.*

Isaiah 66:2 AMPC

Regarding will over emotions, Hannah Whitall Smith wrote:
> *In how many souls at this very moment is there nothing but confusion,
> simply because the feelings are allowed to govern instead of the will?*
>
> *The real thing in your experience is what your will decides, not
> your emotions. You are far more in danger of hypocrisy and untruth
> in yielding to the assertions of your feelings than in holding fast to the
> decision of your will.*

Be aware of who is ruling your nursery—your mother-like will or childlike emotions.

EVENING - *Reigned by Peace*

God is not the author of confusion, but of peace.

1 Corinthians 14:33 KJV

My soul is no longer full of confusion, Lord, because I am allowing my will—which is under *Your* will—to reign over my emotions. Help me to stay strong in that decision. For I no longer want to be swayed by the untruths of my feelings. I put all this into Your hands. For You are not the author of confusion, but the writer of peace.

DAY 117

MORNING - *A Captivating Woman*

We demolish arguments and every pretension that sets itself up against the knowledge of God, and we take captive every thought to make it obedient to Christ.
2 CORINTHIANS 10:5 NIV

Are your emotions leading you astray? Are your thoughts convincing you that you are a hypocrite, making you feel ashamed? If so, stop. Take a deep breath and rein in your feelings. Then take those thoughts of hypocrisy away, captive to the obedience of Christ.

EVENING - *Living in Divine Power*

Though we walk (live) in the flesh, we are not carrying on our warfare according to the flesh and using mere human weapons. For the weapons of our warfare are not physical [weapons of flesh and blood], but they are mighty before God for the overthrow and destruction of strongholds.
2 CORINTHIANS 10:3–4 AMPC

All day, Lord, I've been tapping into the divine power You have given me, using it to destroy every thought that wasn't worthy of You. With every emotion or thought of my being a hypocrite, I stopped in my tracks, took a deep breath, and reined in my feelings and thoughts, which, once I became aware of them, I realized were usually based on untruths. And I brought them to You. Thank You for walking with me today. Continue to keep me in this place of power, while awake and asleep.

DAY 118

MORNING - *A Singing Woman*

*"I will instruct you. I will teach you the way that you should go.
I will advise you as my eyes watch over you. Don't be stubborn
like a horse or mule. They need a bit and bridle in their mouth
to restrain them, or they will not come near you."*
PSALM 32:8–9 GW

Your powerful emotions are strongholds that can be pulled down by the truth of the Gospel through the power, grace, mercy, and love of God. When you say to the Lord, "You are my hiding place. You protect me from trouble. You surround me with joyous songs of salvation" (Psalm 32:7 GW), He will teach you the way to go, give you advice, and watch over you. Your job is to let Him do His job!

EVENING - *In Prayer*

*Let everyone who is godly pray—pray to You in a time
when You may be found; surely when the great waters
[of trial] overflow, they shall not reach [the spirit in] him.*
PSALM 32:6 AMPC

Lord, the idea—no, the *fact*—that as a believer, I can pray to You at any time, brings me such confidence and assurance. Knowing that when I do, no trouble can touch my spirit, floods me with peace! Help me to just give up everything—my thoughts, my feelings, my will, my entire being—to You and You alone. For then I will truly be Your daughter, filled with joy, hidden wholly in You.

DAY 119

MORNING - *A Once-Stubborn Woman*

The joy of the Lord is your strength and stronghold.
NEHEMIAH 8:10 AMPC

You may be wondering, *Exactly what happens if I do not cling stubbornly to my own will?* You'll be surrounded by mercy! You'll "be glad and find joy in the Lord" (Psalm 32:11 GW). You'll find yourself bursting out in song, so great will your happiness be!

Thus, your joy will be found when you remain in God's will. But how do you find God's will for your life? By continually coming to Him in prayer, by consistently immersing yourself in His Word, by constantly seeking Him first! And the joy you find will become your ultimate strength!

EVENING - *Climbing a Mountain of Strength*

The mountain of the house of the LORD will be established as the chief of the mountains. . . . And many peoples will come and say, "Come, let us go up to the mountain of the LORD. . .that He may teach us concerning His ways and that we may walk in His paths."
ISAIAH 2:2–3 NASB

Oh, what a mountain of strength You are, Lord. I run to You each morning, searching Your Word for grounding, for truth. I look to You for wisdom during the day, knowing I can stand firm in Your will for me. And in the evening, I reflect upon the day, seeing Your hand in and on my life. I am in harmony with You—every step of the way! I give You a mountain of praise!

DAY 120

MORNING - *The Consistent Woman*

*Ask and keep on asking and it shall be given you; seek and keep on
seeking and you shall find; knock and keep on knocking and the door
shall be opened to you. For everyone who asks and keeps on asking
receives; and he who seeks and keeps on seeking finds; and to him
who knocks and keeps on knocking, the door shall be opened.*
LUKE 11:9–10 AMPC

God does not ask you to seek His will and then go on your merry way. It is a
constant, consistent practice on your part. You are to continue asking, seeking,
and knocking. In doing so, you will continue to receive God in your hearts and
find His will for your life. He will keep on opening doors that had been shut!

EVENING - *Keeping on!*

*And Judah gathered together to ask help from the Lord;
even out of all the cities of Judah they came to seek
the Lord [yearning for Him with all their desire].*
2 CHRONICLES 20:4 AMPC

I want to live a life where I am consistently seeking You, Lord, seeing You in
all things, longing for You with all that I am. Keep this fresh in my mind and
heart, my soul and spirit, God. For when I continue to seek You, I know the
right doors will be open!

DAY 121

MORNING · *A Seeking Woman*

Do not seek what you will eat and what you will drink, and do
not keep worrying. For all these things the nations of the world
eagerly seek; but your Father knows that you need these things.
But seek His kingdom, and these things will be added to you.
LUKE 12:29–31 NASB

But you may ask, if I follow God's will, how will my family, my friends, my loved ones fare? Not to worry. All you need to do is seek God's kingdom first; everything else will fall in line! When you live in God's will and are hidden in Christ, you take up residence in the worry-free zone, a place where emotions amount to naught, where they become mere specks of dust floating on the surfaces of your mind.

EVENING · *Filled with Assurance*

You'll find all your everyday human concerns will be met.
Don't be afraid of missing out. You're my dearest friends!
The Father wants to give you the very kingdom itself.
LUKE 12:31–32 MSG

Jesus, Your words, Your assurance that You will take care of everything when I come to You, seeking You above all else, fills me with such peace and praise to Abba God! Thank You, Jesus, for revealing this to my heart once again. I can rest in confidence that I am the daughter of the King and well provided for in every way!

DAY 122

MORNING - *A Harmonious Woman*

Jacob stayed behind by himself, and a man wrestled with him until daybreak. When the man saw that he couldn't get the best of Jacob as they wrestled, he deliberately threw Jacob's hip out of joint.
GENESIS 32:24–25 MSG

You cannot wrestle with God's will for your life. If you do, you'll end up limping around like Jacob. But when your will works with God's, you're indeed a power to be reckoned with! And this is amazing because it's what you were created to do from the very beginning. Before the Fall, your natural state was in total harmony with God. You're just getting right back to the beginning!

EVENING - *Staying in Tune with God*

Then you will live a life that honors the Lord, and you will always please him by doing good deeds. You will come to know God even better. His glorious power will make you patient and strong enough to endure anything, and you will be truly happy.
COLOSSIANS 1:10–11 CEV

Jesus, I so long to please You. I want my life to be worthy of Your response, "Well done, good and faithful servant" (Matthew 25:23 KJV). I want to be faithful to You, to know You more, to be strong in all things. Give me power, patience, and peace for this day. Keep me consistent in my faith and persistently seeking You first in all things. For Your way is my way.

DAY 123

MORNING - *A Near-Sighted Woman*

The angel told him: "Don't be afraid, Zechariah!
God has heard your prayers."
LUKE 1:13 CEV

In following God's will for your life, you may not always see the picture or the outcome He has in mind. Consider Zachariah. One day while he was serving in the temple, the angel Gabriel appeared. "When Zachariah saw him, he was troubled, and fear took possession of him" (Luke 1:12 AMPC). But the angel told him not to fear. Zachariah's prayers had been heard. He and his wife, Elizabeth (well past child-bearing age), would have a son. Zachariah was to call the boy John. He would have the power of Elijah and help turn the people back to God. Because Zechariah couldn't "see" the whole picture, he was filled with disbelief! Can you relate?

EVENING - *Trusting in God's Guiding*

Many people have tried to tell the story of what God has done among us.
LUKE 1:1 CEV

Many times, Lord, I have heard the stories in Your Word. Yet still, like Zachariah, I sometimes hesitate to do what You want me to do because I don't know what You're up to. Help me to remain true to Your will for me, to remember that You know and see all that lies behind and before me. And that I can trust in You to lead me the right way!

DAY 124

MORNING - *A Once-Silenced Woman*

Zachariah said to the angel, by what shall I know and be sure of this?
For I am an old man, and my wife is well advanced in years.
LUKE 1:18 AMPC

Stunned by the angel's words that he and his wife would become parents, Zachariah expressed his disbelief! In response, the angel silenced him, saying, "You will be and will continue to be silent and not able to speak till the day when these things take place, because you have not believed what I told you" (Luke 1:20 AMPC).

How many times has God silenced you in some way because you didn't believe? Listen for God. Believe what He says. Have faith—and then watch what amazing things God's words create for You!

EVENING - *Open to God Speaking*

The angel replied to him, I am Gabriel. I stand in the [very] presence of
God, and I have been sent to talk to you and to bring you this good news.
LUKE 1:19 AMPC

God, help me to always keep an open ear and an open mind to what You are speaking into my life—even if it comes from the angel Gabriel himself! Help me not to react with shock and/or disbelief, or to ask for a sign, but to trust in all You do and say. For I know that Your will—when I hear and follow it—never fails to bring good news into my life.

DAY 125

MORNING · *A Believing-before-Seeing Woman*

When he did come out, he was unable to speak to them; and they [clearly] perceived that he had seen a vision in the sanctuary; and he kept making signs to them, still he remained dumb.
LUKE 1:22 AMPC

Zachariah, now "dumb," was given no further knowledge between his doubting in Luke 1:18 and the moment when, "filled with and controlled by the Holy Spirit" (Luke 1:67 AMPC), he sang his song of praise on the day of his son's birth. Zachariah really didn't understand what was happening, but that didn't matter. He knew that God, after being somewhat silent for four hundred years, was moving.

EVENING · *No Longer "Dumb"*

My words are of a kind which will be fulfilled in the appointed and proper time.
LUKE 1:20 AMPC

I don't want to be "dumb," Lord, but instead filled with the truth and assurance that whatever words or visions You give me will be fulfilled—in *Your* time, way, and place, not mine! And I know that when those words of Yours do come true, I will be as filled with the same praise that came out of Zachariah—and, most likely, his now-fruitful wife Elisabeth! You truly are a miracle worker!

DAY 126

MORNING - *A Woman in the Midst*

*Here is the new agreement that I, the LORD, will make with
the people of Israel: "I will write my laws on their hearts
and minds. I will be their God, and they will be my people."*
JEREMIAH 31:33 CEV

In the midst of your daily activities, you don't need to know or understand all that God is doing. You need merely to take a step back and focus on Jesus. You need not fear God's will but trust Him, resting in the truth that He knows what He's doing. As Eva Marie Everson wrote in *Oasis*, "Before Moses went up the mountain, he chiseled out the stones on which God's laws would be written. Our hearts are the new stones. We must bring them to God in our hands, ready for him to write upon them His will for our lives." Are you ready to let God write on your heart?

EVENING - *Enheartened by God's Will*

*Your very lives are a letter that anyone can read by just looking at you.
Christ himself wrote it—not with ink, but with God's living Spirit;
not chiseled into stone, but carved into human lives.*
2 CORINTHIANS 3:3 MSG

I'm keeping my eyes on You, Jesus, trusting in God's will, knowing that I am Your love letter to those around me. Here is my heart. Write on it what You will!

DAY 127

MORNING · *An Extraordinary Woman*

So here's what I want you to do, God helping you: Take your everyday, ordinary life—your sleeping, eating, going-to-work, and walking-around life—and place it before God as an offering.
ROMANS 12:1 MSG

So consider your emotions as merely servants and regard your will in God's as the real master of your being. When you do, you'll find that you can ignore your emotions and simply pay attention to the state of your will. Each day, present yourself to God as a living sacrifice. Trust Him to move in your life. Hannah Whitall Smith tells faithful females to remember that they are not giving up their wills but are simply substituting the "higher, divine, mature will of God for our foolish, misdirected wills of ignorance and immaturity."

EVENING · *Embracing an Extraordinary God-Willed Life*

Embracing what God does for you is the best thing you can do for him.
ROMANS 12:1 MSG

Because of all You have done, are doing, and will do for me, Lord, I am bringing myself to You. That is the best way I know to worship You. So here I am. Your living sacrifice. Trusting You as You move in my life, giving up my ignorant and immature will to Your higher, divine nature. I can't wait to see what You will do in me next!

DAY 128

MORNING · *A Woman with an Attitude*

You must have the same attitude that Christ Jesus had. . . . When he appeared in human form, he humbled himself in obedience to God.
PHILIPPIANS 2:5, 7–8 NLT

Hannah Whitall Smith wrote:

> *He wills that you should be entirely surrendered to Him and that you should trust Him perfectly. If you have taken the steps of surrender and faith in your will, it is your right to believe that no matter how much your feelings may clamor against it, you are all the Lord's, and He has begun to "worketh in you both to will and to do of his good pleasure"* (Philippians 2:13 KJV).

EVENING · *Empowered to Do God's Will*

Work hard to show the results of your salvation, obeying God with deep reverence and fear. For God is working in you, giving you the desire and the power to do what pleases him.
PHILIPPIANS 2:12–13 NLT

I am Yours, Lord—heart, soul, body, mind, spirit, and will! No matter what my emotions or thoughts are telling me, I know that I cannot be taken out of Your hand. I thank You for allowing Your Son to save me. And I take peace in the knowledge that You are helping me, giving me the longing and power to do what You will me to do. In all this I give You all the pleasure and praise. Amen.

DAY 129

MORNING - *The Joy-Filled Woman's Path Marker: Promise No. 7*

This is the agreement (testament, covenant) that I will set up and conclude with them after those days, says the Lord: I will imprint My laws upon their hearts, and I will inscribe them on their minds (on their inmost thoughts and understanding).

HEBREWS 10:16 AMPC

God, through His Word, has made an agreement with you. Because You believe in Him, He has promised to imprint upon your heart His laws. He will also engrave them onto your mind. So you need no longer look to the world's ways or to your own will. Simply look to Him above, Jesus next to you, and the Spirit within. Believe in God's promise. And you will find not only rest from your emotions but joy in the Spirit of the Lord.

EVENING - *Joyfully Doing God's Will*

"I take joy in doing your will, my God, for your instructions are written on my heart."

PSALM 40:8 NLT

You have already planted within me, Lord, the Spirit that will lead me to the path and ways You have already laid out to me. Help me to imprint this thought on my mind, to make it my own. And when my emotions look like they're about to career out of control, get me back to You by taking a deep breath, seeking Your face, and listening to Your Spirit within.

DAY 130

MORNING - *The Joy-Filled Woman's Path Marker: Proof No. 7*

Paul and his friends went through Phrygia and Galatia, but the Holy Spirit would not let them preach in Asia. After they arrived in Mysia, they tried to go into Bithynia, but the Spirit of Jesus would not let them. So they went on through Mysia until they came to Troas. During the night, Paul had a vision of someone from Macedonia who was standing there and begging him, "Come over to Macedonia and help us!" After Paul had seen the vision, we began looking for a way to go to Macedonia. We were sure that God had called us to preach the good news there.

ACTS 16:6–10 CEV

The Word proves God's will can be found as you move through life. Claim that proof and, like Paul, you will not only be protected but rewarded with the amazing vision God has for your life.

EVENING - *Moved in Spirit*

The Holy Spirit said to Philip, "Go over and walk along beside the carriage." . . . The Spirit of the Lord snatched Philip away. . . . Meanwhile, Philip found himself farther north. . . . He preached the Good News there.

ACTS 8:29, 39, 40 NLT

Lord, I want to be so in tune with Your will for my life that, as I obey, I not only clearly see Your vision for me but hear Your voice and am moved. For when I trust in You, I know that no matter where I land, it'll be good news!

DAY 131

MORNING - *The Joy-Filled Woman's Path Marker: Provision No. 7*

I am telling you nothing but the truth when I say it is profitable (good, expedient, advantageous) for you that I go away. Because if I do not go away, the Comforter (Counselor, Helper, Advocate, Intercessor, Strengthener, Standby) will not come to you [into close fellowship with you]; but if I go away, I will send Him to you [to be in close fellowship with you].
JOHN 16:7 AMPC

Before He shed His human form, Jesus promised you a Helper—the Holy Spirit. He is closer than you think! So tap into His presence and power every moment of every day. And you will never lose your way in God's will. Believe in this provision and watch God's will keep your misdirected thoughts and feelings at bay.

EVENING - *Holy Spirit Empowered*

*As for me, I am filled with power—
with the Spirit of the LORD.*
MICAH 3:8 NLT

Lord, I'm tapping into the power of the Holy Spirit right here, right now. I feel His presence. And with Him in my life, mind, heart, spirit, and soul, I know I will never lose my way. Thank You for giving me this amazing gift.

DAY 132

MORNING - *The Joy-filled Woman's Path Marker: Portrait No. 7*

And this is the confidence (the assurance, the privilege of boldness) which we have in Him: [we are sure] that if we ask anything (make any request) according to His will (in agreement with His own plan), He listens to and hears us.

1 JOHN 5:14 AMPC

God has not only *promised* His will for your life is written on your heart (see Hebrews 10:16) and presented living *proof* of such guidance (see Acts 16:6–10), He has *provided* you access to it by giving you the Holy Spirit (see John 16:7). All you need to do is seek God above all things—be constantly tuned into Him—and you will have total access to God's will! Claim this *portrait* statement (based on 1 John 5:14) by taking it totally to heart!

In Christ, I have access to God's will.

EVENING - *Walking in His Will*

Remember the LORD in all you do, and he will give you success.

PROVERBS 3:6 NCV

Every moment of every day, Lord, I walk in Your will, and it's awesome! I no longer give in to fear, stress, or anxiety offered by this fallen world. I love Your peace, strength, and power as they move through me via the Holy Spirit. I look forward to each day, never knowing where You will be working but on the lookout for it all the same. Life is an adventure with You at the helm!

DAY 133

MORNING - *A Guided Woman*

Teach me to do your will, for you are my God.
PSALM 143:10 NLT

You've given yourself to God. You're in His hands, and He's shaping you into a new creature with a divine purpose. You've determined to keep your will in agreement with His. You are, in effect, trusting Him with everything. But now you may be unsure of the next step. You know God has a purpose for your life, but which direction should you go? How can you follow His leading if you are unsure which voice is His? You must now be certain of two things: that you intend to obey God in all things and that He will make His will known to you.

EVENING - *Aligned with God*

May your gracious Spirit lead me forward on a firm footing.
PSALM 143:10 NLT

I am Yours, Lord. And I feel so good and secure in Your hands. Continue to grow me up into the woman You would have me be. Align my will with Yours. For I trust You to lead me, to speak into my ears, to show me the pathway to You. Of Your direction, I am sure.

DAY 134

MORNING - *The Inquiring Woman*

If any of you is deficient in wisdom, let him ask of the giving God [Who gives] to everyone liberally and ungrudgingly, without reproaching or faultfinding, and it will be given him.
JAMES 1:5 AMPC

It's not just God the Father that will make His will known to you. Jesus the Son and the Holy Spirit are determined to do so as well! They are going to guide you down the right path—every step of the way. In fact, they have promised to do so!

God, Guide No. 1, has promised to give you wisdom—if you only ask!

EVENING - *Gaining Wisdom*

For the LORD grants wisdom! From his mouth come knowledge and understanding.
PROVERBS 2:6 NLT

Lord, so many times I forget to ask for Your input when it comes to making decisions. Yet I know You will tell me all I need to know—if only I would come to You first! So here I am, Lord, in Your presence. Speak to me! Tell me what I need to know. I will listen for Your infinite knowledge. And I will take Your direction without question because I know You understand far more than I ever will.

DAY 135

MORNING - *The Shepherded Woman*

The watchman opens the door for this man, and the sheep listen to his voice and heed it; and he calls his own sheep by name and brings (leads) them out. When he has brought his own sheep outside, he walks on before them, and the sheep follow him because they know his voice.

JOHN 10:3–4 AMPC

Not only God the Father, but Jesus the Son, Guide No. 2, is also ready to lead you. He is the Great Shepherd who goes before you. He is the one whose voice you are familiar with. He may be calling you this very minute. Trust Him enough to follow Him—wherever He leads.

EVENING - *Guided Along the Right Paths*

The LORD is my shepherd; I have all that I need. He lets me rest in green meadows; he leads me beside peaceful streams. He renews my strength. He guides me along right paths, bringing honor to his name.

PSALM 23:1–3 NLT

Jesus, what peace fills my heart when I realize that with You in my life, I lack nothing. You give me rest, lead me, renew me, and guide me. And all to bring honor to Your glorious name. Thank You for always looking after me. Help me not to wander but to listen to Your voice and follow You wherever You lead.

MORNING - *The Woman Open to Teaching*

But the Comforter (Counselor, Helper, Intercessor, Advocate, Strengthener, Standby), the Holy Spirit, Whom the Father will send in My name [in My place, to represent Me and act on My behalf], He will teach you all things. And He will cause you to recall (will remind you of, bring to your remembrance) everything I have told you.
JOHN 14:26 AMPC

Besides God the Father and Jesus the Son, you have another amazing ally: the Holy Spirit, Guide No. 3. With the Father, Son, and Holy Spirit on your side, you cannot get lost. You need not fear anything! If you confidently believe in God the Father, His Son, Jesus, and the Holy Spirit, if you determine to look for and expect their guidance, you will receive it.

EVENING - *Led by the Spirit*

For those who are led by the Spirit of God are the children of God.
ROMANS 8:14 NIV

How wonderful to have a three-person team looking out for me! Help me, Spirit, to be open to Your teaching. Remind me of what I already know. Open my ears to Your call, whispers, nudging. I rest knowing that with You I will never go astray.

DAY 137

MORNING - *The Unwavering Woman*

Only it must be in faith that he asks with no wavering (no hesitating, no doubting). For the one who wavers (hesitates, doubts) is like the billowing surge out at sea that is blown hither and thither and tossed by the wind.

JAMES 1:6 AMPC

So you've got three main guides to God's will and direction: God the Father, Jesus the Son, and the Holy Spirit. The key here is that you must not doubt!

EVENING - *Delivered to the Promised Land*

If the Lord delights in us, then He will bring us into this land and give it to us, a land flowing with milk and honey.

NUMBERS 14:8 AMPC

Lord, I long to please You. And I have no doubts in Your plan for me. Thus, I am not tossed about by the waves or blown away by the wind. Instead, I am standing firm in You, knowing that You, Jesus, and the Spirit will lead me in the way I am to go. And that my final destination will be the land of promise, a place where I am always provided for. I rest in this knowledge. I revel in this peace.

DAY 138

MORNING - *A Confident Woman*

*For the Lord God is a Sun and Shield; the Lord bestows [present] grace
and favor and [future] glory (honor, splendor, and heavenly bliss)!
No good thing will He withhold from those who walk uprightly.*
PSALM 84:11 AMPC

God will give you guidance if you seek it in faith, with confidence He will give it. In addition, you must keep in mind that God knows absolutely everything! So regardless of how you or those around you see confusion and loss in the path He has chosen for you, He knows exactly what blessings await. Although you may not understand His road map for you, remember that with your human vision, you see only a portion of the map. He sees the entire picture, and in His vision you must trust.

EVENING - *Blessed in Believing*

*O Lord of hosts, blessed (happy, fortunate, to be envied) is the man
who trusts in You [leaning and believing on You, committing all
and confidently looking to You, and that without fear or misgiving]!*
PSALM 84:12 AMPC

Shine Your wisdom on me, Lord God. And shield me from relying on my own knowledge. I am trusting in You above and beyond all things. For I know You have a great plan for me, even if I can't figure out what that is right now. So, I rest in You, confident that all will be well.

DAY 139

MORNING - *The Woman of God*

"Anyone who comes to me but refuses to let go of father, mother, spouse, children, brothers, sisters—yes, even one's own self!—can't be my disciple."
LUKE 14:25 MSG

Upon your pathway, you may discover that to follow Jesus, you are called to forsake inwardly everyone in your life—including yourself! In other words, you may be guided to paths that those you love most will disapprove of. For this you must be prepared. You must continually tell yourself that God is in control. He knows all—including what is best for you.

EVENING - *Steered by the Master Alone*

Our God is in heaven. He does anything he wants to do.
PSALM 115:3 NIrV

God, You are Lord of all. You do anything You want to do, including planning my life. Continually remind me that You, Master of the universe, are in control. And You have amazing things lined up for me. So help me not to be swayed by others but rest in the assurance that You are my Father, the one who knows what's best for me.

DAY 140

MORNING - *A Woman with Guideposts*

Thou art my rock and my fortress;
therefore for thy name's sake lead me, and guide me.
PSALM 31:3 KJV

❦

How does God give you His guidance? In four simple ways: through His Word, through providential circumstances, through your spiritually enlightened judgment, and through the inward promptings of the Holy Spirit upon your mind. When these four harmonize, when they are all in sync, you know God's hand is guiding you.

EVENING - *Expecting a Signal*

Wait and hope for and expect the Lord; be brave and of
good courage and let your heart be stout and enduring.
Yes, wait for and hope for and expect the Lord.
PSALM 27:14 AMPC

❦

I seem to be in limbo, Lord, waiting for Your direction. Right now all is unclear. But all that means is that You want me to be patient until You give me the signal. I know You only want what's best for me. So my hope and trust are in You. Show me, Lord—via the scriptures, my intelligence, Your voice, and the Spirit's prompting—when and where to move.

DAY 141

MORNING - *A Word-Inspired Woman: Guidepost No. 1*

All Scripture is inspired by God and is useful to teach us what is true and to make us realize what is wrong in our lives. It corrects us when we are wrong and teaches us to do what is right.
2 TIMOTHY 3:16 NLT

If your road map bypasses scripture, beware—you are headed for a dead end. If you are confused about which path to take, you are to consult God's Word. If the Bible provides guidance in that particular regard, ask the Holy Spirit to make everything clear to you. Then obey. But be careful not to take scripture out of context, just because that's the answer or the guidance you endeavor to have.

EVENING - *Prepared*

God uses it [His Word] to prepare and equip his people to do every good work.
2 TIMOTHY 3:17 NLT

Thank You for Your scripture, Lord. It is so powerful, wise, and helpful to me. It has taught me so much already! Remind me that scripture takes precedence over the traditions of humankind. And help me to not take it out of context but to read the whole, as You intended it. In the morning, show me how to use Your Word to prepare me for the work You lay out before me. And in the evening, may I take rest in its comforting arms.

DAY 142

MORNING - *A Seeking Woman*

*You have been taught the holy Scriptures from childhood,
and they have given you the wisdom to receive the
salvation that comes by trusting in Christ Jesus.*
2 TIMOTHY 3:15 NLT

Although the Bible tells you what kind of person to marry, how you should work, and how to raise your children, it doesn't name your spouse, tell you what job you should take, or how long to ground a teenager. In those cases and others, if you cannot find a clear answer in the Bible, seek guidance using the other three ways mentioned—through circumstances, your intelligence, and the Spirit's prompting. If any of these tests fails, you need to stop. Wait on the Lord. Watch for Him to move. Eventually, He will give you the wisdom you seek.

EVENING - *Longing for a Whisper*

*Your ears shall hear a word behind you, saying, "This is the way, walk in it,"
whenever you turn to the right hand or whenever you turn to the left."*
ISAIAH 30:21 NKJV

Lord, I long to hear Your voice whisper in my ear. I need Your guidance, Your direction. Be my compass, for I don't know which way to go. Lead me out of the darkness I feel surrounding me. Help me look away from my emotions and focus on You and You alone. Lead me on. But if I need to wait, give me patience to do just that.

DAY 143

MORNING - *A Providential Woman: Guidepost No. 2*

*I know that You can do all things, and that no thought
or purpose of Yours can be restrained or thwarted.*
JOB 42:2 AMPC

Next, look at what's happening in your life, the providential circumstances that have come to the forefront. For instance, you may have been somewhat content in a career, only to find yourself laid off. You thought the road was clear but now find yourself stranded, not knowing which way to turn. Sometimes, losing a job can be the best thing that ever happened! For now, you can perhaps do the thing you had wanted to do for a long time. God has, in effect, pushed you out of your comfort zone so that you will be moved to do what He has clearly called you to do, perhaps years ago!

EVENING - *By Providential Circumstances*

*"For I know the plans I have for you," says the LORD. "They are plans
for good and not for disaster, to give you a future and a hope."*
JEREMIAH 29:11 NLT

I love to make plans, Lord—not just for myself but for everyone in my life. And when those plans are ruined, I get frustrated. But I know *You* are concerned with every detail of my life. And I know You have a grand scheme for each and every one of us. Your plan is supreme, so no matter what happens, I can relax in hope, knowing everything and everyone is in Your hands.

MORNING - *A Woman at the Gate*

*"When he brings out his own sheep, he goes before them;
and the sheep follow him, for they know his voice."*

JOHN 10:4 NKJV

If your circumstances are truly providential, God will open doors for you—you won't have to break them down. In other words, if your direction is truly from God, He will go before you and pave the way. Mary Slessor of Calabar wrote, "If I have done anything in my life, it has been easy because the Master has gone before." This is confirmed in John 10:4. Jesus "goes before" to open the gate, and you "follow him."

EVENING - *Opened by the Good Shepherd*

*"I am the good shepherd; and I know My sheep, and am known
by My own. As the Father knows Me, even so I know
the Father; and I lay down My life for the sheep."*

JOHN 10:14–15 NKJV

I know, Jesus, that You have only good things in mind for me. And the fact that You have already laid down Your life for me assures me that if there is one person I can trust, it is You, over and over again! So go before me, Lord. Pave my way. I'm right behind You!

DAY 145

MORNING · *A Spiritually Enlightened Woman: Guidepost No. 3*

I will instruct you and teach you in the way you should go;
I will guide you with My eye. Do not be like the horse or
like the mule, which have no understanding, which must be
harnessed with bit and bridle, else they will not come near you.
PSALM 32:8–9 NKJV

The third test is to use your God-given gifts and intelligence, which God wants you to use to find your pathway. Although you are not to depend on your own reasoning or common sense, you can use spiritually enlightened judgment to find your way. For God will speak to you through the abilities He has given you. In other words, if you have two left feet, He will not call upon you to be a ballet dancer. If you are tone deaf, He won't call you to be on the worship team.

EVENING · *Talents and Desires*

May He grant you according to your
heart's desire and fulfill all your plans.
PSALM 20:4 AMPC

God, You have given me certain talents and abilities, certain desires of my heart. But I'm not sure what You want me to do with them. What's Your game plan, Lord? Please show me in Your Word the direction You want me to go. Fill me with Your wisdom. Help me not to run ahead of You but to wait on Your every signal for direction. In Your pathway, I know I'm safe.

DAY 146

MORNING - *A Spirited Woman: Guidepost No. 4*

They went to Phrygia, and then on through the region of Galatia. Their plan was to turn west into Asia province, but the Holy Spirit blocked that route.

ACTS 16:6 MSG

The fourth and final way to find God's guidance is following the cues given by the Holy Spirit. If you sense the Spirit putting up roadblocks, prompting you to stop dead in your tracks—stop! Wait until all barriers are removed before forging ahead.

EVENING - *By the Inward Promptings of the Holy Spirit*

Trust God from the bottom of your heart; don't try to figure out everything on your own. Listen for GOD's voice in everything you do, everywhere you go; he's the one who will keep you on track. Don't assume that you know it all. Run to GOD!

PROVERBS 3:5–7 MSG

How egotistical of me to think I know exactly what You want for me, Lord! You created this universe—You created me—with a definite plan in mind. So I sprint to You today. Give me wisdom to select the path of Your choosing. I trust You to let me know where and when to go. So here I am, Lord, waiting for Your voice. Speak to me. I am listening.

DAY 147

MORNING - *A Comfortable Woman*

Moses said to the Lord, "Please, Lord, I'm not a good speaker. . . ."
The Lord asked him, "Who gave humans their mouths? Who makes humans
unable to talk or hear? Who gives them sight or makes them blind? It is I,
the Lord! Now go, and I will help you speak and will teach you what to say."
EXODUS 4:10–12 GW

If your barrier is merely fear, if you are uncomfortable about a new endeavor or direction, that may not be the Holy Spirit saying "Stop." It may simply mean that God is about to stretch you spiritually and mentally or is about to pull you back from a path onto which you may have strayed.

EVENING - *Ready to Be Stretched*

And the Lord said to Moses, put forth your hand and take it by the tail. And
he stretched out his hand and caught it, and it became a rod in his hand.
EXODUS 4:4 AMPC

Oh my, Lord, sometimes I am not willing to be stretched. I feel so inadequate that I'm not sure I can do what You want me to do, or go where You are calling me to go. But then I remember You are the Lord of all creation. Nothing is impossible when I put myself in Your hands. And You will be with me, helping me along the way. So here I am, Lord. Put me on the path of *Your* choosing. And I will walk that path in faith!

DAY 148

MORNING - *A God-Influenced Woman*

My child, if sinners entice you, turn your back on them!
PROVERBS 1:10 NLT

Be aware that anything that provokes dissonance of the divine harmony within you must be rejected as not coming from God but from other sources. The strong personalities in your life influence you greatly. So do your temporal circumstances and conditions, which sway you more than you know. In these instances, your worldly desire for a particular thing may override (or threaten to override) God's guiding voice. Be alert to which voices are speaking to you.

EVENING - *In Harmony with Wisdom*

Wisdom shouts in the streets. She cries out in the public square. . . . "Come and listen to my counsel. I'll share my heart with you and make you wise."
PROVERBS 1:20, 23 NLT

I've listened to so many voices, Lord, that I can't seem to figure out what to do. Help me to see all the options, and then hone in to Your voice alone—not the voice of my desires or those people who have influence over me. I want to do what You want me to do. I want You—and You alone—to sway me, to rule me, to show me the right path. So here I am. Listening for Your wisdom for the next step I am to take. Share Your heart with me in this moment.

DAY 149

MORNING - *The Listening Woman*

You will hear a voice behind you saying, "This is the way.
Follow it, whether it turns to the right or to the left."
ISAIAH 30:21 GW

One of the voices speaking into your life may be your spiritual enemy. You know what happened with Eve in the garden. She listened to the wrong voice, which led to her—and the world's—fall. Thus, it's not enough to feel you're being led to a new endeavor or action. You must discern the source of the voice calling before you rush off down the path. Step back. Take the time to find the true voice—no matter how long you may have to wait. Listen carefully. Then when you hear the Spirit say, "This is the way. Follow it," move out. When you do, know for a certainty that Jesus is leading the way.

EVENING - *Waiting for God's Voice*

This is what the Almighty LORD, the Holy One of Israel, says:
You can be saved by returning to me. You can have rest.
You can be strong by being quiet and by trusting me.
ISAIAH 30:15 GW

I'm returning to You, Lord, listening for Your voice—the voice of truth. No matter how long it takes, I will be trusting in You. Speak to me. I want to be sure it is You that are leading the way. Resting in You, assured of Your presence, I am strong, quiet, and trusting.

DAY 150

MORNING - *A Walking Woman*

*"And now, you see, I am going to Jerusalem, bound by the
[Holy] Spirit and obligated and compelled by the [convictions
of my own] spirit, not knowing what will befall me there."*
ACTS 20:22 AMPC

Endeavor to discern God's guidance by using (along with the four tests through
God's Word, your circumstances, your intelligence, and the Spirit's prompting)
what Smith calls "a divine sense of 'oughtness' derived from the harmony of all
God's voices." When you do, you will have nothing to fear. If you have faith
in God, if you trust Him with all, you will have the courage and strength to
walk the way He is leading, your hand in His.

EVENING - *With No-Fall Assurance*

*If you do what the LORD wants, he will make certain each step you take is
sure. The LORD will hold your hand, and if you stumble, you still won't fall.*
PSALM 37:23–24 CEV

I'm hanging on to You for dear life, Abba. Keep a tight grip on me. Squeeze my
hand if I'm walking out of Your will for me. I don't want to stray, for whenever
I step out on my own, I always trip up. But You'll never let me fall. You are
my refuge and my strength. You are my guiding light. So I'm determined to
stick to You like glue and to praise Your name with each step!

DAY 151

MORNING - *A Fearless Woman*

Thus says the Lord: Stand by the roads and look;
and ask for the eternal paths, where the good, old way is;
then walk in it, and you will find rest for your souls.
JEREMIAH 6:16 AMPC

There is no fear for you living this higher life if you live each moment of every day under God's guidance. It is the most wonderful privilege and promise that you have been given and leads to a myriad of rewards.

"Rejoice in it. Embrace it eagerly," Smith wrote. "Let everything go that it may be yours."

EVENING - *Living the Higher Life*

Our inner selves wait [earnestly] for the Lord; He is our Help
and our Shield. For in Him does our heart rejoice, because we
have trusted (relied on and been confident) in His holy name.
PSALM 33:20–21 AMPC

I have no fear because I am walking with You, Lord, relying on Your Word, my providential circumstances, my intelligence, and the Spirit's prompting, as well as that "divine sense of oughtness" when I obtain the harmony derived from all Your voices. Thank You for the chance to live this higher life in You. What joy it gives me!

DAY 152

MORNING - *The Joy-Filled Woman's Path Marker: Promise No. 8*

I [the Lord] will instruct you and teach you in the way you should go; I will counsel you with My eye upon you.
PSALM 32:8 AMPC

Through His Word, God promises that He will be there to teach you, direct you in the way you should go. In fact, He's got His eye on you—and so sees so much more than you! Believe in this amazing promise. And you will realize the joy this reassurance gives you!

EVENING - *Guided Day and Night*

I will bless the LORD who guides me; even at night my heart instructs me. I know the LORD is always with me. I will not be shaken, for he is right beside me.
PSALM 16:7–8 NLT

Even in the twilight hours, Lord, You shine Your light of wisdom so that I can see where You would have me go. You are right beside me, so I need fear nothing. With You in my life, I know I will never be lost because You are the beacon my spirit craves and with Your eye upon me, You are continually giving light to my path. Thank You, Lord, for all Your attention and love.

DAY 153

MORNING - *The Joy-Filled Woman's Path Marker: Proof No. 8*

At the command of the LORD the children of Israel would journey, and at the command of the LORD they would camp; as long as the cloud stayed above the tabernacle they remained encamped. . . . Whether it was two days, a month, or a year that the cloud remained above the tabernacle, the children of Israel would remain encamped and not journey; but when it was taken up, they would journey. At the command of the LORD they remained encamped, and at the command of the LORD they journeyed; they kept the charge of the LORD.

NUMBERS 9:18, 22–23 NKJV

～

The Word proves God is continually guiding you. Just wait on Him, then, when He gives you the signal, move on to the next part of your journey. Keep the charge of the Lord and you'll be continually led to your Promised Land.

EVENING - *Following God's Lead*

For You are my rock and my fortress; for Your name's sake You will lead me and guide me.

PSALM 31:3 NASB

～

I want to glorify Your name, Lord, but I'm not sure exactly what You want me to do. Perhaps You want me to remain where I am. If so, that's okay. But if You want me to move out, give me the word, and I'll step out like Abraham, even though I don't know where You're taking me. In the meantime, I'm hiding in You, my rock, my strength, my love.

DAY 154

MORNING - *The Joy-Filled Woman's Path Marker: Provision No. 8*

Every Scripture passage is inspired by God. All of them are useful for teaching, pointing out errors, correcting people, and training them for a life that has God's approval.

2 TIMOTHY 3:16 GW

God not only gave you His Son and Holy Spirit to help guide you. He also gave you His Word. By reading and applying His Word to your life, you will be trained up in the way you should go. Believe in this provision—as well as providential circumstances, spiritually enlightened judgment, Holy Spirit promptings, and the divine "oughtness" leading within you. Use them! And you will be getting a clearer and firmer hold of that higher life!

EVENING - *Having a Mountaintop Experience*

The LORD gave me the two tablets on which God had written with his own finger all the words he had spoken to you from the heart of the fire when you were assembled at the mountain.

DEUTERONOMY 9:10 NLT

Father God, from Your fingertip to mine are the words You wrote so many years ago. Whenever I am in Your Word, I find myself having my own mountaintop experience. Continue to guide me and teach me, Lord. Give me Your wisdom so that I can understand what You are speaking into my heart.

DAY 155

MORNING - *The Joy-Filled Woman's Path Marker: Portrait No. 8*

You are partners with Christ Jesus because of God. Jesus has become our wisdom sent from God, our approval, our holiness, and our ransom from sin.

1 CORINTHIANS 1:30 GW

God has not only *promised* His guidance and wisdom (see Psalm 32:8) and *proven* that, if you are patient and keep your eye on Him, such guidance is always available (see Numbers 9:18, 22–23), He has *provided* access to it—not just through His Word (see 2 Timothy 3:16), but also through providential circumstances, spiritually enlightened judgment, Holy Spirit promptings, and the divine "oughtness" sense within you! Ask for access to His wisdom and direction. He can't help but give it to you! Now take this eighth *portrait* statement and allow it to lead your heart and life.

In Christ, I have access to God's wisdom and direction.

EVENING - *Relying on God as Compass*

I know, LORD, that our lives are not our own.
We are not able to plan our own course.

JEREMIAH 10:23 NLT

I am a little, lost lamb without Your wisdom and guidance, Lord. So I humbly come to You now. Teach me what I should know. Show me the way in which I should walk. Lead me to You, the Rock that is higher than any other. The Master who loves, watches over, and leads me.

DAY 156

MORNING - *A Certain Woman*

Peter went over the side of the boat and walked on the water toward Jesus. But when he saw the strong wind and the waves, he was terrified and began to sink.
MATTHEW 14:29–30 NLT

Even though you're a believer, you may have doubts. Although you know God exists, you may be uncertain He loves you. Or, although certain of your future, you may have doubts about your present. Or being a modern woman, you may doubt the promises God made thousands of years ago can apply to your life today! Thus, you have no peace, joy, or hope for your present day. So you live in the future instead. When you live your life outside of the promises God made to *you*, you're no longer focused on Jesus. You're like Peter, sinking in the sea because you've turned your sight to the wind and water. You've taken your eyes off Jesus. But there is hope—no doubt!

EVENING - *Saved by Jesus*

"Save me, Lord!" he shouted. Jesus immediately reached out and grabbed him. "You have so little faith," Jesus said. "Why did you doubt me?"
MATTHEW 14:30–31 NLT

I need You, Lord, to save me from the doubts that keep me from trusting in You, from living in this present moment. I know You can still both the wind and the waves. Still the tumults in my heart right now. Grab me and hold me tight. Help me to live in the now with You, buoyed by Your promises.

DAY 157

MORNING - *A Faithful Woman*

When they climbed back into the boat, the wind stopped.
MATTHEW 14:32 NLT

The instant you let doubts enter your mind, your fight of faith ends and your spiritual rebellion begins. In fact, when you doubt, you are calling God, Jesus, and the Holy Spirit liars, for "he that believeth not God hath made him a liar" (1 John 5:10 KJV)! What sorrow you must give your Abba God. What pain your doubting must cause your Savior. And what a barrier you put up against the working of the Holy Spirit in your life. Climb back into the boat of faith today!

EVENING - *Breaking Down Barriers*

Then the disciples worshiped him.
"You really are the Son of God!" they exclaimed.
MATTHEW 14:33 NLT

I want to be in the boat of faith today, Lord, in this very moment—and stay there! For I know You truly are the Son of God. And there is no promise You won't keep. Break down the barrier erected by my doubts so that Your Spirit may work unrestricted. I praise You, Lord, as the God of truth. The God of my life.

DAY 158

MORNING - *A Saved Woman*

"Who needs a doctor: the healthy or the sick?"
LUKE 5:31 MSG

Perhaps you feel unworthy of receiving the promises of God. Perhaps temptations have gotten the best of you; you have sinned to the point of believing God would be well rid of you. After all, why should He have any love for an undeserving sinner such as you? Perhaps you have undergone numerous trials that have convinced you that for some reason God has forsaken you and no longer cares about you or your life. If you have entertained thoughts and doubts such as these, be assured: Jesus came to save you!

EVENING - *Up for a Change*

"I'm here inviting outsiders, not insiders—
an invitation to a changed life, changed inside and out."
LUKE 5:32 MSG

I have accepted Your invitation in the past, Lord. But because I've made so many mistakes, slipped up so many times—even today, in fact—I feel unworthy. But my feelings often lead me astray. Continually remind me, Lord, that You love me no matter what. That You came to save me—while I was still missing the mark. Change my life, Lord, inside and out!

DAY 159

MORNING - *A Claimed Woman*

We love him, because he first loved us.
1 JOHN 4:19 KJV

Hannah Whitall Smith wrote, "Your very sinfulness and unworthiness, instead of being a reason why He should not love you and care for you, are really your chief claim upon His love and His care!" What a wonderful truth to meditate on. God truly does care for and love you, and shame on you for doubting such lavish attention. Know that no one has greater love for you than your Abba God.

EVENING - *Filled with Affection*

No one has greater love [no one has shown stronger affection] than to lay down (give up) his own life for his friends.
JOHN 15:13 AMPC

I thank You, Lord, for loving even before I came into existence. And for showing that love by dying for me on the cross. No one has ever sacrificed his or her life for me—except for You. I am humbled, amazed, and filled with affection for You. The idea that You are my Friend—through thick and thin—astounds me. Help me never to doubt Your love but to simply accept it for the wonderful gift it is. And one that keeps on giving!

DAY 160

MORNING - *The Prodigal Woman*

*When he was yet a great way off, his father saw him,
and had compassion, and ran, and fell on his neck, and kissed him.*
LUKE 15:20 KJV

Remember the tale of the prodigal son and the joy of the father upon his son's return? If not, reread Luke 15:11–32. You are not perfect; at times, you wander; yet in spite of your faults, while you are still a long way off, your Father God sees you and is "moved with pity and tenderness" for you. He runs to you, embraces you, and kisses you "fervently" (Luke 15:20 AMPC). Then He celebrates your return! This happens each time you stray.

EVENING - *Welcomed Home*

*When he came to himself, he said, How many hired servants of my
father's have bread enough and to spare, and I perish with hunger!*
LUKE 15:17 KJV

Jesus, what a wonderful story! Whenever I stray and then "come to myself," I realize that I have strayed so far away from You that I am spiritually starving, when all I need to do is come to You and You will fill me up! You will *love* me up! You are my manna. My living water. I'm running to You now. Do You see me? Have compassion, Lord, as I fall into Your arms and You welcome me home!

DAY 161

MORNING - *A Woman Charged*

*It has come at last—salvation and power and the Kingdom
of our God, and the authority of his Christ. For the accuser
of our brothers and sisters has been thrown down to earth—
the one who accuses them before our God day and night.*

REVELATION 12:10 NLT

Any accusations that come into your head about your behavior and mistakes come from one source—the enemy. He brings charges against you day and night (see Revelation 12:10). And if you listen to—and believe—his case against you, you find yourself in agreement with him. The only things then left are doubt and discouragement. You need to remember that Jesus has overcome the enemy. The latter's accusations are null and void.

EVENING - *Stands Triumphant in Christ*

*Through God we shall do valiantly:
for he it is that shall tread down our enemies.*

PSALM 60:12 KJV

Help me, Lord, to become more aware of the accusations hurled against me in my own mind! And to remember every moment of the day that You never gave in to the enemy. In fact, You have already defeated him—and will someday get rid of him altogether! Knowing this, my mind is at peace. I am putting all my faith, hope, and trust in You. Because with You in my life—and mind—I can do anything!

DAY 162

MORNING - *The Lord's Daughter*

I will give you the keys to the kingdom of heaven,
and God in heaven will allow whatever you allow on earth.
But he will not allow anything that you don't allow.
MATTHEW 16:19 CEV

In John Bunyan's *The Pilgrim's Progress*, characters Christian and Hopeful, having been beaten and tortured, are prisoners of Giant Despair in Doubting Castle. When all seems lost, Christian suddenly has an *aha!* moment. He finds he has in his possession a key called Promise. It opens any lock in the giant's castle! By using it, he not only finds freedom from Doubting Castle but escapes from Giant Despair *and* finds himself back on the King's highway! You, too, have such a key! So rid yourself of any doubts, which only lead to despair. Sink your teeth into God's promises.

EVENING - *With Keys to the Kingdom*

I rise before the dawning of the morning, and cry for help;
I hope in Your word. My eyes are awake through the night watches,
that I may meditate on Your word. Hear my voice according to Your
lovingkindness; O LORD, revive me according to Your justice.
PSALM 119:147–149 NKJV

Here I am, Lord, hoping in Your Word from dawn to dusk, knowing that's what will protect me from the doubts that threaten to rise within my mind. I know You've given me the keys to Your kingdom. I'm Your daughter, so there's no need to fear. You'll do as You've promised. And I rejoice in that fact!

DAY 163

MORNING - *A Seeking Woman*

The Lord asked Abraham, Why did Sarah laugh, saying,
Shall I really bear a child when I am so old?
Is anything too hard or too wonderful for the Lord?
GENESIS 18:13–14 AMPC

Perhaps you're embarrassed, even ashamed, to admit to Jesus that you have doubts. So instead of praying about them, you suppress them. On this despairing heap, you add guilt as a sort of cherry on top, making yourself even more miserable and distancing yourself further from God. Or perhaps you're afraid, like Sarah, who laughed when God told her she would be a mother. Do you, too, think yourself irredeemable? Do you deny—even to God—that you have doubts in His ability to do the impossible? Look to the promises in God's Word. They are for *you*, and they never fail.

EVENING - *Knows the Power of God's Promises*

Not a single one of all the good promises the LORD had given to the family
of Israel was left unfulfilled; everything he had spoken came true.
JOSHUA 21:45 NLT

Your Word, Lord, has such power. Everything that comes out of Your mouth takes on a life of its own. All of Your promises have come true—since before the beginning of time. I know You can do the impossible because You have said it over and over again. Help me to get that into my head. May I fall asleep tonight, praying, "You are my God. And in You, all things are possible. For You are the ultimate promise keeper!"

DAY 164

MORNING - *A Surrendered Woman*

For with God nothing is ever impossible and no word from God shall be without power or impossible of fulfillment.

LUKE 1:37 AMPC

If you have doubts, surrender them to Jesus. Tell Him, "I do believe; help me overcome my unbelief!" (Mark 9:24 NIV). He will remind you that not only is nothing impossible for Him, that "no word from God will ever fail" (Luke 1:37 NIV), but also that "everything is possible for one who *believes*" (Mark 9:23 NIV, emphasis added)!

EVENING - *Promised Wisdom*

But if any of you lacks wisdom, let him ask of God, who gives to all generously and without reproach, and it will be given to him. But he must ask in faith without any doubting, for the one who doubts is like the surf of the sea, driven and tossed by the wind.

JAMES 1:5–6 NASB

Lord, You know what frightens me. You know what doubts assail me and make me feel like I'm sinking in quicksand. So I ask You today, Lord, as I read Your good Word, to lead me to a promise I need to learn, memorize, and carve into my heart. I need Your wisdom to lead me into the light of understanding. Shine Your Word on me, Lord. I am ready!

DAY 165

MORNING · *A Shielded Woman*

*Take up the shield of faith, with which you can
extinguish all the flaming arrows of the evil one.*
EPHESIANS 6:16 NIV

When doubts begin creeping back in, do not despair. Turn them over to the Lord. Protect yourself with the shield of faith. Arm yourself with "the sword of the Spirit, which is the word of God" (Ephesians 6:17 NIV). By reciting God's promises (mentally or aloud), you will be putting your focus back where it belongs—on Jesus. And although the doubts, arrows of the enemy, may clamor against your shield, they will not be able to hurt you. Stand firm in Christ.

EVENING · *Armed with God's Word*

*Fear ye not, stand still, and see the salvation of the LORD,
which he will shew to you to day: for the Egyptians whom ye
have seen to day, ye shall see them again no more for ever.
The LORD shall fight for you, and ye shall hold your peace.*
EXODUS 14:13–14 KJV

Jesus, because You are with me, I will not fear. I will stand still, calmly and quietly trusting in Your Word. I know You will rescue me today, once again. The doubts assailing me will be like the Egyptians—I will see them no more. Because I am hiding in You, You will make them disappear. Thank You for always being here, fighting for me as I continue to rest in You, holding my peace.

DAY 166

MORNING - *A Praying Woman*

So God has given both his promise and his oath. These two things are unchangeable because it is impossible for God to lie. Therefore, we who have fled to him for refuge can have great confidence as we hold to the hope that lies before us. This hope is a strong and trustworthy anchor for our souls.
HEBREWS 6:18–19 NLT

For further defense against demon doubts and discouragement, pray the prayer below as soon as you awaken every morning and evening. Be confident in God's promise and truth. Make Him your refuge. Use your hope and faith in Him as the anchor for your soul.

EVENING - *Standing Firm*

Be ready! Let the truth be like a belt around your waist, and let God's justice protect you like armor.
EPHESIANS 6:14 CEV

Good morning, Lord. You are my Abba Father. I am Your daughter whom You dearly love and have forgiven, every moment of every day—even before I was born. Because Jesus has saved me, I am Yours completely. On Him I remain focused. I stand firm in my faith with You, God, as my divine supplier, Christ as my rock and refuge, and the Holy Spirit as my Comforter and guiding light. In this I have peace and joy. Amen.

DAY 167

MORNING · *The Joy-Filled Woman's Path Marker: Promise No. 9*

*"God is not like people. He tells no lies. He is not like humans.
He doesn't change his mind. When he says something,
he does it. When he makes a promise, he keeps it."*

NUMBERS 23:19 GW

Through His Word, God promises He is like no human. He always tells the truth. And He never changes His mind. When He says He'll do something— He does it! He always, always, always keeps His word. You need never doubt His promises! Engrave this fact upon your mind.

EVENING · *A Lifeboat of Promises*

*Remember your promise to me; it is my only hope.
Your promise revives me; it comforts me in all my troubles.*

PSALM 119:49–50 NLT

Lord God, Your promises are my only hope. I cling to them as I tread these deep waters. They keep my head above the flood of doubt that threatens without. I breathe in Your promises and they calm me—mind, body, and spirit. They are my greatest comfort and strength. I climb into them like a lifeboat. Keep me from looking to the world for rescue. I put all my hope in You.

DAY 168

MORNING - *The Joy-Filled Woman's Path Marker: Proof No. 9*

[The boy's father said], "If you can do anything, take pity on us and help us." "'If you can'?" said Jesus. "Everything is possible for one who believes." Immediately the boy's father exclaimed, "I do believe; help me overcome my unbelief!" When Jesus saw that a crowd was running to the scene, he rebuked the impure spirit. . . . Jesus took him [the boy] by the hand and lifted him to his feet, and he stood up.

MARK 9:22–25, 27 NIV

God's Word provides you with proof that everything is possible for believers. Just take what faith you have and believe! When doubts begin creeping in, admit them to God and ask Him for help to overcome them. Then watch Him begin to do the impossible in your own life!

EVENING - *Rising with Renewed Hope*

I cried out, "I am slipping!" but your unfailing love, O LORD, supported me. When doubts filled my mind, your comfort gave me renewed hope and cheer.

PSALM 94:18–19 NLT

Abba God, I'm slipping into doubts again. Support me with Your love—love that never fails. Remove the doubts from my mind. You've done it before—please, do it again! Comfort me with Your Word. Support me on this slippery slope. Ensure my footing. I need the cleats provided by Your promises. They renew my hope. Oh Lord, in You alone I surmount doubt and rise into joy.

DAY 169

MORNING - *The Joy-Filled Woman's Path Marker: Provision No. 9*

The faithful love of the LORD never ends! His mercies never cease. Great is his faithfulness; his mercies begin afresh each morning. I say to myself, "The LORD is my inheritance; therefore, I will hope in him!" The LORD is good to those who depend on him, to those who search for him. So it is good to wait quietly for salvation from the LORD.

LAMENTATIONS 3:22–26 NLT

God is faithful to you in all ways. Him and all His promises are yours for the asking. As a kingdom daughter, they are part of your inheritance. Depend on His coming through for you. Believing is your part. The work is His. Just be patient. Before long, you'll see Him move in amazing ways.

EVENING - *Committed to Promises*

Commit thy way unto the LORD; trust also in him; and he shall bring it to pass. And he shall bring forth thy righteousness as the light, and thy judgment as the noonday. Rest in the LORD, and wait patiently for him: fret not.

PSALM 37:5–7 KJV

Lord, I am committing my way to You, trusting in You and Your promises, knowing that You cannot help but fulfill them for me. You will bring me through this. I yearn for Your light. I rest in You, waiting patiently, keeping Your Word in my mind. What strength there is in each of Your promises! Your Word is like a sonnet meant just for me. Write it on my heart.

MORNING - *The Joy-Filled Woman's Path Marker: Portrait No. 9*

By his divine power, God has given us everything we need for living a godly life. . . . And because of his glory and excellence, he has given us great and precious promises. These are the promises that enable you to share his divine nature and escape the world's corruption caused by human desires.

2 PETER 1:3–4 NLT

God has not only *promised* He keeps all His promises (see Numbers 23:19) and *proven* that He can do the impossible, even help you overcome any doubts (see Mark 9:22–25, 27), He has also *provided* you with His promises as your inheritance (see Lamentations 3:22–26)! And the great thing about that is your belief in His promises will make you more and more like Him every day! In Christ, I have inherited God's promises.

EVENING - *Above the Fray*

Yes, and the Lord will deliver me from every evil attack and will bring me safely into his heavenly Kingdom.

2 TIMOTHY 4:18 NLT

I know You will deliver me from these doubts, Lord. Every time one attacks, I feel the power of Your promises come against it. Meanwhile, I will remain in You, above the doubts this world presents. Because of Your promises, I have victory! And all the glory goes to You! Thank You, Lord! You are worthy of so much praise!

DAY 171

MORNING - *An Overcoming Woman*

Now to Him who is able to keep you from stumbling, and to make you stand in the presence of His glory blameless with great joy, to the only God our Savior, through Jesus Christ our Lord, be glory, majesty, dominion and authority, before all time and now and forever. Amen.

JUDE 1:24–25 NASB

You may have the misconception that once you enter the life of faith, temptations and your yielding to them will cease. Or that any temptation—whether you act on it or not—is itself a sin and that you're at fault for the suggestions of evil that entered your mind. This may inevitably lead you into condemnation and discouragement, the continuing of which can result, at last, in actual sin. Hannah Whitall Smith wrote, "Sin makes an easy prey of a discouraged soul, so that we fall often from the very fear of having fallen." But fear not. God can keep you from stumbling.

EVENING - *Held Up in the Lord*

When I said, My foot is slipping, Your mercy and loving-kindness, O Lord, held me up.

PSALM 94:18 AMPC

Lord, I know that temptation lies all around me. And my thoughts can lead me astray. But no matter what happens in my life, God, I know You will hold me up when I begin slipping because You love me like no other. May the only thing that preys upon me be Your infinite affection as I stand firm in You.

DAY 172

MORNING - *The God-Loving Woman*

For all that is in the world—the lust of the flesh, the lust of the eyes, and the pride of life—is not of the Father but is of the world. And the world is passing away, and the lust of it; but he who does the will of God abides forever.
1 JOHN 2:16–17 NKJV

What exactly is temptation, and how does the evil one lure you into his net? First of all, you must understand that the evil one tempts you to look to him, the world, or your flesh to meet your needs. In other words, he tempts you to act independently of God. Such temptation approaches you via three worldly channels, as noted by the apostle John in the verse above. But if you love God more than the things of the world, God will help you find a way out.

EVENING - *Keeps Focused*

Do not love the world or the things in the world.
If anyone loves the world, the love of the Father is not in him.
1 JOHN 2:15 NKJV

Help me keep my focus on You, Lord. To love You above anything else that I can see in this world. For I know when my eyes are on You alone, I will not sink into temptation but rise to victory.

DAY 173

MORNING - *The Abiding Woman: Temptation Channel 1*

Walk in the Spirit, and you shall not fulfill the lust of the flesh. For the flesh lusts against the Spirit, and the Spirit against the flesh; and these are contrary to one another, so that you do not do the things that you wish.
GALATIANS 5:16–17 NKJV

Neil Anderson, author of *The Bondage Breaker*, says that three channels—"the lust of the flesh, the lust of the eyes, and the pride of life"—were the ones Satan used when he tempted Eve in the garden. First "the woman saw that the tree was good for food" (Genesis 3:6 NKJV). This lust of the flesh draws you away from the will of God (see Galatians 5:16–17) and destroys your dependence upon Him (see John 15:5). But God will provide a way out.

EVENING - *Grafted into Jesus*

"I am the vine, you are the branches. He who abides in Me, and I in him, bears much fruit; for without Me you can do nothing."
JOHN 15:5 NKJV

I know I can do nothing without You, Jesus. So help me to not be tempted by the flesh. For when I am, I am drawn away from You. I want to remain in You, focus on You, and live in You. You are the power, the source, that fills me up and helps me to grow. I graft myself into You this moment as I seek Your face.

MORNING · *The Abiding Woman: Temptation Channels 2 and 3*

*They looked to Him and were radiant;
their faces shall never blush for shame or be confused.*

PSALM 34:5 AMPC

There are two other channels through which Satan tempted Eve in the garden. The second, the lust of the eyes—"it was a delight to the eyes" (Genesis 3:6 NASB)—draws you away from the Word of God (see Matthew 16:24–26), lessening your confidence in Him (see John 15:7). And the third, the pride of life—"the tree was desirable to make one wise" (Genesis 3:6 NASB)—draws you away from the worship of God (see 1 Peter 5:5–11) and destroys your obedience to God (see John 15:8–10). But God can help you cancel your subscription to these channels.

EVENING · *Growing in Confidence and Obedience*

*If you abide in Me, and My words abide in you,
you will ask what you desire, and it shall be done for you.*

JOHN 15:7 NKJV

Help me, Lord, to not be distracted by the lust of my eyes but to be focused on Your Son, the Word. For when my eyes are looking in the right place—at Jesus—my confidence in You grows. For I know, that if I am living and looking to You and Your Word, You and Your Word live in me. And whatever I desire will be done for me through You. What an amazing praise!

DAY 175

MORNING - *The Humbled Woman*

Be sober, be vigilant; because your adversary the devil walks about like a roaring lion, seeking whom he may devour. Resist him, steadfast in the faith.
1 PETER 5:8–9 NKJV

Notice that in each method—the lust of the flesh, the lust of the eyes, and the pride of life—Satan's temptations draw you away from and attempt to destroy your relationship with God. When you allow food to rule your life, you have fallen for the lust of your flesh. When you've a craving for material things and do everything in your power to get them, you are bowing to the lust of your eyes. And when you attempt to be your own god, to no longer bow to the true God, to refuse to seek His direction and commands, you are drawn away from praising Him and are snared by the pride of life. But do not despair! God has a plan to reroute you!

EVENING - *Lifted Up*

Humble yourselves under the mighty hand of God, that He may exalt you in due time, casting all your care upon Him, for He cares for you.
1 PETER 5:6–7 NKJV

I'm bowing down before You right now, Lord, giving myself completely to You. Save me from the power of temptation. I know You care for me. And that as I lower myself in my own estimation, You rise in my own eyes and I am lifted up with You and am able to stand firm in my faith.

DAY 176

MORNING · *The Rerouted Woman*

God did not lead them along the main road that runs through Philistine territory, even though that was the shortest route to the Promised Land. God said, "If the people are faced with a battle, they might change their minds and return to Egypt."
EXODUS 13:17 NLT

The severity and power of your temptations—no matter what channel Satan has used to reach you—may be the strongest proof that you're in the land of promise you've sought. After all, when the Israelites first left Egypt, God took the former slaves the long way, around the Philistines, "lest perhaps the people change their minds when they see war, and return to Egypt" (Exodus 13:17 NKJV). But later, when they had more faith in God, He allowed them to be involved in a few skirmishes while in the wilderness, perhaps to test their mettle. It was not until they were entering the Promised Land that the real battles began.

EVENING · *On the Way to the Promised Land*

So God led them in a roundabout way through the wilderness toward the Red Sea.
EXODUS 13:18 NLT

Thank You, Lord, for always leading me the right way. Increase my faith so that I can, with You, face up to whatever channel the enemy uses to bring me down. Even if I have to go the long way around, I know You are merely increasing my strength on my way to Your land of promise.

DAY 177

MORNING · *A Traveling Woman*

*The Lord went ahead of them. He guided them during the day with
a pillar of cloud, and he provided light at night with a pillar of fire.
This allowed them to travel by day or by night.*
EXODUS 13:21 NLT

So if you are facing a myriad of temptations, some stronger than others, you can know, oddly enough, that you are headed in the right direction and that God will get you through. All you need is to remain confident in Him, focused, joyful, firm in faith, patient, prayerful, planted in the Word, and steadfast in Christ. That seems like a tall order. But don't worry. God will guide you through. He's already gone ahead to prepare the way!

EVENING · *With a Constant Companion*

*And the Lord did not remove the pillar of cloud or
pillar of fire from its place in front of the people.*
EXODUS 13:22 NLT

Thank You, God, for always being with me. It is reassuring to know You will never leave or desert me—even when I'm going through the wilderness of life. With You, I know I'm heading in the right direction—straight for the land of Your promises. And there is no better place to be!

MORNING · *The Overcoming Woman: Remaining Confident*

Be strong and of a good courage. . . . Be not afraid, neither be thou dismayed. . . . Only be thou strong and very courageous.
JOSHUA 1:6, 7, 9 KJV

Someone once said that in overcoming temptations, confidence is the first thing, confidence is the second thing, and confidence is the third thing. In other words, you cannot let the fact that you're facing temptation discourage you but must stand confident in your faith and its strength instead. When Joshua was about to enter the Promised Land and face many foes, God repeatedly told him to be strong, courageous, and fearless. And Jesus reinforces this command to you in John 14:27.

EVENING · *Soaking in God's Command for Courage*

Do not let your hearts be troubled, neither let them be afraid. [Stop allowing yourselves to be agitated and disturbed; and do not permit yourselves to be fearful and intimidated and cowardly and unsettled.]
JOHN 14:27 AMPC

What powerful words, Lord! Whenever I forget who You are or fall out of abiding in You, I feel agitated, afraid, intimidated, and unsettled. So here I am, in Your Word, soaking in it, abiding in it. You are the God who will never leave me but always provide for me. In this, I remain confident.

DAY 179

MORUNG - *The Overcoming Woman: Remaining Focused*

> *"My thoughts are not your thoughts,*
> *nor are your ways My ways."*
> ISAIAH 55:8 NKJV

Do not become discouraged when you face temptations. Instead, turn away from them and look for God to deliver you. Understand that He might not do it when or in the way you expect, for He has told you that He doesn't think like humans. But know and understand that He will do it! Put your confidence on the believing side—God's side, the winning side! He has overcome the world! Keep your eyes on the Champion.

EVENING - *On the Mighty Power of God*

> *"Be strong and courageous; do not be afraid nor dismayed before*
> *the king of Assyria, nor before all the multitude that is with him;*
> *for there are more with us than with him."*
> 2 CHRONICLES 32:7 NKJV

I feel so outnumbered, Lord. I am feeling weak and discouraged. So I am putting all my focus on You. Give me strength and courage. Help me to be brave before the temptations assailing me. I am looking to You for help, knowing that You are more powerful than anything I may ever face. I'm putting my faith in You and You alone. Save me, Jesus. Save me now!

MORNING - *The Overcoming Woman: Remaining Joyful*

Consider it pure joy, my brothers and sisters,
whenever you face trials of many kinds.
JAMES 1:2 NIV

Above all, be joyful during trials and temptations. Don't be brought low in your attitude, thoughts, and demeanor in the midst of the battle. The joy in the Lord will give you the strength you need in the midst of your weakness. Want to really catch the devil off guard? When temptation whispers in your ear, start worshiping the Lord! The evil one won't know what hit him!

EVENING - *In God's Stronghold*

And be not grieved and depressed,
for the joy of the Lord is your strength and stronghold.
NEHEMIAH 8:10 AMPC

It seems strange, Lord, to be joyful in the midst of trials and temptations, yet that is exactly how You want us to be! Help me to adopt the mindset You want me to have no matter what is happening in my life. Give me the power to praise You when temptation whispers in my ear. And I know the joy I find in praise will be exactly what makes me strong! Thank You for being my Stronghold. What would I do without You?!

DAY 181

MORNING - *The Overcoming Woman: Remaining Firm in Faith*

"You will not have to fight this battle. Take up your positions; stand firm and see the deliverance the LORD will give you. . . . Do not be afraid; do not be discouraged. Go out to face them tomorrow, and the LORD will be with you."

2 CHRONICLES 20:17 NIV

Keep your faith that God will deliver you from whatever temptations you face. Believe His promises to fight your battles are true. In fact, "the Lord your God walks in the midst of your camp, to deliver you and give your enemies over to you" (Deuteronomy 23:14 NKJV). But you must stand there with Him, for "the Lord is with you when you are with Him" (2 Chronicles 15:2 NASB). If you suddenly can't find God, *you're* the one who's moved—not Him!

EVENING - *Sticking with God*

"Do not be afraid or discouraged because of the king of Assyria and the vast army with him, for there is a greater power with us than with him. With him is only the arm of flesh, but with us is the LORD our God to help us and to fight our battles."

2 CHRONICLES 32:7–8 NIV

Lord, how many times must I read Your Word before I truly believe—and never forget—You'll deliver me by fighting my battles. All I have to do is stand my ground because You're always with me. So help me to stick with You and keep this idea in my head. What joy Your constant presence gives me!

DAY 182

MORNING · *The Overcoming Woman: Remaining Patient*

*When your faith is tested, your endurance has a chance to grow.
So let it grow, for when your endurance is fully developed,
you will be perfect and complete, needing nothing.*

JAMES 1:3–4 NLT

To remain firm in faith, you must practice patience. Give God time to work. He will not fail, for He has told you that "no weapon that is formed against thee shall prosper" (Isaiah 54:17 KJV). He will help you find a way out. Do not trust in yourself, for you are not strong enough. You need the power of His Holy Spirit working through you (see Acts 1:8). It is God who will arm you with the strength you need (see Psalm 18:32, 37 below). So step aside and let Him take up the battle.

EVENING · *Armed with Strength*

God arms me with strength, and he makes my way perfect. . . . I chased my enemies and caught them; I did not stop until they were conquered.

PSALM 18:32, 37 NLT

I love the psalms, Lord, because they speak in my voice. You are the one who gives me all the strength I need to conquer whatever comes up against me. It is You who steers me in the right direction. With You on my side, I am assured with victory. What peace and joy this revelation gives me as I seek my rest and strength in You!

DAY 183

MORNING - *The Overcoming Woman: Remaining Prayerful*

If you don't know what you're doing, pray to the Father. He loves to help.
You'll get his help, and won't be condescended to when you ask for it.
Ask boldly, believingly, without a second thought.

JAMES 1:5 MSG

Back up all this—your confidence, focus, joy, faith, and patience in God—with prayer, perhaps not so much for the removal but for the wisdom and strength to face your temptations and learn from them. Remember, God has a plan for your life, for good and not evil.

EVENING - *Delivered from Temptations*

"Because he has set his love upon Me, therefore I will deliver him;
I will set him on high, because he has known My name. He shall
call upon Me, and I will answer him; I will be with him in trouble;
I will deliver him and honor him."

PSALM 91:14–15 NKJV

God, I need You! Deliver me from my temptations. Beam me up, Lord, out of this world. Set me on high; bring me to Your side. I am calling on You now. Please answer me. You have said You will be with me in trouble, and I feel I am sinking in deep. But I know of Your power. I have read of Your strength in Your Word. You are my only hope. Save me, I pray!

DAY 184

MORNING - *The Overcoming Woman: Remaining Planted in the Word*

The Word that God speaks is alive and full of power [making it active, operative, energizing, and effective]; it is sharper than any two-edged sword.
HEBREWS 4:12 AMPC

Scripture is great soil. You are bound to wither and weaken amid temptation—and in many other ways—if you remove yourself from it. You'll also be standing somewhere in the dark and without water. Jesus' greatest weapon when tempted in the desert was the Word of God (see Matthew 4:1–11). When you feel yourself being enticed, dig yourself deep in the Word. Memorize whatever verses will help you build the strongest barbed wire fence of protection to keep the evil one from nibbling at your resolve.

EVENING - *Energized by the Good News*

This Good News about Christ. . . . Is the power of God at work, saving everyone who believes.
ROMANS 1:16 NLT

Lord, Your Word is the most powerful weapon in the world—seen and unseen. Thank You for gifting it to me. Show me what verses I need to memorize to help defend me. Make Your Word alive in me, full of power. When it flows through me—mind, heart, body, soul, and spirit—I feel energized. I'm digging deep, Lord, in Your Word. Plant it within me!

DAY 185

MORNING - *The Overcoming Woman: Remaining Steadfast in Christ*

Be sure that your faith is in God alone. Do not waver,
for a person with divided loyalty is as unsettled as a wave
of the sea that is blown and tossed by the wind.

JAMES 1:6 NLT

Finally, be sure and steady in your intentions to stand firm in Christ (see James 1:6–8), for you can do all things through Christ who strengthens you (see Philippians 4:13). "For the Lord will be your confidence, and will keep your foot from being caught" (Proverbs 3:26 NKJV). So flee from the evil one and run to God. Stand still. Stand firm. And you will not only escape but be blessed (see James 1:12 below).

EVENING - *Blessed in Endurance*

God blesses those who patiently endure testing and temptation.
Afterward they will receive the crown of life that
God has promised to those who love him.

JAMES 1:12 NLT

I am facing my temptations and trials while standing sure and steady in You, Jesus. You are my confidence. You keep my foot out of the snare. So I'm running to You, hiding beneath Your Father's wings. There I will be safe. There I will not doubt. There I will endure. And there I am truly blessed.

DAY 186

MORNING - *The Choosey Woman*

Now therefore fear the LORD, and serve him in sincerity and in truth: and put away the gods which your fathers served on the other side of the flood, and in Egypt; and serve ye the LORD. And if it seem evil unto you to serve the LORD, choose you this day whom ye will serve; whether the gods which your fathers served that were on the other side of the flood, or the gods of the Amorites, in whose land ye dwell.
JOSHUA 24:14–15 KJV

Although you may encounter temptations, if you are wholly in God's camp—mind, body, spirit, and soul—you will abhor them. Thus, you must especially guard against those temptations you love to indulge. For as George Eliot wrote, "No evil dooms us hopelessly except the evil we love, and desire to continue in, and make no effort to escape from." So make up your mind, now, today, whose camp you are living in, whose side you are on.

EVENING - *On God's Side*

As for me and my house, we will serve the LORD.
JOSHUA 24:5 KJV

I'm choosing here and now, Lord, to be on Your side of the flood. It is You—and You alone—that I will serve. I'm in Your camp—mind, body, spirit, and soul. Here nothing can touch me. Here I will live forever and a day!

MORNING - *The Encamped Woman*

I the LORD thy God will hold thy right hand,
saying unto thee, Fear not; I will help thee.
ISAIAH 41:13 KJV

If you're looking to the things of this world to save you—chocolate or french fries, a new dress or purse or shoes, riches or fame—or to the worldlings themselves, you've taken your eyes off God. You've strayed from your base camp and entered a wilderness. So remember to choose the One who has overcome the world! Pull up stakes and pitch your tent on God's side once again! "We must then commit ourselves to the Lord for victory over our temptations, as we committed ourselves at first for forgiveness," Hannah Whitall Smith wrote. "And we must leave ourselves just as utterly in His hands for one as for the other."

EVENING - *Power to Save*

Behold, all they that were incensed against thee shall be ashamed and
confounded: they shall be as nothing; and they that strive with thee shall perish.
ISAIAH 41:11 KJV

Lord, I am tired of trying to fight temptation in my own power. I don't know what I was thinking, for Your Word tells me You'll fight my battles. You're on my side and I'm on Yours! So I'm stepping back and letting Your power come through me. Already I feel relief. I know You'll give me victory over this temptation, and that someday this will all be but a recollection of Your power to save.

DAY 188

MORNING - *The Joy-Filled Woman's Path Marker: Promise No. 10*

No temptation has overtaken you except what is common to mankind. And God is faithful; he will not let you be tempted beyond what you can bear. But when you are tempted, he will also provide a way out so that you can endure it.

1 Corinthians 10:13 niv

Remember that God is faithful. Through His Word, He has promised to put up an exit sign just for you, and you'll find it if your eyes are open. He will show you a way to escape temptation—even when there seems to be no way. You need merely keep your eyes, heart, thoughts, spirit, and soul on Him, and your faith *in* Him. He—and He alone—is your confidence (see Psalm 71:5). Live Your life with this promise as part of your very being!

EVENING - *Filled with Great Expectations*

Wait [expectantly] for the Lord, and He will rescue you.

Proverbs 20:22 ampc

I'm running out of patience, Lord. I'm not sure how much more I can take, how much longer I can hold on. I run to You. Shelter me in Your presence. Be my rock and refuge—a boulder that can neither be destroyed nor removed. I am expecting Your deliverance from temptation. I remain steadfast in You, knowing You will rescue me. In that fact alone, I have peace.

DAY 189

The devil came to him and said, "If you are God's Son, tell these stones to turn into bread." Jesus answered, "The Scriptures say: 'No one can live only on food. People need every word that God has spoken.' " . . . The devil said, "If you are God's Son, jump off. The Scriptures say: 'God will give his angels orders about you. They will catch you in their arms, and you won't hurt your feet on the stones.' " Jesus answered, "The Scriptures also say, 'Don't try to test the Lord your God!' " . . . The devil said to him, "I will give all this to you, if you will bow down and worship me." Jesus answered, "Go away Satan! The Scriptures say: 'Worship the Lord your God and serve only him.' " Then the devil left Jesus, and angels came to help him.

MATTHEW 4:3–11 CEV

God's Word proves that scripture repels and disempowers the tempter's wily ways. To tap into the power His Word provides, engrave it upon your heart and mind. Then stand back and watch God take over the battle.

EVENING - *Access to Courage*

"In the world you will have tribulation; but be of good cheer, I have overcome the world."

JOHN 16:33 NKJV

Jesus, I am again facing temptation. Turn my head, Lord. Help me to focus on your Word alone.

DAY 190

MORNING - *The Joy-Filled Woman's Path Marker: Provision No. 10*

Surely He shall deliver you from the snare of the fowler. . . . He shall cover you with His feathers, and under His wings you shall take refuge; His truth shall be your shield and buckler. You shall not be afraid.
PSALM 91:3–5 NKJV

God provides you with a place to hide while He delivers you from temptations and trials. Your job is to run to Him. He'll give you cover. Under His wing, you need not fear anything or anyone—seen or unseen! What joy that gives you—if you believe!

EVENING - *Ready for Rescue*

"What does the LORD your God require of you? He requires only that you fear the LORD your God, and live in a way that pleases him, and love him and serve him with all your heart and soul."
DEUTERONOMY 10:12 NLT

I know that what You have done for me in the past, Lord, You will do again. You have rescued me from temptations so many times. And now here we are again. You know I love You, God. I want to live in a way that pleases You. I want to serve You—and no one else—with all my heart, soul, and mind. So help me again today, Lord. Fight my battles. Give me courage to go on.

MORNING - *The Joy-Filled Woman's Path Marker: Portrait No. 10*

Overwhelming victory is ours through Christ, who loved us.
ROMANS 8:37 NLT

❦

God has not only *promised* He will provide a way out of temptations (see 1 Corinthians 10:13) and *proven* that His Word can defeat any foe you come up against (see Matthew 4:1–11), but He has also *provided* you with refuge while He goes out and fights your battles (Psalm 91:3–5)! With Him and His Word in your life, you cannot be anything but a conqueror (see Romans 8:37)! In fact, you already are!

In Christ, I am more than a conqueror (see Romans 8:37).

EVENING - *Powerful in Divine Strength*

So for the sake of Christ, I am well pleased and take pleasure in infirmities, insults, hardships, persecutions, perplexities and distresses; for when I am weak [in human strength], then am I [truly] strong (able, powerful in divine strength).
2 CORINTHIANS 12:10 AMPC

❦

When I abide in You, nothing can touch me—no sin, no temptation, no evil. When I am weak, unable to fend for myself, You come alongside and win my battles. I find myself powerful in Your divine strength. I take joy in watching my enemy run away. No one can stand against You. What would I do without You, Lord? You amaze me. I praise Your name, over and over again!

DAY 192

MORNING - *The Redeemed & Forgiven Woman*

For everyone has sinned; we all fall short of God's glorious standard. Yet God, in his grace, freely makes us right in his sight.
ROMANS 3:23–24 NLT

Although hidden in Christ you can win the battle, even saints do weaken at times in the face of temptation. Because you are not perfect, you do sometimes fall short of the standards God has set for you—you miss the mark, or sin. (*Sin* under discussion here is intentional sin [conscious, overt acts in defiance of God] as opposed to unintentional [through ignorance, with no malice or forethought]. Examples of intentional sin are stealing, lying, gluttony, and adultery.) But don't lose hope! Jesus makes all things right.

EVENING - *Given Hope*

Yet God, in his grace, freely makes us right in his sight. He did this through Christ Jesus when he freed us from the penalty for our sins.
ROMANS 3:24 NLT

I realize, Lord, that I don't always do the right thing. I miss the mark of perfection. Yet instead of getting discouraged, I will rise up in praise, thanking You, God, for allowing Your Son Jesus to die on the cross for my sins, making me right in Your eyes. That fact gives me hope, allowing me to rest easy in the assurance You have provided at great cost to You.

DAY 193

MORNING - *The Awakened Woman*

"When he finally came to his senses, he said to himself, 'At home even the hired servants have food enough to spare, and here I am dying of hunger!'"
LUKE 15:17 NLT

On your pathway to holiness, you may find yourself suddenly and unexpectedly encountering temptation and, before you know it, swept into sin. When you, like the prodigal son, suddenly come to your senses, you may then be tempted to be discouraged and give up everything as lost or to cover up the sin completely. Either option is lethal to you if you want to grow and progress in your Christian life. The only real pathway available is to face the fact that you have indeed sinned, confess it to God, and discover, if possible, the reason and the remedy. Your divine union with God requires absolute honesty with Him and with yourself.

EVENING - *Comes Home*

"I will go home to my father."
LUKE 15:18 NLT

I want to be honest with You, Lord, and with myself as well. I don't want to lose the closeness I have with You. So when I sin, may my first act be to come home to You, Father God, and tell You all about it. When I do, help me find the reason and the remedy so that I can avoid this misstep in the future.

DAY 194

MORNING · *The Highway Woman*

Watch the path of your feet and all your ways will be established.
PROVERBS 4:26 NASB

When you fail, you really have no cause for discouragement and giving up. You must recognize the fact that it's not about a *state* but a *walk* of life with Christ. Hannah Whitall Smith wrote, "The highway of holiness is not a place, but a way." As one hidden in Christ, you are a follower of the Way. When you walk out of the Way, you can immediately check yourself and find your way back. You must be aware of where you are, hour by hour, minute by minute. If you have turned off the path, you must instantly return to the route the Father has mapped out for you and trust Him more than ever!

EVENING · *Standing By*

Thus says the LORD, "Stand by the ways and see and ask for the ancient paths, where the good way is, and walk in it; and you will find rest for your souls."
JEREMIAH 6:16 NASB

Help me, Lord, to watch where I'm going. For I don't want to stray from Your way. But when I do lose my pathway, I pray that I would not rush ahead of You but stand and ask You "where the good way is, and walk in it." For when I do, I will not only be in Your will and way but find the peace that awaits me there.

DAY 195

MORNING - *The Once-Discouraged Woman*

The heart of the people sank, all spirit knocked out of them.
JOSHUA 7:5 MSG

After a disastrous defeat against the city of Ai soon after entering the Promised Land, the children of Israel were so discouraged their hearts sank. Have you ever cried, "Why didn't I stay in my comfort zone instead of stepping out into this walk of faith?" By so saying, you're expressing despair about not only the present but the future as well. You become immobilized, not wanting to step backward or forward. Your discouragement leaves you in a sort of limbo, a place of no growth, progress, or future. After such an overwhelming failure—emotionally, physically, mentally, spiritually—you may find it easier to wallow in your despondency, your face on the ground, than to look up to God. But He, as always, has a better idea. As God told Joshua, He tells you, "Get up!"

EVENING - *Lifted Up!*

The LORD said to Joshua, "Get up! Why are you lying on your face like this?"
JOSHUA 7:10 NLT

Lord, sometimes I get so discouraged with myself, others, and my circumstances, that my heart sinks down into my feet. My spirit knocked clean out of me. Then I hear Your voice saying, "Get up!" Give me the strength to rise up when failure knocks me down! Lift me on my feet again!

DAY 196

MORNING - *A Tell-All-to-God Woman*

*If we confess our sins, he is faithful and just to forgive
us our sins, and to cleanse us from all unrighteousness.*

1 John 1:9 KJV

What keeps your head down? Perhaps it is the thought that God will find it hard to forgive you. In fact, He may not forgive you at all! Or if He does, it may take Him days, perhaps years, to get over it. Thank God your Father is not like some humans. As soon as you come to Him and confess your sins, He forgives! Immediately! There is no silent treatment, no grudge. This you must believe! For if you do not, you have made God out to be a liar (see 1 John 5:10). And you know He is nothing but truth!

EVENING - *Refreshed by the Almighty!*

*Turn to face God so he can wipe away your sins,
pour out showers of blessing to refresh you.*

Acts 3:19 MSG

Lord, I feel so weighed down sometimes by my missteps. And I'm afraid to come to You, thinking You won't forgive me. But that is a totally misled mindset! I want to ease my burden by telling You everything—the good and the bad! For I know You will forgive me immediately! So here I come, Lord, ready to bear my soul and be refreshed in doing so!

MORNING - *The Walking Woman*

Let us lay aside every weight, and the sin which doth so easily beset us, and let us run with patience the race that is set before us, looking unto Jesus the author and finisher of our faith.
HEBREWS 12:1–2 KJV

As soon as consciousness of your sin has set in, you must immediately lift up your face to God and become conscious of His forgiveness. You can only continue walking on this path of holiness by taking your eyes off your misstep and "looking unto Jesus." Otherwise, you will keep tripping up!

EVENING - *Aware of the Misstep*

Have mercy upon me, O God, according to Your lovingkindness; according to the multitude of Your tender mercies, blot out my transgressions. Wash me thoroughly from my iniquity, and cleanse me from my sin.
PSALM 51:1–2 NKJV

Lord, I need Your mercy. You abound in love for me, so please help me, God. Blot out the sins I have committed, the wrongs I have done. I have felt the pangs of the Holy Spirit, Lord. I am now aware of the misstep I took. My heart is so heavy. Lift me up, Lord. Help me not to wallow in discouragement but to bask in Your forgiveness that is everlasting.

DAY 198

MORNING · *An Open Woman*

"This is what the LORD, the God of Israel, says: Hidden among you,
O Israel, are things set apart for the LORD. You will never defeat
your enemies until you remove these things from among you."
JOSHUA 7:13 NLT

Once your eyes are back on Jesus, you can confess what you have done. Within that confession may lie your motives. In Joshua 7:20–21, a man named Achan confessed his missteps to Joshua.

Here's what Achan's path to sin looked like: He saw (spoils of war), coveted, took, then hid. In four steps, Achan, who had taken his eyes off God, had intentionally sinned. Does this progression sound familiar? Eve did the same thing in the garden. She saw the fruit that would make her wise. She coveted it, then took it. Later, she hid from God.

When you misstep and don't confess, you miss out on the victory in God!

EVENING · *Experiencing Amazing Relief*

Joshua said to Achan, "My son, give glory to the LORD,
the God of Israel, by telling the truth. Make your confession
and tell me what you have done. Don't hide it from me."
JOSHUA 7:19 NLT

God, I don't want to miss out on the power that You provide those who come to You with a clean breast. So bring to my mind those sins I am aware and unaware of. In this moment, I confess them to You. With nothing hidden from Your eyes, I feel an amazing relief!

DAY 199

MORNING - *The Encouraged Woman*

*Now the LORD said to Joshua, "Do not be afraid, nor be dismayed;
take all the people of war with you, and arise, go up to Ai."*
JOSHUA 8:1 NKJV

When you have sinned, acknowledge it. Be like the children of Israel in this account in Joshua. Rise up "early in the morning" (Joshua 7:16 KJV), then run to where the sins are hidden, take them from the midst of their hiding places, and lay them before the Lord (see Joshua 7:22–23). Then you can stone them, burn them, and bury them (see Joshua 7:25–26) and immediately receive God's forgiveness, encouragement, and victory, as did Joshua and the Israelites.

EVENING - *Given Victory*

*"See, I have given into your hand the king of Ai,
his people, his city, and his land."*
JOSHUA 8:1 NKJV

You are so amazing, Lord. A part of me thinks that You will like me better if I hide things from You, things I'm ashamed of. But when I do that, I only weaken myself because there's a barrier between You and I. The amazing part is that when I do come to You, confessing all, You end up not only relieving me of a terrific burden, but giving me victory! It boggles my mind. But I praise You for how You work all the same. I don't need to understand—just confess. Thank You, Lord, for Your forgiveness, encouragement, and victory!

DAY 200

MORNING · *An Outspoken Woman*

*My life dissolves and weeps itself away for heaviness; raise me up
and strengthen me according to [the promises of] Your word.*
PSALM 119:28 AMPC

❧

Hannah Whitall Smith wrote:

> *Our courage must rise higher than ever, and we must abandon ourselves
> more completely to the Lord that His mighty power may the more
> perfectly work in us. . . . We must forget our sin as soon as it is thus
> confessed and forgiven. We must not dwell on it and examine it and
> indulge in a luxury of distress and remorse.*

If you do not do as Smith suggests, you will get deeper and deeper into your
sin and further away from God, putting a sin barrier between you and Him.
By breaking the silence of sin, you break the barrier to God and His power!

EVENING · *Leaving Behind All the Missteps*

I considered my ways; I turned my feet to [obey] Your testimonies.
PSALM 119:59 AMPC

❧

I've taken stock of all my ways, all the paths I've taken. I've told You everything,
Lord! And now I turn my feet back onto Your path. I'm leaving behind all the
missteps I've made and am lifting myself up to You. My sins, once confessed,
are forgotten. I refuse to consider them again. Instead, I rise up in Your power,
in the amazing promises of Your Word!

DAY 201

MORNING - *An Imperfect Woman*

David said to Nathan, I have sinned against the Lord. . . .
2 SAMUEL 12:13 AMPC

King David's encounter with Bathsheba is another example of a good person's journey into failure. Instead of being with his men at war, David stayed home. He *saw* a bathing Bathsheba, *coveted* her, *took* her by committing adultery with her, and then sent her home, which means he *hid* her and their sin. Not only was David's commander, Joab, discouraged at the events, but "the thing that David had done displeased the LORD" (2 Samuel 11:27 NKJV). Even though David's sin was unconfessed up to this point, God still knew what David had done! Fortunately, David did confess when the prophet Nathan confronted him. Although David escaped with his life after this sin, it's effects lingered. God will shield us from dying for sin but not from the effects of it.

EVENING - *Receiving Forgiveness*

*And Nathan said to David, the Lord also
has put away your sin; you shall not die.*
2 SAMUEL 12:13 AMPC

Help me to keep in mind, Lord, that although I'm not perfect, and You'll forgive me when I confess my sins, their repercussions will remain. Lord, it's so much better to follow Your commandments from the beginning than to disobey, sin, and have the unintended consequences affect me and all those around me. Help me stay on Your good path, Lord, and avoid the missteps altogether.

DAY 202

MORNING · *The Seen Woman*

Jesus repeated the question: "Simon son of John, do you love me?"
"Yes, Lord," Peter said, "you know I love you."
"Then take care of my sheep," Jesus said.

JOHN 21:16 NLT

Trying to hide your sins is like having a cavity and not attending to it. Hidden in your mouth, it grows deeper and deeper until it becomes abscessed, threatening to infect your entire body unless you have it pulled. If you don't confess your sins and continue to hide them from God (an insane endeavor since He sees and knows everything), not only do you distance yourself from God but your misdeeds will, like David's, take on a snowball effect until you are buried by them or, like Peter, you'll find yourself weeping bitter tears (see Matthew 26:69–75). Instead, confess, be forgiven, and allow God to redeem Your life, just like He did Peter's!

EVENING · *Eyes Jesus*

Let us run with patience the race that is set before us, looking unto Jesus.

HEBREWS 12:1–2 KJV

My eyes are off the mistakes I've made, the failures I've had. I'm looking to You, Jesus, to help me through this life in You. I'm armed with Your patience—for I have none of my own. And with You holding my hand, running beside me, I can conquer any habit, any sin. Thank You, Lord, for never leaving me, for never running out on me. I praise Your name!

DAY 203

MORNING - *A Rescued Woman*

We have been rescued from our enemies so we can serve God without fear,
in holiness and righteousness for as long as we live.
LUKE 1:74–75 NLT

God already knows what you've done. Confessing sins is more for your benefit than His. For when you admit a sin or indulgence, you are bringing it into the light, enabling you to forgive yourself for the deed done in the past, to request God's help in finding its cause in the present, and to help guard against it in the future. Make Psalm 139:23–24 your continual plea before God. If you do, God will rescue you. He'll turn your darkness to light (see Ephesians 5:8 NLT).

EVENING - *Searched and Saved*

Search me, O God, and know my heart; test me and know my
anxious thoughts. Point out anything in me that offends you,
and lead me along the path of everlasting life.
PSALM 139:23–24 NLT

I'm here for a God-scan, Lord. Please examine my body, mind, heart, and soul for anything that is displeasing to You. I don't want to fall into any temptations. So if there is anything You need me to hand over to You—and leave there— point it out to me. With You, the yoke is easy and the burden light. Thank You for saving me from shadows and bringing me into Your Son's light.

MORNING - *The Joy-Filled Woman's Path Marker: Promise No. 11*

If we [freely] admit that we have sinned and confess our sins, He is faithful and just (true to His own nature and promises) and will forgive our sins [dismiss our lawlessness] and [continuously] cleanse us from all unrighteousness [everything not in conformity to His will in purpose, thought, and action].

1 JOHN 1:9 AMPC

Through His divine Word, God promises His faithfulness in forgiving you for your sins. Day after day, minute by minute, He's also promised to cleanse you from any wrongdoing. So don't let things pile up. Instead, come clean with God without fear! Believe this promise and you'll be whiter than snow!

EVENING - *Honesty, the Blessed Policy*

Behold, You desire truth in the inward parts, and in the hidden part You will make me to know wisdom.

PSALM 51:6 NKJV

Lord, I can no longer lie to myself. I need to come to You in truth. My misdeed is weighing me down, Lord. I bring it now into Your light so that You can blast it away. Give me wisdom, Lord, to handle this situation better the next time. Your Word says that You will help the contrite and brokenhearted, Lord. Right now, that's me. So please, help me, heal me, make me whole.

DAY 205

Blessed are those whose transgressions are forgiven, whose sins are covered. Blessed is the one whose sin the LORD does not count against them and in whose spirit is no deceit. When I kept silent, my bones wasted away through my groaning all day long. For day and night your hand was heavy on me; my strength was sapped as in the heat of summer. Then I acknowledged my sin to you and did not cover up my iniquity. I said, "I will confess my transgressions to the LORD." And you forgave the guilt of my sin.

PSALM 32:1–5 NIV

Psalm 32, presumably written by King David after the prophet Nathan confronted him over his sin with Bathsheba, is amazing proof God does forgive one who confesses his or her failures. And, as He did David, God will not only redeem but empower the confessor to continue on and do great things!

EVENING - *Far Removed from Past Failures*

As far as the east is from the west, so far has He removed our transgressions from us.

PSALM 103:12 NKJV

I cannot even fathom, Lord, how far away You remove our sins from us. I want to get back up, walking in Your way. Yet my feet feel stuck. Lift me out of this pit of despair. Help me to understand that You've not only forgiven me of my sin but have forgotten all about it. Bring me back into Your saving grace.

DAY 206

MORNING - *The Joy-Filled Woman's Path Marker: Provision No. 11*

Who is a God like you, who pardons sin and forgives the transgression of the remnant of his inheritance? You do not stay angry forever but delight to show mercy. You will again have compassion on us; you will tread our sins underfoot and hurl all our iniquities into the depths of the sea.

MICAH 7:18–19 NIV

God not only provides forgiveness from your sins and failures. He doesn't get angry! He's thrilled to be merciful to you. He even has compassion for you. And, best of all, He pardons you! Once having confessed your sins, He puts them behind you forever! What joy you have with a God of boundless—and immediate—forgiveness! Now move forward in His will and way!

EVENING - *Boundless and Immediate Forgiveness!*

For I acknowledge my transgressions, and my sin is always before me. Against You, You only, have I sinned, and done this evil in Your sight— that You may be found just when You speak, and blameless when You judge.

PSALM 51:3–4 NKJV

Jesus, no matter where I go, I cannot run from the sin I have committed. It is always right there in front of my face. So I now confess it to You. For it is You I have wronged. Rescue me, Lord, from this awful predicament. Help me to realize that Your forgiveness is not only boundless but immediate. Help me to put this wrongdoing behind me and move forward in Your will and way.

DAY 207

MORNING - *The Joy-Filled Woman's Path Marker: Portrait No. 11*

Because of the sacrifice of the Messiah, his blood poured out on the altar of the Cross, we're a free people—free of penalties and punishments chalked up by all our misdeeds. And not just barely free, either. Abundantly free!
EPHESIANS 1:7–8 MSG

God has not only *promised* He'll forgive you for your confessed missteps (see 1 John 1:9) and *proven* He'll then redeem and empower you (see Psalm 32:1–5), but He's also *provided* you immediate mercy, compassion, and pardon so you can more forward in His will and way (see Micah 7:18–19). What joy this next *portrait* statement (based on Ephesians 1:7) provides!

In Christ, I am not only redeemed but forgiven.

EVENING - *Freed and Forgiven!*

Create in me a clean heart, O God, and renew a steadfast spirit within me. Do not cast me away from Your presence, and do not take Your Holy Spirit from me. Restore to me the joy of Your salvation, and uphold me by Your generous Spirit.
PSALM 51:10–12 NKJV

I feel like I've been wallowing in mud, Lord. I need to calmly yet boldly lift myself up and confess to You. I've got this habit that I've been hiding from others and supposedly from You. But who am I kidding? You know and see all. Work through me, Lord, to help me break this habit. Restore me to Your joy.

DAY 208

MORNING - *The Woman Assured of God's Presence*

With him is an arm of flesh, but with us is the
Lord our God to help us and to fight our battles.
2 Chronicles 32:8 ampc

One of the greatest challenges facing you, a believer, is seeing God's hand in everything. Almost everything you encounter in your life comes to you through human instrumentalities, and most of your trials are the result of some person's failure, ignorance, carelessness, cruelty, or sin. But how could an all-loving God put us through such heartbreak? Hannah Whitall Smith wrote,

What is needed, then, is to see God in everything and to receive everything directly from His hands with no intervention of second causes. And it is to this that we must be brought before we can know an abiding experience of entire abandonment and perfect trust. Our abandonment must be to God, not to man. And our trust must be in Him, not in any arm of flesh, or we shall fail at the first trial.

EVENING - *Simply Trusts*

Behold, the Lord's hand is not shortened at all, that it cannot save,
nor His ear dull with deafness, that it cannot hear.
Isaiah 59:1 ampc

I know, Lord, that no matter what is happening in my life, Your hand is in it. So I won't worry or moan or fuss. I'll simply trust You to work everything out for my good. Because no arm of flesh—no human instrumentality—has more power than You do in Your little finger!

MORNING - *The Woman with God on Her Side*

Steep your life in God-reality, God-initiative, God-provisions. Don't worry about missing out. You'll find all your everyday human concerns will be met.
MATTHEW 6:33 MSG

Scripture supports Smith's claim that there are no "second causes" for the believing Christian—that everything comes to you through your Father's hand and with His knowledge, no matter what person or circumstances may have been the apparent agents. After all. . .

- Not one sparrow falls to the ground without God knowing about it.
- He even knows how many hairs are on your head.
- You need not worry about your needs because the Father knows them.
- You need not seek revenge because God will do it for you.
- You need not fear because God is on your side.

(See Matthew 10:29–30; Matthew 6:32; Romans 12:19; Psalm 118:6.)

EVENING - *Flying Right*

"What is the price of two sparrows—one copper coin? But not a single sparrow can fall to the ground without your Father knowing it. And the very hairs on your head are all numbered."
MATTHEW 10:29–30 NLT

Sometimes I'm such a birdbrain. But even then, God, You love me. Without You, I could never fly right. You know me so well, I sometimes wonder why You put up with me. And then I remember—it's because You love me. I am humbled in Your presence. Thank You, Lord, for giving me such love.

MORNING - *The Well-Provided-for Woman*

*God, my shepherd! I don't need a thing. You have bedded me
down in lush meadows, you find me quiet pools to drink from.*
PSALM 23:1–2 MSG

And there's more evidence of scripture supporting Smith's claim that there
are no "second causes" for the believing Christian—that everything comes to
you through your Father's hand. Because. . .

- No one can stand against you because God is for you.
- Because you have God as your Shepherd, you are never in need.
- When you pass through the waters and the fire, God is with you.
- You are not harmed by lions because God shuts their mouths.
- You need not be concerned by what your fellow humans do to you because
  God is your Helper, and He will neither leave you nor forsake you.

(See Romans 8:31; Psalm 23:1; Isaiah 43:2; Daniel 6:22; Hebrews 13:5–6.)

EVENING - *Unharmed*

*What shall we say about such wonderful things as these?
If God is for us, who can ever be against us?*
ROMANS 8:31 NLT

Everything that comes to me comes from You, Lord—the good and the bad.
And the great thing about it is that You are for me! You love me! You will not
harm me. And that's what I'm trusting in. That everything I need will come
through and from You—the Ultimate Provider!

DAY 211

MORNING - *The God-Created Woman*

*Has not my hand made all these things,
and so they came into being?" declares the LORD.*
ISAIAH 66:2 NIV

⌘

Thus, second causes are under the management of your Father. Not one of them can reach you without God's permission and knowledge. Everything (except your own sinfulness) comes from your Lord. "It may be the sin of man that originates the action, and therefore the thing itself cannot be said to be the will of God," Hannah Whitall Smith wrote, "but by the time it reaches us, it has become God's will for us and must be accepted as coming directly from His hands."

EVENING - *Allowing Things to Be*

"All the people of the earth are nothing compared to him. He does as he pleases among the angels of heaven and among the people of the earth. No one can stop him or say to him, 'What do you mean by doing these things?' "
DANIEL 4:35 NLT

⌘

You do as You please, Lord, as You see fit. Therefore, I will not question where anything comes from or ask You what You mean by allowing certain situations or people to come into my life. I leave it all in Your hands, knowing that there is a reason behind it. And as I stop asking "Why?" and simply allow things to be, I find amazing peace. Thank You!

DAY 212

MORNING · *The Cared-for Woman*

A Samaritan. . .went to him and bandaged his wounds,
pouring on oil and wine. Then he put the man on his
own donkey, brought him to an inn and took care of him.
LUKE 10:33–34 NIV

Never forget that, through it all, God will be with you, laughing with you during times of joy and comforting you through times of trial. Imagine you are the person who has been beaten and robbed and is lying on the side of the road. Others may pass by, but you look up at the One who has paused by your side. It is the face of Jesus. He will put oil on your wounds, bind you up, pick you up, and carry you to a place of warmth and comfort, providing for you until you are back on your feet.

EVENING · *Carried to Safety*

" 'The LORD your God cared for you all along the way as
you traveled through the wilderness, just as a father cares
for his child. Now he has brought you to this place.' "
DEUTERONOMY 1:31 NLT

I am overwhelmed by the love You have for me, Father God. When I am at my lowest, I look up and there You are. Others have passed me by, but You will never leave me. You bind me up, pick me up, and carry me to safety, just as You would a little girl. Thank You for bringing me to this place of warmth and comfort.

DAY 213

MORNING - *The Woman Abandoned to God*

*Neither death nor life, neither angels nor demons, neither our
fears for today nor our worries about tomorrow—not even
the powers of hell can separate us from God's love.*
ROMANS 8:38 NLT

In all things you must be patient and totally abandoned to God's will and way, to His plan for you, through every blessing as well as every trial. For God loved Jesus as much on the cross as He did on Mount Tabor (where Jesus was transfigured). You are like a child in God's arms. Everything that touches you goes through Him first. You must realize that no evil exists—no matter how dark and bleak—that God cannot turn into good.

EVENING - *With an Always-There Protector*

*Yes, I carried you before you were born. I will be your God throughout
your lifetime—until your hair is white with age. I made you,
and I will care for you. I will carry you along and save you.*
ISAIAH 46:3–4 NLT

Lord, it's great to have one constant in my life—an always-there protector, refuge, strength, fortress. Nothing comes to me without it first coming through You. Thank You for carrying me through whatever happens—from this day to the last. I'm safe in Your love and care.

DAY 214

MORNING - *A Woman Sent Ahead*

*"Don't be sad or angry with yourselves that you sold me. . . .
God sent me ahead of you to make sure that you would have
descendants on the earth and to save your lives in an
amazing way. It wasn't you who sent me here, but God."*
GENESIS 45:5, 7–8 GW

Take the case of Joseph. Instead of killing him, his brothers sold him to some merchants. After serving as a slave, being accused of rape and thrown into a dungeon, Joseph became the number-two man in Egypt and was later able to save the lives of his father and his brothers during a famine. He told his siblings not to be upset with themselves. And that it was God, not them, who'd actually sent Joseph ahead. Although their plan had been evil, God made good come out of it! God will make good come out of your life, too!

EVENING - *Where God Plans Good*

*"Even though you planned evil against me,
God planned good to come out of it."*
GENESIS 50:20 GW

Lord, how comforting to think that no matter what is going on in my life, You have a plan for me. You are sending me out ahead so that good will come out of whatever is happening. So no evil can thwart Your purpose! What a relief! I rest easy in this knowledge—and in You!

DAY 215

MORNING - *A Woman Close to God*

The LORD was with Joseph, so he became a successful man.
GENESIS 39:2 GW

Through all Joseph's trials and successes, our Father God was with Joseph—and Joseph stayed with God. "While Joseph was in prison, the Lord [the great I Am] was with him. The Lord reached out to him with his unchanging love and gave him protection. . . . The Lord was with Joseph and made whatever he did successful" (Genesis 39:20–21, 23 GW). Because Joseph stayed close to the Lord, our Creator God turned Joseph's trial into a blessing—not only for Joseph himself but for the sons of Israel! And He promises to do the same for us!

EVENING - *Living in God Reality*

When you pass through the waters, I will be with you; and through the rivers, they shall not overflow you. When you walk through the fire, you shall not be burned, nor shall the flame scorch you.
ISAIAH 43:2 NKJV

Lord, I feel as if I am being tossed from floodwaters to the furnace and back again. But that's only how I feel—I know it is not reality. My reality is that You are here beside me—through fire and water. There is no need for me to freak out about anything. My comfort is that You are with me no matter where I land, and that You will work all things out to my good. And in that fact I not only find peace but know I'll succeed.

DAY 216

MORNING · *The Trusting Woman*

It is just as the Scriptures say, "What God has planned for people who love him is more than eyes have seen or ears have heard. It has never even entered our minds!"

1 CORINTHIANS 2:9 CEV

God is not the author of sin, but He uses His creativity and His wisdom to work the design of His providence to His—and your—advantage. All you need to do is trust Him to work things out to your good. He will overrule events, trials, and tragedies in your life to His glory!

Being a woman, you may often try to fix things and get frustrated when you can't. Those are times when you need to let go and let God. Because *He* is the "Great Fixer."

EVENING · *Looking Up*

I will set My eyes upon them for good, and I will bring them again to this land; and I will build them up and not pull them down, and I will plant them and not pluck them up.

JEREMIAH 24:6 AMPC

I know, Lord, that somehow You are looking around, searching for a way to make good come out of everything that is happening in my life. In the meantime, I am looking to obey You every step of the way. So keep me in Your sights, Father God, as I continue to seek You and Your presence, Your will and Your way, around every corner I encounter. See You there!

DAY 217

MORNING - *The Creative Woman*

God is able to do far more than we could ever ask for or imagine.
He does everything by his power that is working in us.
EPHESIANS 3:20 NIRV

❧

Oftentimes, God sees solutions that you cannot even imagine! After all, He is the *Creator* God. As the great I Am, He has everything under His power. Are you allowing God to work in the events of your life—or are you too busy "fixing them" to let Him into the situations, thus blocking His way? When you are walking in God's will and in His way, trusting Him to come through for you, He will create a wonderful solution, in *His* time. Granted—it may take much patience and faith on your part. But are these not the cornerstones of your belief?

EVENING - *Out Imagined*

I am the LORD God. I rule the world, and I can do anything!
JEREMIAH 32:27 CEV

❧

Every time I turn around, God, You are coming up with a solution I never would have imagined in a thousand years! You are amazing! You, the ruler of the world, can do anything. And I am a witness to that fact, over and over again! Help me to let go and let You work, to be patient, have faith, and wait expectantly for the good You are bringing into my life.

DAY 218

MORNING - *A Traveling Woman*

When the king ordered the search for beautiful women, many were taken to the king's palace in Susa, and Esther was one of them.
ESTHER 2:8 CEV

Like Dorothy in *The Wizard of Oz*, you sometimes may have to go quite a distance down that long, yellow-brick road of loss, grief, tragedy, and trials before you find your way home. And the amazing thing about this is that many times you have incredible life-changing experiences and learn valuable lessons along the way.

EVENING - *On the Road with God*

"If you keep quiet at a time like this, deliverance and relief for the Jews will arise from some other place, but you and your relatives will die. Who knows if perhaps you were made queen for just such a time as this?"
ESTHER 4:14 NLT

Esther is a great example, Lord, of a girl caught up in a whirlwind of events beyond her control. When her story begins, she is orphaned, brought into the king's harem, chosen to be the next queen, and then faced with having to risk her life to save her people. Talk about life-changing experiences! I, too, have gone through trials and tragedies. But I've learned a lot, too, mostly to trust in You to make everything come out right. Give me the courage to do what You call me to do at such a time as this I'm living in. Thanks for being with me as I travel down this road of life!

DAY 219

MORNING - *The Focused Woman*

"God will surely come to help you. He'll take you up out of this land. He'll bring you to the land he promised to give to Abraham, Isaac and Jacob."
GENESIS 50:24 NIrV

Your God is an awesome God! He leads you through desert places. But if you keep your eyes on His pillar of light and follow the cloud He sends before you, you will have the living water you need to continue along the way. He will provide you with manna—His wonderful Word. He will continue to take care of you and will one day lead you to the Promised Land.

EVENING - *Nourished along the Way*

"God will surely come to help you."
GENESIS 50:25 NIrV

God, when something is repeated in Your holy Word, I pay attention! In Genesis 50:24 and 25, the word is that You will surely come to help me get to the Promised Land. That leaves no room for doubt that You are here already, with Your hand in mine, ready to take me up out of where I am and plant me down in good soil. I praise You for the living water of Jesus and manna of Your Word that keeps me fit along the way!

DAY 220

MORNING - *A Woman Never Alone*

I am with you all the days (perpetually, uniformly, and on every occasion), to the [very] close and consummation of the age. . . .
MATTHEW 28:20 AMPC

Your part is to trust that everything you experience—good and bad—comes through God to you. You are not to be beguiled by the darkness of doubts, what-ifs, and trials but to understand that He is with you in the midst of your storms and will find an awesomely creative way to turn whatever evil confronts you into your eventual good. You need not enjoy your trials but simply understand that you must trust God's will, wisdom, and creativity in the midst of them and impress the certainty upon your mind that He is with you through it all until the end of the age.

EVENING - *Letting It Be*

Amen (so let it be).
MATTHEW 28:20 AMPC

I am believing, Lord, that You are with me all the time. Every second of my life. From the beginning to the end. On every occasion. I feel Your very presence beside me and am overwhelmed with Your love, compassion, kindness, sweetness. So I will not worry but simply trust that whatever is happening now—whether it be fair or foul—comes from You and will always be good for me! So let it be!

DAY 221

MORNING - *The Knowing Woman*

I will confess, praise, and give thanks to You, for You have heard and answered me; and You have become my Salvation and Deliverer.
PSALM 118:21 AMPC

Knowing everything is in God's hands, you can simply let go with abandon and let God work His marvels in good times and bad, praising Him all the way. As Bill Gillham writes in *What God Wishes Christians Knew about Christianity*:

> For by praising Him in and for your circumstance,
> you leave God two alternatives: Change the circumstance,
> or give you so much grace that you'll actually become glad for the
> experience. Either way, you're the winner.

EVENING - *Rejoicing*

We can rejoice, too, when we run into problems and trials, for we know that they help us develop endurance. And endurance develops strength of character, and character strengthens our confident hope of salvation.
ROMANS 5:3–4 NLT

I'm determined to rejoice in the midst of this trial, Lord. Through my tears and pain, I give You praise and sing Your name. In this life, Lord, I want to glorify You. You will give me the strength and courage to face anything—any man, woman, or child. Through You I can love them unconditionally and forgive any misdeeds. Praise, praise, praise!

MORNING - *The Joy-Filled Woman's Path*
Marker: Promise No. 12

We are assured and know that [God being a partner in their labor] all things work together and are [fitting into a plan] for good to and for those who love God and are called according to [His] design and purpose.
ROMANS 8:28 AMPC

In His Word, God promises that He will work all things out for your good. Everything is working out according to His plan. He's partnering with you as you live your life. Why? Because you love Him—and He's crazy about you! So just relax. Take joy in simply living with Him, knowing He's got you in His hands.

EVENING - *God's Grand Plan*

The LORD is on my side; I will not fear. What can man do to me?
PSALM 118:6 NKJV

I'm in a tough spot, God. I feel fear rising up within me. But I know You are on my side. And although it's hard for me to fathom how this will turn out, I know You have something up Your sleeve. I don't need to know the details. All I need is to look to You. To trust that in Your wisdom and creativity, You will work this into Your grand plan. That gives me courage and great peace.

DAY 223

MORNING - *The Joy-Filled Woman's Path Marker: Proof No. 12*

[Shadrach, Meshach, and Abednego] were cast into the midst of the burning fiery furnace. . . . [Then Nebuchadnezzar said], "I see four men loose, walking in the midst of the fire; and they are not hurt, and the form of the fourth is like the Son of God." . . . Then Shadrach, Meshach, and Abednego came from the midst of the fire. . . . The fire had no power; the hair of their head was not singed nor were their garments affected, and the smell of fire was not on them.

DANIEL 3:21, 25–27 NKJV

God's Word provides the proof that when you stick with Him, He sticks with you. In fact, He walks with you in the midst of fire! With Him, you will come away from any test spiritually unsinged! You won't even smell like fire!

EVENING - *On the Other Side*

"Give your entire attention to what God is doing right now, and don't get worked up about what may or may not happen tomorrow. God will help you deal with whatever hard things come up when the time comes."

MATTHEW 6:34 MSG

The future is so uncertain, Lord. I find myself wishing my life away, just so I can get on the other side of this trial I am going through. Help me to find Your peace. Take my hand and lead me into Your light. Change my thoughts from panic to praise!

MORNING - *The Joy-Filled Woman's Path Marker: Provision No. 12*

Blessed be the God and Father of our Lord Jesus Christ, the Father of sympathy (pity and mercy) and the God [Who is the Source] of every comfort (consolation and encouragement), Who comforts (consoles and encourages) us in every trouble (calamity and affliction), so that we may also be able to comfort (console and encourage) those who are in any kind of trouble or distress, with the comfort (consolation and encouragement) with which we ourselves are comforted (consoled and encouraged) by God.

2 CORINTHIANS 1:3–4 AMPC

God provides all the comfort you need to get through whatever you are going through. He has so much compassion for you! And remember Jesus? He knows what it's like to be hurt, bruised, afflicted, rejected, and more! So snuggle up to the Great I Am. He's always on your side!

EVENING - *Back in the Light*

I may walk through valleys as dark as death, but I won't be afraid. You are with me, and your shepherd's rod makes me feel safe.

PSALM 23:4 CEV

Thank You, Great Shepherd, for walking through the darkest valleys with me and for always bringing me back into the light. I'm not afraid with You by my side. With Your rod for protection and Your staff to guide me, I'll always be protected and on the right road! Thank You for walking this path with me.

DAY 225

MORNING - *The Joy-Filled Woman's Path Marker: Portrait No. 12*

When you pass through the waters, I will be with you, and through the rivers, they will not overwhelm you. When you walk through the fire, you will not be burned or scorched, nor will the flame kindle upon you.
ISAIAH 43:2 AMPC

God has not only *promised* He will work all things out for your good (see Romans 8:28) and *proven* that He will be with you in flood and fire (see Daniel 3:21, 25–27), but He has also *provided* you with all the comfort and compassion you need along the way (see 2 Corinthians 1:3–4). Imbue yourself with this next *portrait* statement (based on Isaiah 43:2) and revel in the peace that follows.

In Christ, I am assured of God's presence in any and all situations.

EVENING - *God as a Constant Companion*

They should seek the Lord, if haply they might feel after him, and find him, though he be not far from every one of us: for in him we live, and move, and have our being.
ACTS 17:27–28 KJV

You are never far away from me, Lord. Thank You, God! I cannot take a step without You knowing, guiding, leading. You take such good care of me. I need never fret or moan or fear. In Your presence, I am in the best hands ever!

DAY 226

MORNING - *The Free Woman: Result No. 1 of the Higher Life*

Now the Lord is the Spirit. . . .
2 CORINTHIANS 3:17 AMPC

You have a choice. You can live in bondage or experience the freedom that life in Christ affords.

In the first scenario, your soul is controlled by an unyielding obligation to obey the laws of God, either because you fear God's punishment or you expect some kind of remuneration for duties performed. In the second scenario, the controlling authority is a new *inner* woman who works out the will of the divine Creator without fear of punishment or an expected reward. In the first, you are a slave, walking in the flesh, hoping your actions please your overseer. In the second, you are free in Christ, a daughter of the King, an heir to His promises, walking in the Spirit, and working simply for God's love. Your true pathway, of course, is that of the free woman.

EVENING - *Walking and Working in Christ*

And where the Spirit of the Lord is, there is liberty (emancipation from bondage, freedom).
2 CORINTHIANS 3:17 AMPC

I want to live a life of freedom in You, Jesus. I don't want to be controlled by fear of punishment, nor expect reward for the things I do. Instead, I just want to walk and work in Your spirit, freedom, and love.

MORNING - *A Trusting Woman*

We know that a person is made right with God not by following the law, but by trusting in Jesus Christ.
GALATIANS 2:16 NCV

Once you've begun your initial walk, you may be led astray, falling back into your former life of bondage to the world. This misstep from freedom back into bondage occurred in the Galatian Church. In his letter to that congregation, the apostle Paul addressed the fact that some Jewish believers were insisting Gentile believers obey the ceremonies and rites of Jewish law. On one occasion, even Peter and Barnabas, attempting to please men instead of God, had sided with these legalistic Jews. Apparently, even the best of men (and women) can fall back into bondage by stumbling off the true path. But Paul, who'd confronted Peter, set his readers straight in Galatians 2:16 above.

EVENING - *Looking to Please God*

I want to please God. Do you think I am trying to please people? If I were doing that, I would not be a servant of Christ.
GALATIANS 1:10 CEV

Help me not to be led down the wrong path, Jesus, especially the one of living to please people instead of You! For if I go down that road, I'll find myself in bondage again. And I so don't want to go there. So help me to live by trusting in You and the freedom You offer, looking to please You alone in all I say and do.

DAY 228

MORNING - *A Woman Saved*

So if the Son makes you free, you will be free indeed.
JOHN 8:36 NASB

You are saved through your faith in Christ, and Christ alone. Anything you add to that formula is not of God and puts you in bondage. The Judaizers added ceremonial law. You may add your religious routines and your own ego (glorifying yourself instead of God). Sometimes you may add your Christian works, substituting them for faith. But make this clear in your mind: God is not so much interested in what you *do* as He is in what you *are*. God has His eye on your inner woman, the new creature born when you first accepted Christ.

EVENING - *New, Inside and Out!*

"For behold, I create new heavens and a new earth;
and the former things will not be remembered or come to mind."
ISAIAH 65:17 NASB

Having come to You, Christ, I am a new woman. Re-created in You! Free in You! So help me to not get trapped by the bondage of religious traditions or routines, or of glorifying myself and my own ego instead of You. I am a new woman, inside and out! A woman who lives for You alone. And, as such, I'm as free as a bird, knowing You will take care of whatever comes my way. . . because I'm walking in the Way!

MORNING - *A New Freedwoman*

*The Jerusalem above (the Messianic kingdom
of Christ) is free, and she is our mother.*
GALATIANS 4:26 AMPC

In Galatians 4:24–31, Paul presents an analogy to help you understand that you are a free woman and not a slave. It's the story of Abraham, who had two sons, one by his wife, Sarah, and the other by her slave, Hagar. In Paul's analogy, Hagar represents the law while Sarah represents God's grace. Ishmael, Hagar's son, was born as a result of human conniving. Isaac, Sarah's son, was born as a result of God's good promise. As a spiritually reborn child of God's promise, you, a freedwoman, cannot go back to a life of slavery under the law! Remember, Ishmael was sent away once the promised son had arrived— because law and grace cannot exist together!

EVENING - *With God as Your Main Focus*

*After starting your Christian lives in the Spirit, why are
you now trying to become perfect by your own human effort?*
GALATIANS 3:3 NLT

Lord, I feel like such a fool. I've been trying to become perfect by doing things. But the reality is that all I need to do is be Your daughter. Help me to live my life as Your servant—not as a slave to the law. You are to be my main focus—not the approval of others, not my pride. I want to walk in freedom and in Your Spirit. I want to live for You—and You alone!

MORNING - *A Woman of the Gospel*

To help you understand the difference between the bondage of the law and the freedom-filled Gospel of Christ and to perhaps discover where your own bondage or freedom lies, here are a few comparisons:

The law says. . .
"*Do* this and you will live."
(Luke 10:28 NASB)
"*Pay* me what you owe."
(Matthew 18:28 KJV)

The Gospel says. . .
"*Live* and then you will do."
(see Galatians 5:16–18)
"I *forgive* you everything."
(see 1 John 1:9)

EVENING - *Brand-New in Christ!*

"I will give you a new heart and put a new spirit within you."
EZEKIEL 36:26 NASB

Lord, the law says "*Make* yourselves a new heart and a new spirit!" (Ezekiel 18:31 NASB, emphasis added). But I am a freed woman in Christ! So You have given me a new heart and put a new spirit within me! I am amazed at the difference between the law and the Gospel. And I am so glad I am no longer under bondage. Help me to stay on the path of freedom. Because I am loving this new heart and spirit You have given me!

MORNING - *A Woman of the Gospel*

Here are some more differences between the bondage of the law and the freedom-filled Gospel of Christ. Again, read them with the intention of perhaps discovering where your own bondage or freedom lies:

The law says. . .
"You *must* love the LORD your God with all your heart, all your soul, and all your strength." (Deuteronomy 6:5 NLT)
"*Cursed* is everyone who does not obey commands that are written in God's Book of the Law." (Galatians 3:10 NLT)

The Gospel says. . .
"This is real love—not that we loved God, but that he *loved* us and sent his Son as a sacrifice to take away our sins." (1 John 4:10 NLT)
"*Blessed* are those whose lawless deeds are forgiven, and whose sins are covered." (Romans 4:7 NKJV)

EVENING - *Gifted with Eternal Life*

*The wages of sin is death, but the gift of
God is eternal life in Christ Jesus our Lord.*
ROMANS 6:23 NKJV

What a disparity, Lord, between the law and the Gospel! My missteps led me down into Death Valley. But You have given me the gift of eternal life when I believe in, trust, hide myself in, and follow Christ Jesus! Thank You for this free gift of eternal freedom!

MORNING - *A Woman of the Gospel*

Here are more differences between the bondage of the law and the freedom-filled Gospel of Christ. Where does your own bondage or freedom lie?

The law says. . .
"You *must* be holy."
(Leviticus 20:26 NIrV)
"*Do* these things."
(Numbers 15:13 NASB)
"Blessings are the result of *obedience*."
(see Deuteronomy 11:27)
"The *seventh* day is the
sabbath of rest."
(Leviticus 23:3 KJV)

The Gospel says. . .
"Christ's death has *made* you holy."
(Colossians 1:22 NIrV)
"Everything is *done*!"
(John 19:30 CEV)
"Obedience is the result of *blessings*."
(see James 1:25)
"The *first* day of the week,
we gathered."
(Acts 20:7 NLT, emphasis added)

EVENING - *Set Free*

Christ Jesus has set you free from the law.
ROMANS 8:2 NASB

Lord, Your Word says that "The Law. . .once restrained and held us captive" (see Romans 7:6 AMPC). I praise You to the heavens that this is no longer so! Because of Jesus, I have been set free. Help me to live as that free woman. No chains for me! I am in Jesus—and He has released me! That makes Him *first* in my book! Thank You, Lord!

DAY 233

MORNING - *A Loving Woman*

Jesus said, " 'Love the Lord your God with all your passion and prayer and intelligence.' This is the most important, the first on any list. But there is a second to set alongside it: 'Love others as well as you love yourself.' "
MATTHEW 22:37–39 MSG

Whew! How exhausting to live in bondage! Thank God Christ came to save you from the law of Moses, for there was no way you could satisfy its demands. Instead, He gave you two new laws to replace all others. The first is to love God with everything you've got. That's the most important order of the day. The second law is to love others as you love yourself. Show Jesus how much you love Him by obeying these great commandments!

EVENING - *Under a New Commandment*

"If you love me, show it by doing what I've told you."
JOHN 14:15 MSG

I come to You today, Lord, with all the love in my heart. The core of my spirit melts in adoration of You. My mind is not on earthly things but on the one thing that will get me through this life, this day, this moment—love for my Father God. In these moments, as I bask in my love for You, I find I am made whole and overflowing with love for others and myself. What amazing love!

DAY 234

MORNING - *A Woman of Love*

When you attempt to live by your own religious plans and projects,
you are cut off from Christ, you fall out of grace.
GALATIANS 5:4 MSG

When you are living in accordance with the law, you become severed from Christ. You find yourself having fallen out of grace. But be very clear upon this point: You are no longer under the law of Moses but under the law of Christ—to love God and others. As you obey this law in Christ, you find yourself walking not in the flesh but in the Spirit, a recipient of God's great grace and a bearer of good fruit!

EVENING - *Experiencing Amazing Grace*

In Christ, neither our most conscientious religion nor
disregard of religion amounts to anything. What matters
is something far more interior: faith expressed in love.
GALATIANS 5:6 MSG

Lord, I sure don't want to fall out of grace with You by trying to live under the law of Moses. Instead, I embrace the law of Christ. I will love You, Father God, with all my heart, soul, and mind. And I will love others—including myself! Help me to do just that, Lord. To live and breathe love! And, in doing so, experience amazing grace!

DAY 235

MORNING - *The Reflecting Woman*

Before Christ came, Moses' laws served as our guardian.
Christ came so that we could receive God's approval by faith. . . .
GALATIANS 3:24 GW

God's law told you where you were falling short. And although it served to bring you to Christ, it can never save you. Only Christ can do that. It may not be law that you have added to Christ but a certain ritual you believe will please others. Or it may be some work of which you are very proud (thus glorifying your own ego). Hannah Whitall Smith wrote that "a religion of bondage always exalts self. It is what *I* do—*my* efforts, *my* wrestlings, *my* faithfulness." You are in bondage if what you hope to see in the eyes of others is your own reflection. Better that you be a freedwoman, looking to leave the reflection of Christ in the eyes of others.

EVENING - *Looking to Christ Alone*

But now that this faith has come, we are
no longer under the control of a guardian.
GALATIANS 3:25 GW

I want to reflect and exalt You and You only, Jesus. Give me the strength to seek only Your approval. May all I do be because of Your power, Your battling, Your faithfulness to me. Help me to step aside and let You be my Source of everything—and give You the glory in all that I say and do!

DAY 236

MORNING · *A Daughter of the King*

You are no longer a slave, but God's child;
and since you are his child, he has made you also heir.

GALATIANS 4:7 NIV

The secret to your freedom is to be as God sees you—a little child. Get God's view of you set in your mind. Walk as if you're a king's daughter—because you are! Children of good parents need not struggle to survive. They need not earn or carry around their own money, for their fathers and mothers provide for them. Parents feed, clothe, shelter, and love the heirs of their own little kingdom. In such a way, your spiritual Father cares for you. He not only provides everything you need but gives you blessings besides. And if you keep in mind that God views you as a child, you'll bear the fruit of His Spirit—"love, joy, peace, patience, kindness, goodness, faithfulness, gentleness and self-control. Against such things there is no law" (Galatians 5:22–23 NIV).

EVENING · *Serving in Love*

"Unless you change and become like little children,
you will never enter the kingdom of heaven."

MATTHEW 18:3 NIV

Father God, I needn't worry, stress, or strain about the future. I needn't become desperate for riches other than the ones You provide in Christ. I needn't try to please anyone except You—not others, not myself—but only to serve You with great love and affection. You're not a hard master but an affectionate and a loving Father, who I'm proud to call Abba God.

DAY 237

MORNING - *An Accepting Woman*

Christ has set us free! This means we are really free. Now hold on to your freedom and don't ever become slaves of the Law again.
GALATIANS 5:1 CEV

Because God has sacrificed His Son, as God's heir you can "walk about in freedom" (Psalm 119:45 NIV), unfettered by the opinions of others—including your own. You are God's willing servant, not a slave. And because He works in you "to will and to act in order to fulfill his good purpose" (Philippians 2:13 NIV), all you need to do is accept Him as your Father, become as a little child, and allow Him to take over your life—to put Him in the driver's seat. And you must not try to grab for the steering wheel, because whenever you do, you're bound to swerve off your path.

EVENING - *Daughter and Heir*

I am the least of all God's people. Yet, God showed me his kindness by allowing me to spread the Good News of the immeasurable wealth of Christ.
EPHESIANS 3:8 GW

Sometimes it seems so unfathomable that You, Father God, would want me as Your daughter and heir, that You would think I am worthy of Your infinite riches. You amaze me, Lord. What grace (unmerited favor) You have entrusted to me! I am blessed in so many ways, just because I believe and have given myself over to Your Son. It is more than I ever asked or imagined.

DAY 238

MORNING - *The Woman with the Key*

*Since we are living by the Spirit, let us follow
the Spirit's leading in every part of our lives.*
GALATIANS 5:25 NLT

The entire key to your Christian life is to become as a little child, living and walking by the Spirit and "[not in your own strength] for it is God Who is all the while effectually at work in you [energizing and creating in you the power and desire], both to will and to work for His good pleasure and satisfaction and delight" (Philippians 2:13 AMPC). What a precious Daddy God you have!

EVENING - *No Greater Blessing*

*[Jesus] said, "I tell you the truth, unless you turn from your sins and become
like little children, you will never get into the Kingdom of Heaven."*
MATTHEW 18:3 NLT

Oh Father God, it's so nice not to have to be in control. I see You as my Father, smiling at me, keeping a tight hold on my hand, leading me in the right direction. I know that You will take care of everything I need and that You intend only good for me—no matter what others may say or how things may appear. My spirit is one with Yours. There is no greater blessing.

DAY 239

MORNING - *A Daughter of Promises*

Live freely, animated and motivated by God's Spirit.
Then you won't feed the compulsions of selfishness.
GALATIANS 5:16 MSG

As God's daughter of the promises, having put aside all self-effort and self-dependence, you will receive endless riches of Christ (see Ephesians 3:8). With your adoring eyes upon your Father—not on yourself, others, or material things—you can relax. So rest in Daddy God. Recognize that you are His child, a beautiful daughter and heir, a free woman, a new creature in Christ. Allow His Spirit to have His way. Sit back and leave the driving to Him. And let the fun—and joy—begin!

EVENING - *Claiming Freedom*

You cannot live at times one way and at times another way according to how you feel on any given day. Why don't you choose to be led by the Spirit and so escape the erratic compulsions of a law-dominated existence?
GALATIANS 5:17–18 MSG

Father God, I am so wrapped up in works and my own self-interest that I have lost my footing on Your pathway. My free spirit is snared in these earthly trappings. I know my ego and my spirit are like oil and water—they do not mix! So help me, Jesus, not to live according to my feelings but according to my faith. Break these chains, Lord. I now claim the freedom found only in You.

MORNING - *The Joy-Filled Woman's Path Marker: Promise No. 13*

And I will give you a new heart, and I will put a new spirit in you. I will take out your stony, stubborn heart and give you a tender, responsive heart.
EZEKIEL 36:26 NLT

In His Word, God promises He will give you a new heart. He'll remove your heart of stone, the one that will not move His way, and give you a tender heart, one that will respond to His very touch, His every whisper. Allow Him to do that for you, and watch the joy begin to flow in and through you! Take this promise to heart!

EVENING - *Made Anew*

Cast away from you all your transgressions which you have committed and make yourselves a new heart and a new spirit!
EZEKIEL 18:31 NASB

Lord, there was no way I could make myself a new heart. No matter what I did, I couldn't live up to the law. But then Jesus came into my life. Now I do have a new heart—and a new mind and soul as well! Thank You for allowing Your Son to die so that He could do for me what I could not do for myself. I am eternally grateful and will eternally praise Your name!

DAY 241

MORNING - *The Joy-Filled Woman's Path Marker: Proof No. 13*

Christ's love controls us. Since we believe that Christ died for all, we also believe that we have all died to our old life. He died for everyone so that those who receive his new life will no longer live for themselves. Instead, they will live for Christ, who died and was raised for them. So we have stopped evaluating others from a human point of view. At one time we thought of Christ merely from a human point of view. How differently we know him now! This means that anyone who belongs to Christ has become a new person. The old life is gone; a new life has begun!

2 CORINTHIANS 5:14–17 NLT

God's Word provides the proof that, if you believe, Jesus will give you a new life! With this proof in your pocket, love Christ and live in Him!

EVENING - *Living and Loving Christ*

This is real love—not that we loved God, but that he loved us and sent his Son as a sacrifice to take away our sins.

1 JOHN 4:10 NLT

Lord, I cannot imagine the boundlessness of Your everlasting, unconditional love—the fact that You gave up Your precious Son for me even while I was still so far away from You. I am humbled that You would do that just so You could restore our relationship. I feel Your arms around me, Lord, giving me the courage to be all You want me to be, in spirit and in love.

DAY 242

MORNING · *The Joy-Filled Woman's Path Marker: Provision No. 13*

It is God Who is all the while effectually at work in you [energizing and creating in you the power and desire], both to will and to work for His good pleasure and satisfaction and delight.
PHILIPPIANS 2:13 AMPC

Through Jesus Christ, God is at work in you, providing you with energy and creating in you all the power and desire you could possibly need to not only become a new creation, a new woman in Christ, but to be a child of God, an heir to His promises, looking to your Abba Father for all that you need. He, His presence, and His promises are yours forever!

EVENING · *Protected*

While Joseph was in prison, the LORD was with him. The LORD reached out to him with his unchanging love and gave him protection. . . . The LORD was with Joseph and made whatever he did successful.
GENESIS 39:20–21, 23 GW

I feel so alone and unloved, Lord. But as I lie here, I am imagining You reaching out to me with everlasting love. I see You surrounding me with Your light. You are my rock, my refuge, my fortress. In You, nothing can ever harm me. With You, I have success, because You are working in me and through me, energizing me. To Your glory, Lord.

DAY 243

MORNING - *The Joy-Filled Woman's Path Marker: Portrait No. 13*

So you are no longer a slave, but God's child; and since you are his child, God has made you also an heir.

GALATIANS 4:7 NIV

God has not only *promised* He will give you a new heart (see Ezekiel 36:26) and *proven* that His love makes you a new person in Christ with all the freedom that entails (see 2 Corinthians 5:14–17), but He has also *provided* you with all the energy and power you need to live your new life (see Philippians 2:13). Because of all God has promised, proven, and provided, claim this new part of your *portrait* (based on Galatians 4:7):

In Christ, I am a free woman, a daughter of God, and an heir of His promises.

EVENING - *From Beginning to End*

"I am the Alpha and the Omega, the Beginning and the End. To the thirsty I will give water without cost from the spring of the water of life. Those who are victorious will inherit all this, and I will be their God and they will be my children."

REVELATION 21:6–7 NIV

Lord, You were here at the beginning and You will be here at the end. You knew me from before the world was formed and You loved me before I was born. In You, I will have victory.

MORNING - *The Woman of Unlimited Growth: Result No. 2 of the Higher Life*

You are God's garden and vineyard and field under cultivation.
1 CORINTHIANS 3:9 AMPC

Dr. Frank Crane, minister and essayist, wrote, "Growth is the key word that unlocks the universe. Growth is God's plan." You are, in fact, God's field. Thus, it is clear that God created you to grow—physically, mentally, emotionally, and spiritually. If you look at yourself and the people around you, you can see that everyone is in a different stage of growth in a myriad of areas. In this journey through life, each person is working at becoming what he or she believes God has called that person to be. And because all are still works in process, in the midst of growth, not one is perfect.

EVENING - *A Work in Progress*

And the boy Samuel continued to grow in stature and in favor with the LORD and with people.
1 SAMUEL 2:26 NIV

I understand, Lord, that I am a work in progress. And, as such, I have a lot of growing up to do. Show me the way. Shed Your light upon my path. You've made me what You already envisioned me to be. So I have all I might need to do what You would have me do. Help me to remember that, Lord. I want to grow up well in Your eyes!

DAY 245

MORNING - *An Imperfect Woman*

*Now we see things imperfectly, like puzzling reflections in a mirror,
but then we will see everything with perfect clarity.*
1 CORINTHIANS 13:12 NLT

Because you know you are a work in progress, you can banish the grief, shame, self-doubt, and self-condemnation that come upon you after you make choices that lead you in the wrong direction. These missteps are merely part of your growth process. Thus, you should take care not to succumb to constant and consistent thoughts of your failings. For as Dr. Crane wrote, "There is no failure in my life. There is a lot of imperfection, but growth implies imperfection."

EVENING - *Seeking the Perfect God*

*All that I know now is partial and incomplete, but then I will know
everything completely, just as God now knows me completely.*
1 CORINTHIANS 13:12 NLT

Lord, I know You know all. That You are the only one truly perfect. Someday, I'll know the whole story. But for now, help me not to be discouraged by my missteps. Help me to understand that they are only part of my growing up in You.

MORNING - *The Woman in Flow*

He struck the rock, and water gushed out, streams flowed abundantly.
PSALM 78:20 NIV

As you grow up in Christ, embarking on the pathway God has marked out for you, He intends for you not to stagnate like the Dead Sea but to flow ever on to the place He bids you, nestled deep in His grace. You are not to have your flow impeded by getting hung up on your faults and failings. Instead, you can simply perceive any growing pains resulting from your missteps and imperfections as blessings, because for those who have not yet arrived, it's all about the journey. As Robert Louis Stevenson wrote, "Little do ye know your own blessedness; for to travel hopefully is a better thing than to arrive, and the true success is to labour."

EVENING - *Traveling Hopefully*

"The Lord, before whom I have walked faithfully,
will send his angel with you and make your journey a success."
GENESIS 24:40 NIV

I am on Your pathway, Lord, the one You have mapped out for me. I'm not going to let my journey be sidetracked by discouragement around my missteps for we both know I have a lot of growing up to do. So whatever mistakes I make I will consider blessings. Because it's all about my journey to You!

DAY 247

MORNING - *A Woman in Waiting*

*Grow in grace (undeserved favor, spiritual strength) and
recognition and knowledge and understanding of
our Lord and Savior Jesus Christ (the Messiah).*
2 PETER 3:18 AMPC

Your joy is found in the process of your growth! And finding that joy, amid your imperfection and immaturity, is what it's all about! *Growth*, here, doesn't mean physical growth, of course. *Growth* in this context is about spiritual growth.

Second Peter 3:18 says you are to "Grow in grace and understanding of our Master and Savior, Jesus Christ" (MSG). When you're first saved, you're an infant in this new life in Christ. As such, you are given milk because you cannot yet handle the meat of the Word (see 1 Corinthians 3:1–3). But thank the Lord, you need not remain a mere babe.

EVENING - *Joyful in the Journey*

*When I was with you I couldn't talk to you as I would to spiritual people.
I had to talk as though you belonged to this world or as though you were
infants in Christ. I had to feed you with milk, not with solid food,
because you weren't ready for anything stronger.*
1 CORINTHIANS 3:1–2 NLT

I don't want to be an infant about my spiritual growth, Lord. I want to start eating the solid food of Your Word. But even more importantly, I await Your timing, remaining joyful in You.

DAY 248

MORNING - *A Flowering Woman*

Then all your people will do what is right. The land will belong to them forever. They will be like a young tree I have planted. My hands have created them. They will show how glorious I am.

ISAIAH 60:21 NIrV

Earthly parents become alarmed and seek medical advice if their babies do not grow physically. So would God your Father be alarmed if you, His child, did not continue to grow spiritually. Yet you may feel as if you can accomplish this growth in your own power. Perhaps you believe that if you try to do greater and greater things, you will reach the epitome of spirituality. Yet like the flowers and trees, you cannot *make* yourself grow. That job has been left in the hands of your Father. You are a mere planting of the Lord—for His glory.

EVENING - *A Mere Planting of the Lord*

They will be like oak trees that are strong and straight. The LORD himself will plant them in the land. That will show how glorious he is.

ISAIAH 61:3 NIrV

You have created me, Lord. And You are my sole source of energy, power, and strength. I am in Your hands, a mere planting of You. Help me to understand this deep down within me, at my very core. For only by being truly rooted in You will I become what You envision for me—for Your glory!

DAY 249

MORNING - *A Mature Woman*

Sisters, stop thinking like children. Be like babies as far as evil is concerned. But be grown up in your thinking.
1 CORINTHIANS 14:20 NIrV

Can you just imagine an impatient child trying to increase her physical height? It's possible, of course, to have a limb-lengthening surgery. But not only is this procedure expensive, it's also very painful. Yet do you not attempt to do something similar when you feel you've lost your passion for your faith? When you feel you haven't gotten anywhere, that your life hasn't improved one iota? In this I-want-it-now culture, you may feel discouraged if you aren't where you think you should be in your spiritual growth. So how do you remedy this situation? Stop trying to grow *into* grace but endeavor to grow *in* grace.

EVENING - *Patient in God's Work*

God began a good work in you. And I am sure that he will carry it on until it is completed. That will be on the day Christ Jesus returns.
PHILIPPIANS 1:6 NIrV

Lord, I know You've started something good in me. Help me to be patient, not looking for solutions outside of You that will make me taller in Your eyes— or even mine or those of others! Help me to be grown up in my thinking as You work in my life!

DAY 250

MORNING - *The Rerouted Woman*

God did not lead them along the main road that runs through Philistine territory, even though that was the shortest route to the Promised Land.
EXODUS 13:17 NLT

Hannah Whitall Smith provides a wonderful analogy to help you understand the concept of growing *in* grace instead of trying to grow *into* grace:

[Some Christians] are like a rosebush planted by a gardener in the hard, stony path with a view to its growing into the flower-bed, and which has of course dwindled and withered in consequence instead of flourishing and maturing.

She likens such Christians to the Hebrews in the wilderness. All the fighting and wandering they did there did not help them obtain one inch of God's Promised Land. To get possession of it, they needed to actually *enter* it. Once they did, they quickly began winning battles.

EVENING - *Growing in Grace*

God said, "If the people are faced with a battle, they might change their minds and return to Egypt."
EXODUS 13:17 NLT

I know, Lord, that You have planted me exactly where You want me. And it's a good place to grow strong for whatever lies ahead. Help me to continue growing as You would have me grow—in grace instead of into it! For when I do enter into Your grace, I will begin winning all the battles before me under Your power, not my own!

DAY 251

MORNING - *A Beloved Woman*

I love those who love me. Those eagerly looking for me will find me.
PROVERBS 8:17 GW

Once you *enter into God's grace* and take possession of it, your spiritual growth will take off, and you will progress beyond your imagination. For as Kay Arthur wrote in *Beloved*, "Only you will ever limit what you are for God." But again, how do you accomplish such spiritual growth in grace? First, you need to understand what grace is. It is not just God's unmerited favor, a gift He freely gives, requiring no action on your part. It is also His boundless, divine love poured out in a multitude of ways.

EVENING - *Gifted with and Rejoicing in God's Grace*

The LORD your God is with you. He is a hero who saves you.
He happily rejoices over you, renews you with his love,
and celebrates over you with shouts of joy.
ZEPHANIAH 3:17 GW

Your love, Lord God, is amazing. You truly are my hero! It boggles my mind that You actually rejoice over me, that You energize me, make me over with Your love. Your joy in doing that gives me joy overwhelming! Thank You for Your gift of grace, Your boundless love. There is nothing I cannot do with You in my life!

DAY 252

MORNING - *A Soulful Woman*

We know how much God loves us, and we have put our trust in his love. God is love, and all who live in love live in God, and God lives in them.

1 JOHN 4:16 NLT

God's love is an abundant, unconditional love, almost beyond human comprehension. Think of the best mother you've ever known or the best husband or the best friend. Take all of their love and multiply it by infinity, and you may have scratched the surface of God's grace to you and love for you. The only thing you need to do to receive such grace is accept it from God's loving hand! Thus, to grow in grace, your soul must be planted in the very heart of God's love.

EVENING - *Planted in God's Very Heart*

No one has greater love [no one has shown stronger affection] than to lay down (give up) his own life for his friends.

JOHN 15:13 AMPC

Your love is so amazing, Lord. You laid down Your life to save mine, and I am humbled by that amount of unconditional, abundant love. I cannot even fathom it. Thank You for Your sacrifice. Thank You for the gift of love and grace. I want to grow in You. So in this very moment, I plant my soul in the very heart of Your love.

DAY 253

MORNING - *A Fielded Woman*

Therefore I tell you, stop being perpetually uneasy (anxious and worried) about your life, what you shall eat or what you shall drink; or about your body, what you shall put on. . . .
MATTHEW 6:25 AMPC

You must steep yourself in grace and allow it to surround you. God has it in His plan that you grow in such a way. You are to "consider the lilies of the field and learn thoroughly how they grow; they neither toil nor spin. Yet I tell you, even Solomon in all his magnificence (excellence, dignity, and grace) was not arrayed like one of these" (Matthew 6:28–29 AMPC). In other words, it's all about allowing God to be in control and trusting Him to grow you as He desires, continually being open to His promptings.

EVENING - *Opening to the Creator*

Is not life greater [in quality] than food, and the body [far above and more excellent] than clothing?
MATTHEW 6:25 AMPC

Help me to change my mindset—and heart-set—Lord Creator. I want to be steeped in grace, to be enveloped by it. I want to be disentangled from worry and anxiety and just rest in You. Take control of my life, mind, body, heart, soul, and spirit. Help me to trust You in all things—big and little. Open me up to Your Word and ways. Speak! Your servant's ears are listening!

MORNING - *A Fretless Woman*

*"Has anyone by fussing in front of the mirror
ever gotten taller by so much as an inch?"*
MATTHEW 6:27 MSG

Yet this is difficult for you who may find yourself seemingly unable to stop worrying about things past, present, and future. But the Word tells you not to fret about the necessities of life, that no one by worrying and being anxious can add one inch to her stature. In fact, worrying and spinning your wheels, like a frenzied and harried gerbil, actually impedes your growth, for it reveals your doubts that God will, as promised, take care of you, just as He takes care of His lilies.

EVENING - *Flourishing in Grace*

*He who leans on, trusts in, and is confident in his riches shall fall,
but the [uncompromisingly] righteous shall flourish like a green bough.*
PROVERBS 11:28 AMPC

Father God, there have been times I worried about everything—my clothes, finances, relationships, work, children. But living a life hidden with Your Son, I am putting those anxieties behind me and resting in You. I know the plans You have for me are for a hope and a future. Thus, I will flourish as You would have me do. Thank You for loving me so. Thank You for always watching over me.

DAY 255

MORNING - *A Lovely Lady Bird*

*Look at the birds of the air; they neither sow nor reap nor gather
into barns, and yet your heavenly Father keeps feeding them.
Are you not worth much more than they?*
MATTHEW 6:26 AMPC

Your worrying signals to God, and others, that since you doubt His provision, you must take things into your own hands. But in doing so, you end up fighting or resisting or impeding God's work, instead of yielding to Him and allowing Him to grow you up into the woman He wants you to be. This does not mean you are to remain idle in your spiritual growth. But it does mean you need to trust God. Take it as fact that He will give you the light, water, food, and clothes you need to live physically, and everything you need spiritually. Growth will come as you wait upon Him, then peaceably and obediently do as He asks.

EVENING - *Leaning on the Lily Maker*

*Trust in the LORD with all thine heart; and lean not unto thine own
understanding. In all thy ways acknowledge him, and he shall direct thy paths.*
PROVERBS 3:5–6 KJV

Okay, Lord, this time I mean it! I'm putting all my concerns, worries, calamities into Your hands. And I'm doing so wholeheartedly! I'm not going to try to figure things out but lean on You and Your understanding, Your plan for my life. In so doing, I know You will keep me on the right pathway. Grow me up, Lord! I'm trusting *You* to provide what I need!

DAY 256

MORNING - *The Chosen Woman*

"You didn't choose me, remember; I chose you, and put you in the world to bear fruit, fruit that won't spoil. As fruit bearers, whatever you ask the Father in relation to me, he gives you."
JOHN 15:16 MSG

To be like the lily, you must understand that you have not chosen Christ but He has chosen you. He says that He has "[planted you], that you might go and bear fruit and keep on bearing" (John 15:16 AMPC). That is how you got into His grace in the first place! So He has planted you as He has the lily, which revels in and responds to God's sunshine, water, and soil. The lily grows naturally. There is no stretching or straining to get something it has already been given. There is no unwarranted and fruitless toiling involved at all!

EVENING - *Eased*

Even as [in His love] He chose us [actually picked us out for Himself as His own] in Christ before the foundation of the world.
EPHESIANS 1:4 AMPC

It staggers my mind, Lord, to think You chose *me* as Your very own woman to serve You. And You have not just picked but planted me so that I could grow into the woman You already envision me to be. I need not strain or stretch or make myself grow. But just allow You to grow me up spiritually. Thank You for the ease of mind, body, spirit, heart, and soul this knowledge of living in Your soil gives me!

DAY 257

MORNING - *The Graceful Woman*

I am the true vine, and my Father is the husbandman.
JOHN 15:1 KJV

You need to learn the lily's secret. Acknowledge that you are planted in grace and then let God—the divine husbandman—have His way with you. You're to put yourself in the light of the Son of Righteousness, allowing the dew from heaven to quench your thirst. And just be pliable and yielding to what He would have you be! If you expend effort trying to make yourself grow spiritually, fussing and straining at every turn, your fruit will bear witness to your unnecessary toiling. You'll be burned out—a common malady in church workers. You'll wilt under stress. You'll look for relief in all the wrong places instead of looking to God. Your eyes will be on your own self or your self-dependence and self-effort. Instead, turn your eyes to the divine husbandman.

EVENING - *Tended by the Divine Husbandman*

Abide in me, and I in you. As the branch cannot bear fruit of itself, except it abide in the vine; no more can ye, except ye abide in me.
JOHN 15:4 KJV

Divine Husbandman, I cannot bear any good fruit except by resting in and abiding in You. Remind me of this daily. For I don't want to be wilted but blossoming under Your care! My eyes are in You, my soul planted in the soil of Your making.

DAY 258

MORNING - *The Expectant Woman*

*I planted, Apollos watered, but God [all the while]
was making it grow and [He] gave the increase.*
1 CORINTHIANS 3:6 AMPC

As you try to take on the world under your own power, God is watching your futile efforts, shaking His head as you run around like a chicken with its head cut off. Why do you feel you must do it all on your own? Does a woman create the baby that grows within her womb? Does she, through some effort on her part, form its tiny fingernails, its crop of hair, its heart, lungs, and eyes? No! God does it all. The only effort she expends is to take care of her body while the baby grows within her. Then in God's timing (and with a bit of pushing on her part), the baby comes forth and into her arms.

EVENING - *Waits for God to Grow Her*

*So neither he who plants is anything nor he who waters,
but [only] God Who makes it grow and become greater.*
1 CORINTHIANS 3:7 AMPC

You, Father God, are the one who grows every child in its mother's womb, through no effort on her part. In the same way, You are the only one who can grow me—through no effort on my part! So help me just to let You work through me as You will. And in Your time, I know that all things will come out right into my arms!

DAY 259

MORNING - *The Helpless Woman*

[Not in your own strength] for it is God Who is all the while effectually at work in you [energizing and creating in you the power and desire], both to will and to work for His good pleasure and satisfaction and delight.
PHILIPPIANS 2:13 AMPC

As God makes the baby grow without it even being aware that it is indeed growing, He has planted you to grow spiritually. And you are utterly helpless to do anything but allow Him to do so and not hinder His work within you. For when you hinder Him, you expend all your energy, grow exhausted, and suddenly find yourself growing backward rather than forward. You would be wise to tap into the lily's secret and grow in God's way.

EVENING - *Strong in Christ*

And He [Jesus] said to me, "My grace is sufficient for you, for My strength is made perfect in weakness." Therefore most gladly I will rather boast in my infirmities, that the power of Christ may rest upon me.
2 CORINTHIANS 12:9 NKJV

Lord, allowing You to live Your life through me is so wonderful. For whenever I am weak, Your glorious strength shines through. In this lily-life, there is no longer a barrier between You and me. Thank You, Lord, for all You have done, all You are doing, and all You will do in my life—to Your glory!

MORNING · *The Surrendered Woman*

The life I now live in the body I live by faith in (by adherence
to and reliance on and complete trust in) the Son of God,
Who loved me and gave Himself up for me.

GALATIANS 2:20 AMPC

Of course, you are not actually a lily. You are a human being with a modicum of intelligence. You have a certain degree of power and personal responsibility. Yet that's just where your hindrance to God's work comes in. Smith wrote:

What the lily is by nature we must be by an intelligent and free
surrender. To be one of the lilies means an interior abandonment of
the rarest kind. It means that we are to be infinitely passive, and yet
infinitely active also: passive as regards self and its workings, active as
regards attention and response to God.

EVENING · *Abandoned to God*

So here's what I want you to do, God helping you: Take your everyday,
ordinary life—your sleeping, eating, going-to-work, and walking-
around life—and place it before God as an offering. Embracing
what God does for you is the best thing you can do for him.

ROMANS 12:1 MSG

I'm totally relying on You, Lord, to do what You will. Just like the lily, I'm putting myself in Your hands as an offering. I lay my life, myself, my ego before You, in total submission. Yet I will be attentive to Your words and respond to whatever You ask of me. In Jesus' name.

DAY 261

MORNING - *The Woman Intimate with God*

"I will love them freely. . . . I will be like the dew to Israel; he shall grow like the lily, and lengthen his roots like Lebanon. His branches shall spread; his beauty shall be like an olive tree, and his fragrance like Lebanon."
HOSEA 14:4–6 NKJV

Step aside and allow God to work while being attentive to what He whispers in your ears and how He wants you to respond. When you do, you will be blessed and become more intimate in your knowledge of Him. You will prosper, bringing forth fruit, "some an hundredfold, some sixtyfold, some thirtyfold" (Matthew 13:8 KJV). Know that whether or not you are conscious of it, God has made you to grow. It's a fact.

EVENING - *Blessed in Trusting*

"But blessed is the one who trusts in the Lord, whose confidence is in him. They will be like a tree planted by the water that sends out its roots by the stream. It does not fear when heat comes; its leaves are always green. It has no worries in a year of drought and never fails to bear fruit."
JEREMIAH 17:7–8 NIV

My confidence is in You, Lord. I'm trusting in You for everything. In so doing, Your Word says I will not fear, nor worry. I will always bear fruit and be ripe for what You would have me to do. Blessings will abound as my spirit rests in You! I am ready to hear You speak into my life.

MORNING - *The Considering Woman*

Consider the lilies, how they grow: they neither toil nor spin.
LUKE 12:27 NKJV

If you find yourself straining once again to be your own gardener, seeding and perhaps even pruning yourself, here's a simple way to refocus yourself.

BE A LILY
Be careful for nothing. Simply pray with thanksgiving and let God's peace reign.
Expect to bear fruit regardless of the storms, wind, and pelting rain.
Abide in the Vine, Jesus Christ. Open a vein and let Him flow into your life.
Let God have His way in everything, understanding that He will make all things right.
Interpose no barrier to His life-giving power working in you.
Look to Jesus, trusting Him to keep you safe in His garden of grace and love.
Yield yourself up entirely to His control, letting your response be "Yes, Lord, yes."

EVENING - *Becoming a Lily*

And God is able to make all grace abound toward you, that you, always having all sufficiency in all things, may have an abundance for every good work.
2 CORINTHIANS 9:8 NKJV

Every day I am becoming more and more of what You want me to be. When my emotions threaten to take control, I "consider the lilies," and Your peace immediately enters in. I am focusing on You, Jesus, knowing that's what I need to do. In You is where I crave to be. Because once I've experienced growth in grace, it becomes a magnificent obsession.

DAY 263

MORNING - *The Joy-Filled Woman's Path Marker: Promise No. 14*

Blessed is the person who. . .delights in the teachings of the LORD and reflects on his teachings day and night. He is like a tree planted beside streams—a tree that produces fruit in season and whose leaves do not wither. He succeeds in everything he does.

PSALM 1:1–3 GW

In His Word, God promises He will grow you up in the grace and knowledge of Him—if you'll just be a lily and let Him do it! Just keep in mind that when you allow God to take over the reins, trusting Him, expecting Him to make you a fruit-bearer in all ways and all days, looking to and yielding to Him in all things, a myriad of blessings will follow. Take this promise to heart!

EVENING - *Blessed by Grace*

Blessed (happy, enviably fortunate, and spiritually prosperous—possessing the happiness produced by the experience of God's favor and especially conditioned by the revelation of His grace, regardless of their outward conditions) are the pure in heart, for they shall see God!

MATTHEW 5:8 AMPC

Lord, I find such joy in Your wonderful gift of grace. I know that what is happening around me is not as significant as what is going on within me. I am rooting myself—heart, body, soul, and mind—in Your soil of grace. I look only to You to meet all my needs. Thank You, Lord, for Your amazing grace!

DAY 264

MORNING - *The Joy-Filled Woman's Path Marker: Proof No. 14*

When I tried to keep the law, it condemned me. So I died to the law—I stopped trying to meet all its requirements—so that I might live for God. My old self has been crucified with Christ. It is no longer I who live, but Christ lives in me. So I live in this earthly body by trusting in the Son of God, who loved me and gave himself for me. I do not treat the grace of God as meaningless. For if keeping the law could make us right with God, then there was no need for Christ to die.

GALATIANS 2:19–21 NLT

In His Word, God provides you with the *proof* that by allowing Him to work through you, all His plans—including those for your life, and grand plans they are—will succeed! Live with the promise of this proof in your minds.

EVENING - *Empowered by the Grace of God*

But the apostles stayed there a long time, preaching boldly about the grace of the Lord. And the Lord proved their message was true by giving them power to do miraculous signs and wonders.

ACTS 14:3 NLT

When my life is hidden in You, Christ, You work miracles. Through You, I am empowered to do mighty deeds. It is amazing how You can use people to do things they never thought possible before. So here I am, Lord. I am offering myself up to You and Your working in, with, and through me. In You, I believe and am fearless.

DAY 265

MORNING - *The Joy-Filled Woman's Path Marker: Provision No. 14*

"Here's what I want you to do: Find a quiet, secluded place so you won't be tempted to role-play before God. Just be there as simply and honestly as you can manage. The focus will shift from you to God, and you will begin to sense his grace."
MATTHEW 6:6 MSG

God provides you with the process to growing in Him in grace and knowledge. Simply get to a place of stillness. A place where you can let go and let be and let God. This need not be a physical place, although that helps, but more importantly a mental, spiritual, and emotional place of quietness. That's where you'll be able to focus on God and sense His grace inside, no matter what's happening on the outside.

EVENING - *An Unfathomable Gift*

For the LORD God is our sun and our shield. He gives us grace and glory. The LORD will withhold no good thing from those who do what is right.
PSALM 84:11 NLT

God, You are everything to me. Because of Your unfathomable gift of grace, I know that I can trust You to meet my every need. I feel Your love within and about me. I bask in the light and peace that You provide me every day. Your living water quenches my thirst. The meat of Your Word nourishes my spirit. I revel in the wonder that is You.

MORNING - *The Joy-Filled Woman's Path Marker: Portrait No. 14*

But grow in the grace and knowledge of our Lord and Savior Jesus Christ. To him be glory both now and forever! Amen.

2 PETER 3:18 NIV

God not only *promises* growth in grace and knowledge of Him as you plant yourself in Him (see Psalm 1:1–3) and *proven* that when you are lily-like, totally yielded to Him, you become a woman after His own heart (see Galatians 2:19–21), but He also *provides* you with the process of getting there (see Matthew 6:6). Because of all God has promised, proven, and provided, claim this new part of your *portrait* (based on 2 Peter 3:18).

In Christ, I am growing in the grace and knowledge of the Lord.

EVENING - *Planted in Grace*

"We believe that we are all saved the same way, by the undeserved grace of the Lord Jesus."

ACTS 15:11 NLT

Jesus, I am humbled that You would give up Your life for me. All I can offer in return is to allow You to live through me now. God has planted me in Your grace. In You, I have the peace of knowing I am safe, that You will provide everything I need, that I need not stretch or strain but simply allow You to grow me into the person You created me to be. Thank You, Jesus, for saving me.

MORNING - *The Woman with Strength in Service:*
Result No. 3 of the Higher Life

And He sat down, called the twelve, and said to them, "If anyone desires to be first, he shall be last of all and servant of all."
MARK 9:35 NKJV

When first entering this life of Christ, you're full of joy and enthusiasm, wanting to do some sort of service for your wonderful Lord, for you've learned the command of Jesus to be the "servant of all" (Mark 9:35 NKJV). But as the days and years pass, you may begin to feel like what was once your delight in serving has become drudgery. You've moved from the freedom you experienced as Christ's workers, with the "May I?" of love to the "Must I?" of duty expressed through gritted teeth. But, after all, as George Eliot wrote, "What do we live for, if not to make life less difficult for each other?"

EVENING - *"May I?"*

"Do you want to stand out? Then step down. Be a servant.
If you puff yourself up, you'll get the wind knocked out of you.
But if you're content to simply be yourself, your life will count for plenty."
MATTHEW 23:11–12 MSG

In the beginning of my serving, Lord, I was so on fire. I couldn't contain my energy. But now I'm really dragging my feet. Show me, Lord, how to change things up so that once again I have a joy-filled life of service and a "May I?" of love on my lips!

DAY 268

MORNING · *The Woman of Breakthrough*

*The Lord has broken through. . .before me, like the bursting
out of great waters. So he called the name of that place
Baal-perazim [Lord of breaking through].*
2 SAMUEL 5:20 AMPC

When you feel anxious, beleaguered, disdainful, exhausted, and tied up in knots about your Christian work, or when you have an impending desire to find your way out of serving others, you can be sure you have stepped off your pathway and embarked upon a route of bondage. You must immediately step back and look at your situation with the means of breaking through to receive the power that awaits a woman hidden in Christ.

EVENING · *In Christ's Power*

*There's the root of our ancestor Jesse, breaking through the earth and growing
tree tall, tall enough for everyone everywhere to see and take hope!*
ROMANS 15:12 MSG

Hidden in You, Jesus, I know I can find the power to break through this current bondage in regard to my service. Speak to my heart. Bring all my duties to mind. Tell me if I have slipped up on my pathway somehow. Am I doing what You would have me do? Or have I merely become a slave to certain roles because I've always done them. Put light upon my path, Lord, and give me the hope that You will make all things clear.

DAY 269

MORNING - *The Freedom-Seeking Servant:*
From Weariness to Strength

This is the covenant that I will make with the house of Israel after those
days, says the LORD: I will put My laws in their mind and write them on
their hearts; and I will be their God, and they shall be My people.
HEBREWS 8:10 NKJV

The first bondage is flagging energy and will to do God's work. You feel as if you're no longer strong enough to accomplish what God has asked you to do. So you either do it begrudgingly or not at all. Yet the fact of the matter is that God has intended you to do what He wills, for He has written it upon your heart and planted the seeds within your mind as part of His new covenant with you. He is working within you and through you to make your work not a duty but a pleasure. And He gives you the energy to do it.

EVENING - *God-Given Energy?*

[Not in your own strength] for it is God Who is all the while effectually at
work in you [energizing and creating in you the power and desire], both to
will and to work for His good pleasure and satisfaction and delight.
PHILIPPIANS 2:13 AMPC

Where is the energy, coming from in each area where I am serving? Is it coming from You or me? If it's coming from You, I should have more than enough. If it's coming from me, that may be why I feel I'm lagging behind. Make all things clear to me, Lord, so that I am serving in Your strength, not my own.

DAY 270

MORNING - *The Woman's Greatest Asset*

He said to me, "My grace is sufficient for you,
for My strength is made perfect in weakness."
2 Corinthians 12:9 nkjv

Your strength is your biggest weakness because it can be a hindrance to what God wants to do through you. You've seen a mother playing patty-cake with her infant who at that age lacks hand-eye coordination and muscular strength. She picks up the baby's arms and claps his hands together, then pats them, rolls them, and opens up his arms for the grand finale. The baby does nothing but yield himself up to his mother's control, and Mom does it all. The yielding is the baby's part; the responsibility, the mother's. The child has neither skill nor capacity to do the motions to patty-cake. His utter weakness is his greatest strength, and it provides his greatest delight!

EVENING - *Heavenly Strength*

"I'm your God. I'll give you strength. I'll help you.
I'll hold you steady, keep a firm grip on you."
Isaiah 41:10 msg

Help me to be weak in You, Lord. For then all Your amazing power can surge through me and accomplish more than I could ever think of doing on my own. Make my weakness my greatest strength, providing my greatest delight in all that I do!

DAY 271

MORNING - *The Freed Servant: Breakthrough of Energy*

Yield yourselves unto God, as those that are alive from the dead,
and your members as instruments of righteousness unto God.
ROMANS 6:13 KJV

To break through this bondage of flagging energy and desire to do God's work, you must go to prayer. Ask God to help you to understand that He has given you the energy and desire to do what He has called you to do. Envision that He is filling you up with everything you need to do the job. Recognize that your strength is your biggest weakness. Yield yourself up to Him.

EVENING - *Getting in the Way*

If we live by the [Holy] Spirit, let us also walk by the Spirit.
[If by the Holy Spirit we have our life in God, let us go forward
walking in line, our conduct controlled by the Spirit.]
GALATIANS 5:25 AMPC

I want to be walking and serving where You want me to be walking and serving, God. So I need Your guidance. Help me to understand that You will give me not just the energy but the desire to do what You have called me to do. So fill me up by Your Holy Spirit, Lord. Help me walk the line, yielding myself to You and Your power, knowing my strength only gets in the way of the Way.

DAY 272

MORNING - *The Freedom-Seeking Servant: Building Up God-Confidence*

Every Scripture is God-breathed (given by His inspiration) and profitable for instruction. . .and discipline in obedience, [and] for training in righteousness (in holy living, in conformity to God's will in thought, purpose, and action).
2 TIMOTHY 3:16 AMPC

The second form of bondage is thinking you're not good enough to serve in a particular way. What you need to understand is that God has already prepared the way for you. The way to break through is to build up your God-confidence by nurturing your spirits in the Word. By reading the Word daily, slowly, prayerfully, you'll feed your mind and spirit with truths that will build you into the woman He wants you to be.

EVENING - *Prepared and Word-Wise*

"He calls his own sheep by name and leads them out. When he has brought out all his own, he goes on ahead of them, and his sheep follow him because they know his voice."
JOHN 10:3–4 NIV

Lord Jesus, help me build up my God-confidence by saturating my mind, soul, and spirit in the word of Your truth. Help me plant it deep in my heart so that I can serve You with confidence, knowing that You, the Great Shepherd, have not only prepared my way but prepared me!

DAY 273

MORNING - *The Freedom-Seeking Servant: Real Master*

Whatever you do, do it wholeheartedly as though you were working for your real master and not merely for humans.
COLOSSIANS 3:23 GW

The third bondage of service is doing things to exult yourself or with the expectation of receiving an external reward. With that kind of pressure, no wonder many Christian workers fall by the wayside. They are so anxious to do something well and right to impress people that they find themselves filled with worry. These kinds of efforts detract from Jesus. If you're exalting yourself, you have taken the glory from Christ.

The remedy is to get your eyes off yourself and back on God. You are to be not human pleasers but *God* pleasers. Forget self. Humility will empower you to go forward, knowing that everything you do is for the Lord—and no one else!

EVENING - *Refocused*

You know that your real master will give you an inheritance as your reward. It is Christ, your real master, whom you are serving.
COLOSSIANS 3:24 GW

I've been so busy trying to please others, myself included, that I've taken my eyes off of You, Jesus. Help me not to be a people-pleaser but a God-gratifier. Take me and my efforts out of the equation, Lord. Help me to simply lean on You for all my energy and power, knowing that all I do, I do for You!

MORNING - *The Freedom-Seeking Servant: Trust over Discouragement*

Commit your way to the Lord [roll and repose each care of your load on Him]; trust (lean on, rely on, and be confident) also in Him and He will bring it to pass.
PSALM 37:5 AMPC

The fourth form of bondage is discouragement and despair. The outreach project that was your idea hasn't brought anyone new into the church. You're ready to step down from being on the committee, to throw in the towel. This attitude indicates a lack of trust in God.

The breakthrough of empowerment for discouragement is rolling every care off on the Lord. Instead of giving up, lean harder on God. It's the evil one who is pointing out your faults and feeding your misgivings. Pray and trust God to give you persistence as well as the courage and care you need.

EVENING - *Courage and Persistence*

"Who knows whether you have not come to the kingdom for such a time as this?"
ESTHER 4:14 ESV

I need Your courage, Lord. Like Esther, I am really stepping out, taking a major leap of faith. Remind me that the success of all my works is in Your hands, not mine. So I give the actual work, the strength to accomplish it, and its results to You. And I take up the mantle of Your peace, power, and perseverance to achieve what You're leading me to do.

DAY 275

MORNING - *The Freedom-Seeking Servant: Joy over Despair*

"For I know the plans I have for you," declares the LORD, "plans to prosper you and not to harm you, plans to give you hope and a future."
JEREMIAH 29:11 NIV

To break through the bondage of despair, cultivate joy within yourself. Recognize that God has a plan for your life. Take joy in that promise! Thank God for all He has done in your life already—and what He plans to do in your future. When you do, you will be so renewed that you will not be able to help expressing God-cheer! For who knows what blessings await you when you persevere!

EVENING - *Blessings Awaiting*

"The LORD your God may tell us the way in which we should walk and the thing that we should do."
JEREMIAH 42:3 NASB

Thank You, God, that You have a plan for me. I've been so pinned down by despair, thinking I had to plan my own way. But I need not worry. You've already laid out my path. So help me to live in the joy of that promise. For I know You've a pot of blessings waiting for me at the end of my rainbow!

Thanks for the above "Atta girl," Lord. It has been a long, sometimes tough road, but the deed has been done. I will not worry about the results but leave them up to You as I reach out for the next task You have for me. Working together with You, there's nothing that can't be accomplished! That's amazing! What joy You give me! Thank You, God. You're the ultimate project manager!

DAY 276

MORNING - *The Freed Servant in the Right Place*

" 'I know your deeds. Behold, I have put before you an open door which no one can shut, because you have a little power, and have kept My word, and have not denied My name.' "

REVELATION 3:8 NASB

So take on your responsibilities in God's strength, under His constant guidance, and by His leading. There is no need to be timid or worried. Just fill one sphere of responsibility, for one door opens to larger things, and another to still larger things, until you find yourself doing, in God's power, tasks you never believed or imagined you'd be doing. And in accordance with His timing, you'll be exactly where He wants you to be.

EVENING - *Secret Blessings*

When you give to the poor, don't let anyone know about it. Then your gift will be given in secret. Your Father knows what is done in secret, and he will reward you.

MATTHEW 6:3–4 CEV

Serving You can be done in so many different ways, Lord. I love giving little secret blessings to those I encounter in my daily endeavors, knowing that You are interested in the little things as well as the big. So each day, Lord, point out to me whom You would like me to secretly serve. Whisper in my ear how You would like me to bless them, which doorway of opportunity lies before me. And thank You for the joy serving You brings!

DAY 277

MORNING - *The Freedom-Seeking Servant: Blessed Efforts*

*But this one thing I do, forgetting those things which are behind,
and reaching forth unto those things which are before.*
PHILIPPIANS 3:13 KJV

The fifth form of bondage concerns the reflections that always follow the completion of any endeavor. These particular afterthoughts come in two varieties. Either you congratulate yourself upon the endeavor's success and are lifted up, or you are distressed over its failure and are utterly cast down. The breakthrough is to put the final results of any task in God's hands—and *leave them there*! Know that God is always pleased with your efforts and move on to the next thing. Refuse to worry. Simply ask God to override any mistakes and to bless your efforts as He chooses.

EVENING - *Pressing Forward*

*I press toward the mark for the prize of the
high calling of God in Christ Jesus.*
PHILIPPIANS 3:14 KJV

I'm not sure how my latest efforts have turned out, Lord, but that's okay. I did my best and so I know *You* will be pleased, and that's all that matters. So no worries! I'm moving on to the next thing You are calling me to do. Just simply override any slipups I may have made and bless what I have done as You choose. So, Lord, what's next?

DAY 278

MORNING - *The Totally Free Servant*

*Each of you as a good manager must use the
gift that God has given you to serve others.*
1 Peter 4:10 gw

Through all your endeavors, be sure that God and His will are your motivating powers. Plug in to His Word to keep you fit and nourished, unfettered of stress, and free of worry. Continually seek His guidance and direction through prayer, then exercise your faith by taking bold steps where no woman has ever gone before—for God's glory and His glory alone. Know that He will never give you a task without giving you the strength, courage, and means to accomplish it. Leave the results with Him, and He will bless you and all your endeavors. When you do, may He say, "Job well done, My good and faithful servant! Rejoice!"

EVENING - *Seeking Guidance*

*Whoever serves must serve with the strength God supplies so
that in every way God receives glory through Jesus Christ.
Glory and power belong to Jesus Christ forever and ever! Amen.*
1 Peter 4:11 gw

I'm not sure what my gift is, Lord, but I want to serve You. So I seek Your guidance. What do You want me to do? Whom do You want me to serve? Lead me to the path You want me to take. Open the doors You want me to enter. I want to do Your will, in Your way and in Your timing. Give me patience to wait for Your call and ears to hear Your instructions.

DAY 279

MORNING - *The Joy-Filled Woman's Path Marker: Promise No. 15*

"For I know the plans that I have for you," declares the LORD,
"plans for welfare and not for calamity to give you a future and a hope."
JEREMIAH 29:11 NASB

God promises He has plans for you! They are plans for your benefit, to give you a future and hope! Not only that, but He's already gone before you to prepare the way! What a great God you have! Take this promise and make it part of your very being—and it will give you such joy.

EVENING - *The Blazed Trail*

He calleth his own sheep by name, and leadeth them out.
And when he putteth forth his own sheep, he goeth before them,
and the sheep follow him: for they know his voice.
JOHN 10:3–4 KJV

Lord Jesus, I need never fear for You always go before me, blazing a trail for me to follow. I am getting to know Your voice very well. The more time I spend with You, the more familiar it becomes. Thank You for giving me the Holy Spirit. With Your strength, His guidance, and the Father's protection, I step into the unknown, sure that You will be with me all the way.

DAY 280

MORNING - *The Joy-Filled Woman's Path Marker: Proof No. 15*

A disciple named Tabitha (in Greek her name is Dorcas). . .was always doing good and helping the poor. . . . She became sick and died. . . . When the disciples heard that Peter was in Lydda, they sent two men to him and urged him, "Please come at once!" Peter went with them. . . . All the widows stood around him, crying. . . . Peter sent them all out of the room; then he got down on his knees and prayed. Turning toward the dead woman, he said, "Tabitha, get up." She opened her eyes, and seeing Peter she sat up.

ACTS 9:36–40 NIV

God's Word provides you with all the proof you need to trust that He will give you, as He did Peter, what you need when you need it to serve Him. Live with the promise of this proof in your deepest heart, soul, mind, and spirit.

EVENING - *One Desire*

Do what the LORD wants, and he will give you your heart's desire. Let the LORD lead you and trust him to help.

PSALM 37:4–5 CEV

God, it's amazing how You work through me to do the things You want me to do. I'm awed at how the things You desire are the things I grow to desire. So lead me on, Lord. I know whatever You have waiting out there for me is what You want me to do. And wherever You lead is exactly where You want me to go!

DAY 281

MORNING - *The Joy-Filled Woman's Path Marker: Provision No. 15*

Keep on doing what you've done from the beginning. . . . Better yet, redouble your efforts. Be energetic in your life of salvation, reverent and sensitive before God. That energy is God's energy, an energy deep within you, God himself willing and working at what will give him the most pleasure.
PHILIPPIANS 2:12–13 MSG

God's Word tells you that He will provide you with all the energy you need to serve Him. Your job is to remember it's not your energy—but His! You'll know that because it will come from deep within, enabling you to please Him in whatever task He gives you to do! Simply persevere, let go and let God—and He will do the work!

EVENING - *God-Given Strength*

My hand is ready to help him. My arm will also give him strength.
PSALM 89:21 GW

Just when I feel like giving up, Lord, I find that then, in that moment, when I go deep within, You are primed to give me all the strength I need to continue on! Then I am able to get my second wind and find the unfathomable re-Source that keeps my hand on the work before me. I thank and praise You for Your arm of strength that consistently pulls me up and gets me back on task!

MORNING - *The Joy-Filled Woman's*
Path Marker: Portrait No. 15

*I have strength for all things in Christ Who empowers me [I am ready
for anything and equal to anything through Him Who infuses inner
strength into me; I am self-sufficient in Christ's sufficiency].*
PHILIPPIANS 4:13 AMPC

God not only *promises* He has a plan for your hope and future (see Jeremiah 29:11) and *proven* that He'll give you what you need in any endeavor that's in line with His plan (see Acts 9:36–40), but He also *provides* you with the process to reenergize and persevere (see Philippians 2:12–13). Because of all God has promised, proven, and provided, claim this new part of your *portrait* (based on Philippians 4:13):

In Christ, I am strong enough to do whatever God calls me to do.

EVENING - *A Tent of Strength and Power*

*He said to me, "My grace is sufficient for you, for my power is
made perfect in weakness." Therefore I will boast all the more
gladly about my weaknesses, so that Christ's power may rest on me.*
2 CORINTHIANS 12:9 NIV

Jesus, Your grace and love are overwhelming. You give me the strength to do all that You have called me to do. Your power shines through my weakness. I am envisioning Your strength and power resting over me like a tent. There is nothing I cannot do! This is a truth that I will emblazon on my heart, for it will give me peace and confidence as I do Your will to Your glory!

MORNING - *The Consistently Transformed Woman: Result No. 4 of the Higher Life*

*Do not conform to the pattern of this world,
but be transformed by the renewing of your mind.*

ROMANS 12:2 NIV

You who have determined to live the higher life, a life hidden in Christ, should be as a result a "peculiar people" (1 Peter 2:9 KJV)—with a mind transformed every day! Yet it seems many believers are so satisfied with lives conformed to the world that there appears to be no discernible difference between Christians and pre-Christians. Or they only assume a Christian mantle when they're with their minister or other Christians. When they get home, they become other persons entirely. If you call yourself a Christian, when others see you they should see Christ, for you are His epistle.

EVENING - *Heart Right!*

*You show that you are a letter from Christ, the result of our ministry,
written not with ink but with the Spirit of the living God,
not on tablets of stone but on tablets of human hearts.*

2 CORINTHIANS 3:3 NIV

Lord, I don't want to give Christ a bad name. Help me to embody Your Good News, not just put on some facade. Show me where I'm falling in with the world. Transform me, Lord, into what You would have me be 24-7! Make my heart right!

MORNING - *A Woman Hidden*

Since, then, you have been raised with Christ, set your hearts on things above, where Christ is, seated at the right hand of God.
COLOSSIANS 3:1 NIV

Hannah Whitall Smith wrote, "The life hid with Christ in God is a hidden life, as to its source, but it must not be hidden as to its practical results." If you are to be Christians who walk the walk and talk the talk, you had best be hidden in Christ 24-7—not just in front of other believers and the minister, but at home, at work, everywhere you go, and in everything you do! A good place to gear yourself up for the day's duties is early in the morning, setting your mind—and heart—on heavenly things, not things of this earth.

EVENING - *With a New Mind-Set*

Set your minds on things above, not on earthly things. For you died, and your life is now hidden with Christ in God.
COLOSSIANS 3:2–3 NIV

Lord, my mind-set is totally off today. So I will be still before You, practicing the presence of God. You are now here. I pray for Your spiritual vision. I reach out with faith that You will do what You have promised to do. I leave my life, my regrets, and my work in Your hands, knowing You will provide all I need every moment of every day.

DAY 285

MORNING - *The Striving Woman*

But seek (aim at and strive after) first of all His kingdom and His righteousness (His way of doing and being right), and then all these things taken together will be given you besides.

MATTHEW 6:33 AMPC

⌒⌒

God's Word tells you to seek God's kingdom and being right with Him before anything else! In his commentary on this verse, Matthew Henry writes, "Seek this first every day; let waking thoughts be of God. Let him that is the First, have the first." Before your feet hit the floor, then, you can determine to clothe yourself in Christ and practice the presence of God.

EVENING - *Seeks God First*

Exercise daily in God—no spiritual flabbiness, please! Workouts in the gymnasium are useful, but a disciplined life in God is far more so, making you fit both today and forever. You can count on this. Take it to heart. This is why we've thrown ourselves into this venture so totally. We're banking on the living God, Savior of all men and women, especially believers.

1 TIMOTHY 4:7–8 MSG

⌒⌒

I'm ready, Lord, to exercise in You. It's a workout I cannot neglect. I love You, and I love seeking Your advice, protection, comfort, peace, and strength every moment of every day. I envision You right beside me. I'm talking to You (mentally and physically) all the time. You help me discern Your voice from others. And it is You I am following—no one and nothing else!

MORNING · *The Woman Practicing God's Presence: Steps 1-3*

And the Lord said, My Presence shall go with you, and I will give you rest.
EXODUS 33:14 AMPC

❧

Bishop John H. Vincent gives you a wonderful, in-the-now explanation of what it means to practice God's presence:

1. To think of God as present—here and now.
2. To repeat the thought, again and again—"God is now here."
3. To practice by concentration of all the faculties of the soul the consciousness of His actual presence here and now, saying over and over again, "God is now here," putting emphasis on every word of the sentence, repeating again and again, each time putting emphasis on one word, and thinking with concentrated attention, and resolving to believe that God is here now.

EVENING · *Groping for God*

*They should seek the Lord, in the hope that they might grope
for Him and find Him, though He is not far from each one of us;
for in Him we live and move and have our being.*
ACTS 17:27–28 NKJV

❧

God, You are here now, right beside me. You are never far from me—ever! In You, I live. In You, I move. In You, the Great I AM, I am. Ah, what a wonderful sensation Your presence gives me. I am conscious of You being in my heart, soul, body, and mind. Spirit to spirit, we are one! Thank You for always being here for me and in me! For in You, I can truly rest.

DAY 287

MORNING · *The Woman Practicing God's Presence: Steps 4-6*

Understand, therefore, that the LORD your God is indeed God. He is the faithful God who keeps his covenant for a thousand generations and lavishes his unfailing love on those who love him and obey his commands.

DEUTERONOMY 7:9 NLT

Bishop John H. Vincent's in-the-now explanation of what it means to practice God's presence concludes here:

4. To ask God, now actually present, to give spiritual vision—the vision calm, intelligent, deliberate, that genuine faith—faith with the will in it—is sure to give.
5. To take for granted, as real faith must do, that what God promises God Himself will do; and then—
6. In cold blood, with intellectual concentration, by an act of willpower leave the entire matter with God—going about your work, business, study, recreation, travel—doing everything you attempt to do with the secret and unchallengeable conviction that all is well and He is near.

EVENING · *Always and in All Ways Near*

*I lay down and slept, yet I woke up in safety,
for the LORD was watching over me.*

PSALM 3:5 NLT

Lord, You give me visions in the night and the faith to see them through. You keep Your promises to me over and over again. I know You will be with me, watching over me. How wonderful it is to live in Your presence.

DAY 288

MORNING - *A Sister Living in Jesus*

*Finally, dear. . .sisters, we urge you in the name
of the Lord Jesus to live in a way that pleases God.*
1 Thessalonians 4:1 nlt

With Christ's mantle without, the Spirit's power within, and God's presence surrounding you here and now, you will be expressing your Lord and Savior to everyone you meet! You will find yourself walking as Christ walked. You will be a peculiar people—empowered, loving, keeping no record of wrongs, returning good for evil, gentle, meek, kind, and yielding. You will not stand up for your own rights but will stand up for those of others, doing nothing for your glory but all for the glory of God. And you will be Christlike in private as well as in public, every hour of every day and not just on special occasions.

EVENING - *Rich in Forbearance*

*Be gentle and forbearing with one another and, if one has a difference
(a grievance or complaint) against another, readily pardoning each other;
even as the Lord has [freely] forgiven you, so must you also [forgive].*
Colossians 3:13 ampc

God, You have forgiven me for so many things. It is quite humbling. If You, in Your infinite mercy, can pardon me, I surely can pardon the person who has wronged me. I leave the situation in Your hands, knowing You will give me peace and the forgiveness I need to extend. Help me keep no record of wrongs and to be rich in forbearance. For that is Your will, Your way.

MORNING - *An Unworried Woman*

So do not worry or be anxious about tomorrow, for tomorrow will have worries and anxieties of its own. Sufficient for each day is its own trouble.
MATTHEW 6:34 AMPC

With Christ's mantle without, the Spirit's power within, and God's presence surrounding you here and now, you will not be plagued with anxieties or what-ifs, because you know that only today is yours. God has given it to you from His loving hand. He has taken back all your yesterdays, and all your tomorrows are still in His hands. You will live happily in the consciousness of here and now. William Osler advises you to "banish the future. Live only for the hour and its allotted work. Think not of the amount to be accomplished, the difficulties to be overcome, or the end to be attained, but set earnestly at the little task at your elbow, letting that be sufficient for the day."

EVENING - *Leaning Back on Jesus*

Do not let your hearts be troubled, neither let them be afraid.
[Stop allowing yourselves to be agitated and disturbed; and do not permit yourselves to be fearful and intimidated and cowardly and unsettled.]
JOHN 14:27 AMPC

Jesus, clothed in You, filled with the Spirit's power, and wrapped in God's presence, I will not be afraid of tomorrow. I'm casting all my troubles at Your feet and taking Your hand. You have everything under control. So any difficulties fly away. I'm happy in the now. . .leaning back against You!

DAY 290

MORNING - *The Courageous Woman Walker*

"Be strong and courageous."
JOSHUA 1:6 NLT

With Christ's mantle without, the Spirit's power within, and God's presence surrounding you here and now, you'll meet challenges bravely and persistently rise above obstacles without discouragement. Remember the story of the farmer's mule? One day, the mule fell into a dry well. Believing he couldn't save the animal, the farmer directed his sons to bury the faithful beast. But each time the boys threw a shovelful of dirt on top of the mule, he simply tramped on it. Soon enough dirt had come down so that the mule just walked out. That which was intended to bury him was the very means by which he was raised up and out of his trouble! May you be such a "mule," overcoming your obstacles and troubles instead of wallowing in an abyss of self-pity and discouragement.

EVENING - *Never Alone*

"This is my command—be strong and courageous! Do not be afraid or discouraged. For the LORD your God is with you wherever you go."
JOSHUA 1:9 NLT

You command me, Lord, never to be discouraged! And why should I, with You right by my side! Any obstacles that come my way, I raise them to You in prayer. Then I call on Your power to help me deal with them or to just put them in Your hands and walk away. Whatever Your will, Lord, becomes my will. What strength and fearlessness I glean from walking with You!

DAY 291

MORNING - *The Tempered Walker*

*Trust in the Lord with all your heart; do not depend
on your own understanding. Seek his will in all you do,
and he will show you which path to take.*
PROVERBS 3:5–6 NLT

David Hume has said that "he is happy whose circumstances suit his temper; but he is more excellent who can suit his temper to any circumstance." How true! Reflect, asking youself if your good temper (attitude) remains, no matter what. Perhaps you are not there yet, but after reading about this higher life, you have begun to hear God's voice whispering in your ear, "This is the way, walk in it" (Isaiah 30:21 NKJV). If so, listen to Him. Heed what He has to say—and only then walk on!

EVENING - *Gaining a God Attitude*

*Your ears will hear a word behind you, saying, this is the way;
walk in it, when you turn to the right hand and when you turn to the left.*
ISAIAH 30:21 AMPC

When I come seeking You, Lord, in every situation, I am happy—no matter what is going on! That's because I'm hidden in, teamed up with You! So what do I need to worry about! Make this good attitude a permanent attitude in me, Lord. Help me to listen to Your voice, obey what You tell me, and then—and only then—continue on the path You have laid out for my life!

DAY 292

MORNING - *The Enlightened Walker*

Tell the older women to behave as those who love the Lord should. . . .
They must teach what is proper, so the younger women
will be loving wives and mothers.
TITUS 2:3–4 CEV

Perhaps you have begun to feel uneasy about certain aspects of your life, attitudes, or habits that are troubling your soul. Perhaps you know of someone who is so Christlike that you envy her expressions, attitude, and behavior, wanting to have what she has. Her face, demeanor, and very being are so filled with the light of Christ that you want to spend time in her presence, basking in the glow she gives off! She is the epitome of the Christian woman whose life is indeed hidden in Christ! Do you want to know her secret? She has an ongoing conversation with God and loves Him with all her being. May you emulate such a woman and share in the joy of such a walker—and become an example for those women coming after you!

EVENING - *A Woman of the Light*

Now you are people of the light because you belong to the Lord.
So act like people of the light and make your light shine.
EPHESIANS 5:8–9 CEV

I am a child of Your light, Lord. I belong to You! So help me to act more like a woman of the light. May I be so filled with You, Your presence, and joy that people see You through my inner glow.

MORNING - *The Word-Wise Talker*

Let everything you say be good and helpful, so that your words will be an encouragement to those who hear them.
EPHESIANS 4:29 NLT

Today there are so many ways through which thoughtless words can injure people. Quick messages—with little forethought on your part—can be transmitted via cell phone, Twitter, e-mail, and Facebook in an instant. Someone reading your message can easily misinterpret your words because she cannot see your face or hear any inflection in your voice. You would be wise to be sure that any words sent with these tools be ones of encouragement only. Any response other than that would best be taken up in a face-to-face encounter. Many times it is better to be a woman of few words. Proverbs 17:28 says that "even fools are thought wise if they keep silent, and discerning if they hold their tongues" (NIV).

EVENING - *Saying the Right Word*

The right word at the right time is like a custom-made piece of jewelry, and a wise friend's timely reprimand is like a gold ring slipped on your finger.
PROVERBS 25:11 MSG

Help me with my words, Lord. May my prayer to You for wisdom in my replies come before my lips start moving or my hands begin typing. May my words only encourage loved ones and strangers alike! I want to be a woman of Your word—not mine! Help me in this endeavor, Jesus!

DAY 294

MORNING - *The Transparent Walker*

And this is the secret: Christ lives in you.
This gives you assurance of sharing his glory.
COLOSSIANS 1:27 NLT

Today's lives are full of anxiety and to-do lists. Endless hours are twittered away as some blog about inanities, telling people how they're spending their days instead of actually living them. Women seem compelled forward only to satisfy their obsession for material things that they end up clinging to instead of God. In the evenings, rather than open up a Bible, they turn to the television, eyes glazed over. A simple Christianity—where truth is sought, others are served, and God's will is done—is more important now than ever before. The only solution to the emptiness of life is a transparent Christianity where others look at you and see Christ alone.

EVENING - *Deep in God's Love*

Christ will make his home in your hearts as you trust in him.
Your roots will grow down into God's love and keep you strong.
EPHESIANS 3:17 NLT

Lord, I want to be so aware of Your abiding in me that when others see me, they see You alone. In fact, when I look in my own mirror, I want to see nothing but Your shining light! Help me to trust You, truly trust You. For then I know I will be deep in God's love and have the strength to do all I am called to do.

DAY 295

MORNING · *The Rejoicing Walker*

Always be full of joy in the Lord. I say it again—rejoice!
PHILIPPIANS 4:4 NLT

Are you tired of trying to live up to the world's expectations? Are you ready for a radical spiritual transformation? You can do it! "With God, all things are possible" (Matthew 19:26 NIV). Put everything you are and hope to be in the hands of the Father of lights, who has promised you "every good and perfect gift" (James 1:17 NIV). And cultivate joy for, as Henry Drummond wrote, "Joy is as much a matter of cause and effect as pain. No one can get joy by merely asking for it. It is one of the ripest fruits of the Christian life, and, like all fruit, must be grown."

EVENING · *In the Secret Place*

In the secret place of His tent will He hide me. . . . In His tent I will offer sacrifices and shouting of joy; I will sing, yes, I will sing praises to the Lord.
PSALM 27:5–6 AMPC

I am ready, Lord, for a radical spiritual transformation! And I know I can get there by trusting in You. In Your secret place, I am hidden. Nothing can harm me. No worries can affect me. Here I see Your shining face and I cannot help but shout with joy! Praises to You, Lord, for all that You are and all that You do in my life!

DAY 296

MORNING - *A Quiet Walker Strengthened*

"Only in returning to me and resting in me will you be saved.
In quietness and confidence is your strength."
ISAIAH 30:15 NLT

❧

Move forward in the power of quietness, knowing that God surrounds you, Christ is within you, and the Holy Spirit guides you. Recognize that your energies should not be used exclusively to pursue worldly means but to seek first His kingdom, knowing that He will provide whatever you need.

You are enfolded in God's love and power. Nothing can harm you, so rest in His care. Leave with Him yesterday. He is guiding you today. He is crowding tomorrow full of blessings and opportunities—so you have only cause for peace and expectancy.

EVENING - *With Peace and Expectancy*

Moses made a serpent of bronze and put it on a pole, and if a serpent
had bitten any man, when he looked to the serpent of bronze [attentively,
expectantly, with a steady and absorbing gaze], he lived.
NUMBERS 21:9 AMPC

❧

Lord, I am seeking You in this moment. My eyes look to You and Your saving power. I am attentive and expectant, steadily focusing on You, knowing You are guiding me today and that tomorrow I will trip over Your blessings and opportunities. Resting in You and Your strength in these quiet moments, I feel You surrounding me and Christ's power within me. May I rest in the Holy Spirit's leadings. All I am and have are Yours!

DAY 297

MORNING - *The Truth-Filled Walker*

*I look to you for protection. I will hide beneath the shadow of
your wings until the danger passes by. I cry out to God Most High,
to God who will fulfill his purpose for me.*
PSALM 57:1–2 NLT

Rejoice in God's safety, for you are His precious child. Know that there is nothing to fear, for behind you is God's infinite power. In front of you are endless possibilities, and you are surrounded by opportunity. Peace and power are yours in Him. Through your trials, He will build you and others into a holy people. Your experiences will lead you to the revelation of His truths. Through His love, you will follow the yearning to serve others. Each unit of your day presents you with an opportunity to build up your Christian character, to strengthen your faith, and to love and praise your God, through whom all your wants, needs, and desires will be met.

EVENING - *Confident in God*

*My heart is fixed, O God, my heart is steadfast
and confident! I will sing and make melody.*
PSALM 57:7 AMPC

God, with You on my journey through life, I need never be afraid. How wonderful to be abandoned to the guidance of a divine Master and fearlessly living my life to His glory. In You I will remain steady of heart, confident of spirit. Reveal Your truths to me in this life. I praise and rejoice in You!

DAY 298

MORNING - *The Empowered Walker*

I will go ahead of you. . .and smooth out the rough places.
ISAIAH 45:2 GW

The best part of your spiritual walk is that you need not do anything in your own power. He will provide all the strength and courage you need. Your part is merely to yield yourself to Him, and His part is to work. He will never give you a command for which He has not equipped you with the power and strength to obey. He will never leave you nor forsake you. In fact, just the opposite, for He always goes before you each little step of the way.

EVENING - *Drawn to God*

*Your mercy and loving-kindness are great, reaching to
the heavens, and Your truth and faithfulness to the clouds.*
PSALM 57:10 AMPC

Pray this beautiful prayer from George MacDonald's *Diary of an Old Soul*:
Afresh I seek thee. Lead me—once more I pray—
Even should it be against my will, thy way.
Let me not feel thee foreign any hour,
Or shrink from thee as an estranged power.
Through doubt, through faith, through bliss, through stark dismay,
Through sunshine, wind, or snow, or fog, or shower,
Draw me to thee who art my only day.

DAY 299

MORNING · *The Joy-Filled Woman's Path Marker: Promise No. 16*

Don't love the world and what it offers. Those who love the world don't have the Father's love in them. Not everything that the world offers—physical gratification, greed, and extravagant lifestyles—comes from the Father. It comes from the world, and the world and its evil desires are passing away. But the person who does what God wants lives forever.

1 JOHN 2:15–17 GW

God promises that when you are focused on Him instead of the world, when you love Him more than anything the world can offer, when you please Him instead of others, you will not only have His love in you but will live in that heavenly love forever! By taking that promise to heart, you cannot help but to rejoice!

EVENING · *A Pledge of Faith*

Light, space, zest—that's GOD! So, with him on my side I'm fearless, afraid of no one and nothing.

PSALM 27:1 MSG

Because of You, Lord, I know I need never be afraid of anyone or anything in this world. You are great, mighty, powerful, and it is to You—and not the things or people of this world—I pledge my undying faith. I refuse to be caught up in the competition for affluence, to worship the almighty dollar. Instead, I come to You, my Master, seated in the heavenlies.

DAY 300

MORNING - *The Joy-Filled Woman's Path Marker: Proof No. 16*

We now have this light shining in our hearts, but we ourselves are like fragile clay jars containing this great treasure. This makes it clear that our great power is from God, not from ourselves. . . . We never give up. Though our bodies are dying, our spirits are being renewed every day. For our present troubles are small and won't last very long. Yet they produce for us a glory that vastly outweighs them and will last forever!

2 Corinthians 4:7, 16–17 nlt

God's Word proves to us that you're not a body with a spirit. You're a spirit with a body. That spirit walking in the light is a great treasure. It proves that your great power is from God, not something you can drum up at will. So no need to worry. God's power provides you with what you need just when you need it!

EVENING - *The True Hidden Treasure*

If we say we are his, we must follow the example of Christ.

1 John 2:6 cev

Lord, I've surrendered myself to You. I want to follow Your path, not that of the world. For You're the true treasure hidden within me, the source of all power as You work through me to reach all.

DAY 301

MORNING - *The Joy-Filled Woman's Path Marker: Provision No. 16*

For we are God's handiwork, created in Christ Jesus to do good works, which God prepared in advance for us to do.
EPHESIANS 2:10 NIV

God, who made you, has re-created you in Christ, transforming you so that you can do the good works God has already planned you will do! So relax! Take courage! Just let go, let be, let God work through you. He's day-by-day equipping, providing you with whatever you need, to do what He wants you to do!

EVENING - *The New Life*

Your old life is dead. Your new life, which is your real life—even though invisible to spectators—is with Christ in God. He is your life. When Christ (your real life, remember) shows up again on this earth, you'll show up, too—the real you, the glorious you. Meanwhile, be content with obscurity, like Christ.
COLOSSIANS 3:3–4 MSG

You are the only reality, Jesus. This world is just a shadow of things to come. I am content in seeking all that You are. Fill me with Your light and power so that I can do the things You are calling me to do—and be! You are my life, my love, my light. You are always beside me, advising, loving, and guiding.

MORNING · *The Joy-Filled Woman's Path Marker: Portrait No. 16*

Present your bodies a living sacrifice, holy, acceptable to God, which is your reasonable service. And do not be conformed to this world, but be transformed by the renewing of your mind.

ROMANS 12:1–2 NKJV

God not only *promises* He loves and has eternal life in line for you who love Him more than the world (see 1 John 2:15–17) and *proven* that your real power comes from Him, not your own being (see 2 Corinthians 4:7, 16–18), but He also *provides* you with everything you need to do what He has already planned you are to do (see Ephesians 2:10). Because of all God has promised, proven, and provided, claim this new part of your *portrait* (based on Romans 12:1–2):

In Christ, I am spiritually transformed with energy, strength, and purpose every day.

EVENING · *Christ-Mind Walker*

We have the mind of Christ (the Messiah) and do hold the thoughts (feelings and purposes) of His heart.

1 CORINTHIANS 2:16 AMPC

This life in Christ is an awesome adventure. I praise God that You, Jesus, live in me. Your thoughts are becoming my thoughts. My will is lining up with Your will. Show me the path You want me to walk. Show me whom You want me to bless. I want to do what You have created me to do.

DAY 303

MORNING - *The Joyfully Obedient Woman: Result No. 5 of the Higher Life*

You are My friends if you keep on doing the things which I command you to do.
JOHN 15:14 AMPC

If you have been fortunate in this life, you've had a friend, lover, sister, brother, or child whom you really and truly loved. Because of that love, you found yourself desiring to do anything and everything for him or her. No sacrifice was too big when it was for this special loved one. When you were separated from this person, you longed for him or her to return to you quickly, if possible. It was almost as if these two separate persons—you and the other—had become one in thought, word, and deed. May you have this kind of loving relationship with Jesus!

EVENING - *No Greater Friend*

No one has greater love [no one has shown stronger affection] than to lay down (give up) his own life for his friends.
JOHN 15:13 AMPC

Lord, You are the greatest Friend I have ever had in my entire life! For no one has done what You've done for me. From You, I never want to part. For you are my very life, my breath, my heart, my soul. I love You like no other. What joy You bring into my heart!

MORNING - *A Woman Utterly Abandoned*

I do not call you servants (slaves) any longer, for the servant does not know what his master is doing (working out).
JOHN 15:15 AMPC

Jesus has given you everything, and He asks for you to wholly surrender to Him in return. Might you have the same type of measureless devotion to Him that He displayed for you on the cross! But perhaps at Jesus' call for utter abandonment to Him, you shrink back. It seems too risky, too difficult, and too scary. You see others going through this life without acknowledging His presence, and they seem to be getting along fine. So why must you surrender yourself to the *n*th degree to this Son of God called Jesus?

Because when you surrender yourself to Christ and obey Him in everything, you will be fulfilling your spiritual destiny.

EVENING - *In Jesus, Your Friend*

But I have called you My friends, because I have made known to you everything that I have heard from My Father. [I have revealed to you everything that I have learned from Him.]
JOHN 15:15 AMPC

You totally surrendered all for me, Jesus. And in turn, I abandon all to You. In doing so, I realize I am suddenly having so many truths revealed to me. I find the paths You have laid out for me. I find the love to embrace and help others. I find serving easy. Thank You, my Friend!

DAY 305

MORNING - *The Happily Obedient Woman*

"I am happy to do your will, O my God."
Your teachings are deep within me.
PSALM 40:8 GW

In wholly binding your life to Jesus, you will discover the reality of the Almighty God! You will be walking in light, not darkness. You will have such an intimate relationship with the Creator that He will tell you things that those who are further away from Him do not know! All you need to do is be totally obedient to Him, to the point where like the psalmist you will declare, "I delight to do thy will, O my God" (Psalm 40:8 KJV), or as Jesus said, "My food (nourishment) is to do the will (pleasure) of Him Who sent Me" (John 4:34 AMPC).

EVENING - *Fed Deep Down Inside*

My food (nourishment) is to do the will
(pleasure) of Him Who sent Me.
JOHN 4:34 AMPC

I long to do what You have already created and prepared me to do, Lord! And I am happy to do Your will! In fact, being obedient feeds me deep down inside. Thank You, Lord, for allowing me to get so close to You. I want to live a life where I don't know where You begin and I end!

DAY 306

MORNING - *The Joyful Woman*

The person who has My commands and keeps them is the one who [really]
loves Me; and whoever [really] loves Me will be loved by My Father,
and I [too] will love him and will show (reveal, manifest) Myself to him.
[I will let Myself be clearly seen by him and make Myself real to him.]
JOHN 14:21 AMPC

This privilege of surrender is one not demanded by God. It's a matter of choice, part of your free will. If you choose not to abandon yourself to Him, the future of heaven will still be available to you, but you'll miss out on the unfathomable joy of this present moment as promised by Jesus!

When you choose to surrender to Him, to obey (or keep) His commands, you prove your love for Him. In return, Christ will not only love what you're doing but will show Himself to you! That leads to even more joy!

EVENING - *Hearing and Heeding*

Blessed (happy and to be envied) rather are those
who hear the Word of God and obey and practice it!
LUKE 11:28 AMPC

Jesus, I'm okay not going the way of the world. That's because I am happy to not only hear Your Word—but heed it! Doing so fulfills me like nothing else this world can offer! I want to be the kind of person that others see and think, *I want what she's having*. What a life You offer me—mind, body, spirit, and soul! Thank You, Jesus!

DAY 307

MORNING - *The Open Woman*

Behold, I stand at the door and knock.
REVELATION 3:20 NKJV

How wonderful that God so desires you to rely on Him instead of yourself! He has such joy in your response to Him as your true love! It is beyond understanding. He's continually knocking on your door, hoping you'll let Him in. And when you do, you'll be like a woman who's built your house not upon the sand, but upon Jesus—the Rock of Ages. With Him as your foundation, obeying Him and His Word every moment of every day, you'll be able to keep your head in times of temptation or persecution. You'll keep your comfort, hope, peace, and joy in the midst of distressing situations; and you'll be kept spurred on by His amazing power! When you keep on obeying Him, He'll keep you safe, strong, resilient, and happy all through your life!

EVENING - *Resilient in Christ*

If anyone hears My voice and opens the door,
I will come in to him and dine with him, and he with Me.
REVELATION 3:20 NKJV

Lord, I want my house to be built on You. I'm opening the door to my heart, mind, and soul in this very moment. Come in, Lord! Sup with me! Teach me what You would have me know. With You, I will be able to have hope, peace, and joy no matter what is happening in my life!

DAY 308

MORNING - *The Passionate Woman*

Blessed are those whose lives have integrity, those who follow the teachings of the LORD. Blessed are those who obey his written instructions. They wholeheartedly search for him. . . . I find joy in the way shown by your written instructions more than I find joy in all kinds of riches.

PSALM 119:1–2, 14 GW

Psalm 119 is a powerful prayer that exalts God's Word and the author's passionate desire to obey it. The psalmist tells God how blessed and happy are those who're wholly devoted to Him and obey His Word. In fact, in the God's Word translation, the word *joy* is used four times (see 119:14, 111, 162) and *happy* nine times (see 119:16, 24, 35, 47, 70, 77, 92, 143, and 174).

God's teachings and commands have kept the psalmist not only from misery but from disaster! Read and obey God's Word and watch your joy increase to infinity and beyond!

EVENING - *Blessed in Reflecting*

I want to reflect on your guiding principles and study your ways. Your laws make me happy.

PSALM 119:15–16 GW

I want to be passionate, Lord, in my desire to study Your ways. I, too, want to be blessed in my devotion and obedience to You and Your Word. I want to have that deep, deep abiding joy in You. Show me the way, Lord! I'm ready to follow!

DAY 309

MORNING · *The Obedient Girl*

*I never forget your word. Be kind to me so that I may live
and hold on to your word. Uncover my eyes so that
I may see the miraculous things in your teachings.*
PSALM 119:16–18 GW

Twelve times the author of Psalm 119 tells his readers of the *new life* (119:25, 37, 40, 50, 88, 93, 107, 149, 154, 156, 159, and 175) he has received through his wonderful relationship with and knowledge of God! The psalmist never brandishes his own opinion but refers only to God and what He has told him. For the only chance he has at a new life is to obey what God says in His Word, whether he understands it or not. Like a child at your father's knee, you are to merely obey God's commands because He says so.

EVENING · *With Cleared Vision*

*I have chosen a life of faithfulness. I have set your regulations in front of me.
I have clung tightly to your written instructions.*
PSALM 119:30–31 GW

I'm hanging on to Your Word for dear life, Lord. Just like a little girl at her Abba Daddy's knees, I'm going to do as You say just because You say so. I'm holding tight to You, Father God. Help me to memorize the scriptures You bring to my mind. Clear my vision so that I see only You and Your Word. Fill me with the overwhelming desire to do all You want me to do!

MORNING - *The Law-Loving Woman*

Oh, how I love your law! I meditate on it all day long. Your commands are always with me and make me wiser than my enemies.
PSALM 119:97–98 NIV

Not only are you instructed to obey God and His commands diligently, but you are to meditate on them. For if you do not bathe yourself in the Word, you will perhaps be unclear as to what He wants you to do. And the more you look to God for answers, the more you will begin to see everything through His eyes 24-7 and keep yourself from immediately looking to others, or yourself, for direction.

EVENING - *Digging Deep*

I have more insight than all my teachers, for I meditate on your statutes. I have more understanding than the elders, for I obey your precepts.
PSALM 119:99–100 NIV

The more I get into Your Word, Lord, the closer I get to You. I am beginning to see things from Your perspective. This world is just a shadow to the light I see in You. I am digging deep, God, wanting to know all about You. I am letting Your Word linger in my mouth. It is the sweetest thing I know. Guide me on the path You want me to travel. I'm packed and ready to go!

DAY 311

MORNING - *The Wholly Loving Woman*

" 'Love the Lord your God with all your heart and with all your soul and with all your mind and with all your strength.' The second is this: 'Love your neighbor as yourself.' There is no commandment greater than these."
MARK 12:30–31 NIV

Be clear. God has chosen many to receive His grace and love and follow Him. But He requests that those who do so love Him with their entire heart, soul, mind, and strength, *and* love others as they love themselves. If only your desire to chase after Him would be as great as your desire for a new pair of shoes or a purse! If you do not yet have that desire, pray that God would grant you passion for His Word, understanding of His love, and a desire to follow Him with everything you are!

EVENING - *Great Desire*

"You are not far from the kingdom of God."
MARK 12:34 NIV

Lord, when I follow Your two greatest commands—to love You with my entire being and to love others as myself, knowing that doing so is more valuable than any other sacrifice I might give You—You have said that I will then not be far from the kingdom of God! What joy that brings my heart! Help me to love like no other!

DAY 312

MORNING - *The Responsive Woman*

I did not confer with flesh and blood [did not consult or counsel with any frail human being or communicate with anyone].

GALATIANS 1:16 AMPC

As you follow God's Word and obey His commands, you must not be concerned about the outcome. Would that you would be like Abraham. When God spoke, he did not ask anyone for advice—he did not consult his own feelings or insights or those of others—but he went where God told him to and did what God told him to do (see Genesis 22). When God spoke, Abraham simply responded, "Here I am" (Genesis 22:1 NKJV). He listened to God's request (to sacrifice his son Isaac) and did as commanded. There was no debate. No argument. No questions. He simply went because God said so. Abraham obeyed, surrendered his son, and God revealed a ram as a substitute for Isaac's life. What joy Abraham's obedience wrought!

EVENING - *No Argument with God*

God tested and proved Abraham and said to him, Abraham! And he said, here I am.

GENESIS 22:1 AMPC

Lord God, I'm not sure what You are going to ask me to do tonight, tomorrow, or even in this moment. I only hope and pray that when You do call, no matter what the request or command You put before me, I will immediately say, "Here I am, Lord!" when You call. No argument. No questions. For simple obedience reaps a myriad of blessings from Your hand.

DAY 313

MORNING - *The Abrupt Pray-er*

Abruptly Jesus broke into prayer: "Thank you, Father, Lord of heaven and earth. You've concealed your ways from sophisticates and know-it-alls, but spelled them out clearly to ordinary people. Yes, Father, that's the way you like to work."
MATTHEW 11:25 MSG

God's revelations, His insights, are revealed to you the moment you obey. May you, like Jesus, abruptly break into prayer when God speaks to you, an ordinary woman, and through your obedience do extraordinary things, not just in your life but in the lives of others. You need not understand what He is doing or why, merely faithfully step out in obedience. Instantly, the next door opens, the sea parts, or the ram appears.

EVENING - *Eager to Obey*

"And all these blessings shall come upon you and overtake you, because you obey the voice of the LORD your God."
DEUTERONOMY 28:2 NKJV

Wow! Being overtaken by blessings is a mind-boggling image. To imagine that You are already working on my future blessings before I've even said, "Here I am, Lord! Ready, willing, and able to do as You ask!" What a concept! Your promises make me so eager to obey. So I come to You today, Lord, to await Your orders. My heart is wholly dedicated to Your desires.

DAY 314

MORNING - *The Patient Woman*

*When He heard that he [Lazarus] was sick,
He stayed two more days in the place where He was.*
JOHN 11:6 NKJV

In this loving relationship with Christ, God may at times be silent. This is a sign of the intimacy you have with Him, like an old couple who sit quietly together at times, comfortable in each other's silent presence. This may be a moment in which you must patiently await His next message, content with remaining with Him and meditating on His Word. For if you run ahead, uncertain of His will, you may miss the miracle He is about to perform.

EVENING - *No Questions Asked*

*As a young man marries a young woman, so will your Builder marry you;
as a bridegroom rejoices over his bride, so will your God rejoice over you.*
ISAIAH 62:5 NIV

Lord, You are building me up to be the woman You want me to be. And You are as happy with me as a bridegroom is with his bride. That's amazing! I feel so loved. Our eternal relationship is something I can hardly grasp. But I can't help but smile. I feel so valued—from my veil to my bridal slippers. Take my hand, Lord. Lead me on. I am ready to follow You, no questions asked.

DAY 315

MORNING - *The Woman Who Follows*

*"Obey the LORD your God. Follow him by
obeying his demands, his commands."*
1 KINGS 2:3 NCV

Your love and devotion to Him are all the Lord asks of you as a reward for all He has done for you. Let yourself go—your entire self—mind, body, soul, strength, talents, spirit, everything you are! Lay it all before Him. Open the lines of communication by praying and digging into His Word, bathing yourself in it each day. Ask Him to help you live out the day in His will, His way. Request His power and spiritual insight to guide you in every task, relationship, and situation—from what to wear to what you read. Consciously recognize His presence in everything, and you will be brimming over with joy in His process as you find yourself lovingly embraced by this tender God, reaping the blessings of hearing His will and keeping it!

EVENING - *Overflowing with Joy*

*"If you do these things, you will be successful
in all you do and wherever you go."*
1 KINGS 2:3 NCV

I love You, Lord, with all that I am and have, bumps and bruises included. I'm open to You, ready to respond and obey. I'm soaking in Your Word, eager to live out each day in Your will and way. Give me Your power and insight to stay in Your presence. In so doing, I find myself overflowing with joy and blessings!

MORNING - *The Joy-Filled Woman's Path Marker: Promise No. 17*

"But this is what I commanded them, saying, 'Obey My voice, and I will be your God, and you shall be My people. And walk in all the ways that I have commanded you, that it may be well with you.'"
JEREMIAH 7:23 NKJV

In His Word, God promises that when you obey His commands, He will not only stick with you but things will be well. In fact, He will delight in you! Imprint this promise firmly in your mind. Write it on your heart. Plant it in your soul. Doing so will help you more firmly state, "Here I am, Lord," when He calls!

EVENING - *A Glorious Mission*

And we know that all things work together for good to those who love God, to those who are the called according to His purpose.
ROMANS 8:28 NKJV

I love You so much, Lord, and although I don't always understand what is happening, I know You will work everything out. All I need to do is stay focused on You and obey all Your commands. For I am here to love You with all my heart, mind, body, soul, and strength and to love others as myself. Serving You is a glorious mission. I want no other master!

DAY 317

MORNING - *The Joy-Filled Woman's Path Marker: Proof No. 17*

[Jesus] appeared to the apostles. . . . He commanded them, "Do not leave Jerusalem until the Father sends you the gift he promised. . . . the Holy Spirit." . . . On the day of Pentecost all the believers were meeting together in one place. Suddenly, there was a sound from heaven like the roaring of a mighty windstorm. . . . Then, what looked like flames or tongues of fire appeared and settled on each of them. And everyone present was filled with the Holy Spirit.

ACTS 1:3–5; 2:1–4 NLT

God's Word provides proof that you are loved by God. For Jesus came through on His promise of the Holy Spirit. What blessings await you who obey!

EVENING - *Patiently Waiting*

If you [really] love Me, you will keep (obey) My commands. And I will ask the Father, and He will give you another Comforter (Counselor, Helper, Intercessor, Advocate, Strengthener, and Standby), that He may remain with you forever.

JOHN 14:15–16 AMPC

I need the Holy Spirit to speak to me, Lord. I am not sure what to do. I need advice. I need the wisdom and strength that He can give me. Your Word says that You hear me when I cry, when I call to You. I'm facing a situation in which I need Your courage. If You remain silent, I'll take that as a signal to wait upon You. Help me not to rush ahead but be patient, for I trust in You.

MORNING - *The Joy-Filled Woman's Path Marker: Provision No. 17*

Work hard to show the results of your salvation, obeying God with deep reverence and fear. For God is working in you, giving you the desire and the power to do what pleases him.
PHILIPPIANS 2:12–13 NLT

God gives you the desires and actions that will please Him. So continue working on your responsive obedience to Him, knowing He's doing His part for you as well, all to your joy and His glory!

EVENING - *Intimate with God*

By faith, Noah built a ship in the middle of dry land. He was warned about something he couldn't see, and acted on what he was told. The result? His family was saved. His act of faith drew a sharp line between the evil of the unbelieving world and the rightness of the believing world. As a result, Noah became intimate with God.
HEBREWS 11:7 MSG

To have the faith of Noah, to build a huge ark in the desert, to ignore the heckling of worldlings as he goes out on a limb in obedience to You—that's the courage I'd like to have. For when we step out in faith, obeying everything You ask us to do, You work miracles, saving more than just us but also others in our lives. I want to be that intimate with You, Lord. Pull me close. I will obey.

DAY 319

MORNING - *The Joy-Filled Woman's*
Path Marker: Portrait No. 17

*"Whoever knows and obeys my commandments is the person
who loves me. Those who love me will have my Father's love,
and I, too, will love them and show myself to them."*

JOHN 14:21 GW

God not only *promises* that when you obey Him, things will be well (see Jeremiah 7:23) and *proven* that when you do His will, His love and amazing promises become your revealed reality (see Acts 1:3–5; 2:1–4), but He also *provides* you with all the desire and power you need to obey Him (see Philippians 2:12–13). Because of all God has promised, proven, and provided, claim this next part of your *portrait* (based on John 14:21):

In Christ, I am loved by God and delight to do His will.

EVENING - *God's Language of Love*

*Your written instructions are miraculous. That is why I obey them. Your
word is a doorway that lets in light, and it helps gullible people understand.
I open my mouth and pant because I long for your commandments.*

PSALM 119:129–131 GW

I love opening Your Word, Lord. It takes me to new places. Even though I may have read the same lines before, You prepare my heart beforehand to grasp their deeper meaning. You are opening doorways to a new life, a new way, a new me. Continue to enlighten me, Lord, as I make my way.

MORNING - *The Woman Divinely United: Result No. 6 of the Higher Life*

"That they all may be one, as You, Father, are in Me, and I in You; that they also may be one in Us, that the world may believe that You sent Me."

JOHN 17:21 NKJV

Growing up, you read fairy tales about beautiful princesses who met or were rescued by princes. Later, you found your beloved was far from the ideal prince. And if you're honest, you're far from being a princess. Yet as a Christian, you've a chance of actually fulfilling the happily-ever-after fairy tale with the one and only true Prince—Jesus Christ, the One who can rescue you from the poverty of ashes and the tower of temptation. With His kiss, you're awakened to a new reality. On Him alone can you rely, for He'll never leave you. He's your comfort, peace, and rock. He's the One with whom you want to become one and live happily ever after. This was God's entire plan for you from the beginning (see 1 Peter 1:20), for your soul and spirit to be united with your ultimate Bridegroom. This divine union is what Jesus prayed for, for all who believe in Him.

EVENING - *A Revealed Mystery*

In the past God hid this mystery, but now he has revealed it to his people.

COLOSSIANS 1:26 GW

Thank You, Lord, for the revelation of this divine union with Your Son. May my soul and spirit be one with Yours, Jesus. Be my Prince! Awaken me to Your very being!

MORNING - *An Embracing Woman*

For we died and were buried with Christ by baptism. And just
as Christ was raised from the dead by the glorious power
of the Father, now we also may live new lives.

ROMANS 6:4 NLT

Because of Christ's death, you are right with God and can be united with Him. It has been disclosed through the scriptures and "is made known to all nations" (Romans 16:26 AMPC). And God has not made your union with Him difficult, nor has He kept it a secret. Yet you may not yet completely grasp the concept of being fully one with God. Perhaps your heart does not fully believe this "oneness" is available to you. Or you may be afraid to trust Him totally. Yet that is where this entire pathway of Christian life is leading to—*voluntarily* embracing a full oneness with God.

EVENING - *Knowing Wonder-Filled Love*

God chose him as your ransom long before the world began,
but now in these last days he has been revealed for your sake.

1 PETER 1:20 NLT

Lord, it is amazing that You planned the sacrifice of Your Son before the world had even begun. And all so that I could be reunited with You and Him! I have never known such wonder-filled love. I believe in the truth of Your Word, Lord. Show me, guide me through the scriptures. Speak to me through Your Word.

DAY 322

MORNING - *The Destined Woman*

*Out of that terrible travail of soul, he'll see that it's worth
it and be glad he did it. Through what he experienced,
my righteous one, my servant, will make many "righteous ones."*
ISAIAH 53:11 MSG

God will not be satisfied until your spirit and soul have reached their destiny of a total and divine union with Him. The usual path of Christian experience mirrors that of the first disciples. Jesus called them, awakening them to their need of Him. Hearing His message, they believed. They left their old lives to follow Him. But they were still so different from Him. At the end, all but one ran from the cross. After His death, they cowered together in a locked room, wondering how they would survive the coming days. These disciples had known only the physical Christ as Teacher and Master, separate from them.

Then while in that upper room, without warning, the disciples were filled with Christ! There was no parting from Him now! They were one with Him, filled with and aware of His life, spirit, and power within them.

EVENING - *Filled with Christ*

*Without warning there was a sound like a strong wind,
gale force—no one could tell where it came from. . . .
Like a wildfire, the Holy Spirit spread through their ranks.*
ACTS 2:2–4 MSG

I want to be completely united with You, Jesus, heart and soul! Make me aware of Your presence, life, spirit, power within me!

DAY 323

MORNING · *The Christ-Only Woman*

*My God will richly fill your every need
in a glorious way through Christ Jesus.*
PHILIPPIANS 4:19 GW

Perhaps you have traveled the disciples' path. You believe that Christ existed. That He was the Father's answer to your final reconciliation with Him. You have confidence that He loves you, that He is beside you and will walk with you through storm and fire, yet you have not given your complete heart, mind, body, and soul to Him but are holding back. Perhaps your will and His are not yet fully enjoined. Hannah Whitall Smith wrote:

You have not yet lost your own life that you may live only in His. Once it was "I and not Christ." Next it was "I and Christ." Perhaps now it is even "Christ and I." But has it come yet to be Christ only, and not I at all?

EVENING · *Knowing the Mystery*

God wanted his people throughout the world to know the glorious riches of this mystery—which is Christ living in you, giving you the hope of glory.
COLOSSIANS 1:27 GW

I want to lose my life in You, Lord, so that I live only in Yours. Help me to understand the glory of You, Christ, living in me. Show me how to make it be You only and I not at all! For I know I won't lose myself—I'll just become the better part of me as You live through me!

MORNING - *The Templed Woman*

You realize, don't you, that you are the temple of God, and God himself is present in you? No one will get by with vandalizing God's temple, you can be sure of that. God's temple is sacred—and you, remember, are the temple.

1 CORINTHIANS 3:16 MSG

This miraculous union of your heart and Christ's has been planned since the beginning of time. In fact, it happened when you accepted Christ. Dwelling within you, a true believer, is the spirit of Christ. You are a temple of the living God. And if you read to whom this applies, you'll see that this scripture pertains to "mere infants [in the new life] in Christ" (1 Corinthians 3:1 AMPC) who are still being fed with milk! So this is not a new dimension to your life as a believer. Christ has been residing in you all along! This is true of every Christian! You have already been transformed into a new creature!

EVENING - *Rising Above*

Put on the new self, which in the likeness of God has been created in righteousness and holiness of the truth.

EPHESIANS 4:24 NASB

Each day, Lord, I remember that it is You living within me. Each hour I surrender myself to Your leading and love. Each moment I sense Your power to rise above this world. The true reality is our divine blending. May I rest in the peace that You are always with me, working through me, loving me—a new world without end, amen.

DAY 325

MORNING - *The Tuned-In Woman*

*Anyone who claims to be intimate with
God ought to live the same kind of life Jesus lived.*
1 JOHN 2:6 MSG

The thing is that you may not yet have tuned in to this fact of God living in you, or accepted it as a spiritual reality. You may not be living in the full power imparted in this divine blending but are living as though it were not true. But as soon as you accept it as a reality through spirit, soul, and mind and devise to give up self, the power of oneness with God manifests itself to its *fullest* extent. When you consciously and consistently recognize Christ within, the evidence of this union comes through in your character. For when you are truly, fully, and intimately one with Christ—allowing Him to have complete and utter reign over you—you are Christlike.

EVENING - *Ablaze in the True Light*

The darkness on its way out and the True Light already blazing!
1 JOHN 2:8 MSG

Lord, when I allow You full rein in my life, when I am living very close to You, when we are totally connected, I feel the darkness leaving me and Your True Light ablaze within! Help me to be consciously and consistently aware of Your being within me. In Your name and power, I pray!

MORNING - *The Christlike Woman*

*You are living the life of the Spirit, if the [Holy] Spirit
of God [really] dwells within you [directs and controls you].*
ROMANS 8:9 AMPC

When you are truly, fully, and intimately one with Christ—you are Christ-like. That means you're walking the walk and talking the talk. It means you're giving Christ not partial but full rein (see Romans 8:9). It means you're being spent in love for others as Christ spent Himself in love for you (see John 21:17). Christ within impels you to feed His sheep, for He has told you, "As my Father hath sent me, even so send I you" (John 20:21 KJV). Jesus said that "every tree is known by its own fruit" (Luke 6:44 NKJV). When living in the full power of a union with Christ, you have a nature that matches His (see Galatians 5:22–23).

EVENING - *Reaping a Cornucopia of Love*

*The spiritual nature produces love, joy, peace, patience,
kindness, goodness, faithfulness, gentleness, and self-control.*
GALATIANS 5:22–23 GW

Your life within me is shining its light into my world. May all who see me really see You through my character and my works. Thank You, Lord, for this overwhelming sense of peace, love, and joy. Thank You for all the fruit You are bearing in my life. I long for a full crop—an abundance of You within me, reaching out. A cornucopia of love within and without!

DAY 327

MORNING - *The Divinely Empowered Woman*

God's divine power has given us everything we need for life and for godliness.
2 Peter 1:3 GW

Because you're fully aware that Christ's living through you, you won't be able to be anything but Christlike, for you've become one of the "partakers of the divine nature" (2 Peter 1:4 NASB). Because He's holy, you'll be holy. The godliness in you, full of light, will shine right through you and into the lives of others! And it's not only your character that reveals you've become united with Christ. The things you do will also be a testament to the truth of your divine union. Jesus said,

> *"The Son cannot do anything on his own. He can do only what he sees the Father doing. Indeed, the Son does exactly what the Father does. . . . If I'm doing those things and you refuse to believe me, then at least believe the things that I'm doing. Then you will know and recognize that the Father is in me and that I am in the Father" (John 5:19; 10:38 GW).*

EVENING - *Partaking in Christ's Light*

This power was given to us through knowledge of the one who called us by his own glory and integrity.
2 Peter 1:3 GW

In You, Lord, I can do anything because You've given me that power. When I'm one with You, Your light shines through me! Make me cognizant of all this, every moment of every day. I want to shine for You!

DAY 328

MORNING · *The United Woman*

Through his glory and integrity he has given us his promises. . . .
Through these promises you will share in the divine nature.
2 Peter 1:4 GW

When you're one with Christ, you're sharing His divine nature will be evident regardless of your emotions on a certain day. Smith says:

> *Pay no regard to your feelings, therefore, in this oneness with Christ, but see to it that you have the really vital fruits of a oneness in character and walk and mind. Your emotions may be very delightful, or they may be very depressing. In neither case are they any real indications of your spiritual state. . . .*
>
> *Your joy in the Lord is to be a far deeper thing than a mere emotion. It is to be the joy of knowledge, of perception, of actual existence.*

God wants you to come to Him willingly. Christ already resides in you, and you already received the Holy Spirit when you accepted Christ. What you need to do is continually, consistently, and completely *recognize* Christ's presence within you and *surrender* yourself to Him.

EVENING · *Finding God's Joy*

"The joy of God is your strength!"
Nehemiah 8:10 MSG

How wonderful to have a joy that's not tied to what happens to me throughout my day, Lord. Knowing that Christ is loving me within, and sheltering me without, is contentment at its best. What joy this gives me!

MORNING - *A Beloved Woman*

God is rich in mercy because of his great love for us.
EPHESIANS 2:4 GW

Although you've known Christ is in you, at times you may have ignored His presence, either through fear or disinterestedness or simply because you were too caught up in the things of this world. Perhaps there have been times you felt unprepared for Him, or perhaps you didn't want Him to see the real you, so to save yourself embarrassment, you've kept Him at bay. While you've left Him waiting, you've missed out on the full peace, power, protection, guidance, insights, and other valuable treasures He could have bestowed upon you and into your life! Be at peace. He's patiently, lovingly waiting for you to look His way. He's already seen all that you are and all that you do—and loves you unconditionally.

EVENING - *Saved by Her Beloved*

We were dead because of our failures, but he made us alive together with Christ. (It is God's kindness that saved you.)
EPHESIANS 2:5 GW

God, I don't want to leave You waiting for me anymore. So here I am. Ready for You to change my life. You know who I am—lumps, bumps, and bruises—and love me anyway! What amazing kindness! Thank You for saving me. Fill me with Your presence—right here, right now!

DAY 330

MORNING - *The Willing Woman*

The LORD your God is with you.
ZEPHANIAH 3:17 GW

So do not fear. Christ has been with you all along. He's ready to help you rest in Him. Allow Him to carry all your burdens, give you insights that only He would have, and empower you to live your life to the fullest 24-7. This is what you have been created for. For it is not you who lives, but Christ lives in you.

Because your partaking of the divine nature is not forced upon you but is something you volunteer to do, you must give your Prince a willing *yes* every minute of every day or the joy of your full and wonderful union with Him will be left wanting. In doing so, you need to acknowledge your oneness with Christ—it's a real thing.

EVENING - *Acknowledging the Hero*

He is a hero who saves you.
ZEPHANIAH 3:17 GW

You are my hero, Lord. I want nothing but You to come rescue me from an ego-driven life. Live in me in this moment. I surrender myself to You and from here on in I believe it as a real thing, happening within my core. This is why I have been created. Here are my burdens. Give me Your insights, power, and love. Live within me, my Hero and Lord!

DAY 331

MORNING - *The Wholly Surrendered Woman*

*I have been crucified with Christ; it is no
longer I who live, but Christ lives in me.*

GALATIANS 2:20 NKJV

Lay down your will, wholly surrendering yourself—mind, body, spirit, and soul—to the Lord. Allow Him to take total possession of you and, in doing so, firmly believe that He has, indeed, taken possession of and is dwelling within you. It is no longer you who live, but Christ who is living in you. Thus, you rely on and trust Him completely. All day and night, steadfastly maintain this attitude, knowing for certain this truth. And what a life with Him you'll have! By surrendering all to Him, you'll possess nothing—and thereby everything! For He is all you truly need. Fully recognizing, acknowledging, and enjoying your union with Christ, you and your Prince can live together happily ever after!

EVENING - *Living Happily with the Prince*

*For a child is born to us, a son is given to us. The government
will rest on his shoulders. And he will be called: Wonderful Counselor,
Mighty God, Everlasting Father, Prince of Peace.*

ISAIAH 9:6 NLT

How wonderful, Lord, to give myself completely to You. All burdens, worries, fears are gone. For everything rests now on Your shoulders. Thank You for rescuing me from the tower of troubles and temptations. Night and day, I'm allowing You to live through me. What joy You give me, my one and only Prince of Peace!

DAY 332

MORNING · *The Joy-Filled Woman's Path Marker: Promise No. 18*

But whoever obeys what Christ says is the kind of person in whom God's love is perfected. That's how we know we are in Christ.
1 JOHN 2:5–6 GW

God's Word promises that when you obey Christ, totally surrendered to His will, God's love is perfected in you! That's how you'll know you are in Christ! Because you are in Him, you'll automatically be like Him. That takes all the pressure off! What a promise to live in and with every moment of the day! Lean back on the power of this promise. Embed it deep within your heart!

EVENING · *Leaning Back*

Those who say that they live in him must live the same way he lived.
1 JOHN 2:6 GW

Lord, I know I am not to believe my feelings. I am not to use them as a barometer of my life hidden with You. But I need Your help this evening. Let me rest in Your arms. Allow me to just lean back and let You take over. Show me the true way, the true life—that You and I are one, the perfect union. Keep me focused on You and Your love.

DAY 333

MORNING - *The Joy-Filled Woman's Path Marker: Proof No. 18*

"I tell you the truth, anyone who believes in me will do the same works I have done, and even greater works, because I am going to be with the Father. . . . I am praying not only for these disciples but also for all who will ever believe in me through their message. I pray that they will all be one, just as you and I are one—as you are in me, Father, and I am in you. . . ."
Peter said to him, "Aeneas, Jesus Christ heals you! Get up, and roll up your sleeping mat!" And he was healed instantly.
JOHN 14:12; 17:20–21; ACTS 9:34 NLT

God's Word proves that when you divinely unite yourself to Jesus, you'll do even greater things than He has done. So get up! Get into Christ!

EVENING - *A Taste of Heaven*

All praise to God, the Father of our Lord Jesus Christ, who has blessed us with every spiritual blessing in the heavenly realms because we are united with Christ.
EPHESIANS 1:3 NLT

This divine union with You, God, is a taste of heaven on earth. My prayer is not for anything but You. A oneness with Christ is my sole desire. With His presence within me, I know I am safe, blessed, loved, and empowered to be all that He wants me to be. Give me the passion, Lord, to extend Your love to others—no matter how I feel. For You are my truth, light, and way.

DAY 334

MORNING - *The Joy-Filled Woman's Path Marker: Provision No. 18*

Through his glory and integrity he has given us his promises that are of the highest value. Through these promises you will share in the divine nature because you have escaped the corruption that sinful desires cause in the world.

2 PETER 1:4 GW

Through His Word, God provides that through His promises you will share in Jesus Christ's divine nature. So give up yourself, your ego, your feelings, your worries, your fears. Consciously and completely unite yourself with Christ. You are free to live and breathe in His power, goodness, and grace. No longer wait! Partake! For God's sake—and for the sake of the lives you will then touch.

EVENING - *Partaking of the Divine Nature*

You surely know that your body is a temple where the Holy Spirit lives. The Spirit is in you and is a gift from God. You are no longer your own.

1 CORINTHIANS 6:19 CEV

I want to partake of Your divine nature, God. So I come to You, surrendering all that I am. I know Your Holy Spirit is within me, a gift from You. So I now give You a gift in return—all my heart, mind, body, and soul. Take possession of me, Lord. I am opening the door to You. Shine Your light throughout my being. Warm me with Your love. Illuminate me!

DAY 335

MORNING - *The Joy-Filled Woman's Path Marker: Portrait No. 18*

All praise to God, the Father of our Lord Jesus Christ, who has blessed us with every spiritual blessing in the heavenly realms because we are united with Christ.
EPHESIANS 1:3 NLT

God not only *promises* that when you obey Him, His love will be perfected in you and Christ will be in you (see 1 John 2:5–6) and *proven* that when you divinely unite yourself to Jesus, you'll be able to do greater things than He did (see John 14:12; 17:20–21; Acts 9:34), but He also *provides* you with the precious promises that will enable you to share Jesus' divine nature (see 2 Peter 1:4). Because of all God has promised, proven, and provided, claim this next part of your *portrait* (based on Ephesians 1:3):

In Christ, I am spiritually blessed because He lives in me.

EVENING - *Divine Union*

I have died, but Christ lives in me. And I now live by faith in the Son of God, who loved me and gave his life for me.
GALATIANS 2:20 CEV

It is no longer I who live, Christ, but You are abiding within me. I am writing this upon my heart, Lord, and repeating it within my mind, for I desire this divine union. You are the Prince of my life, and I give You my hand. I do! I am now living by faith that You have taken total possession of me and You are the true life within. Thank You for Your love, power, and sacrifice.

DAY 336

MORNING - *The Chariot-Riding Woman: Result No. 7 of the Higher Life*

He was taken up before their very eyes, and a cloud hid him from their sight.
ACTS 1:9 NIV

Harriet Beecher Stowe said, "Earthly cares are a heavenly discipline." Hannah Whitall Smith wrote, "They are even something better than discipline—they are God's chariots, sent to take the soul to its high places of triumph." Yet often your earthly woes don't at all resemble God's chariots. Instead, they manifest themselves as stresses, heartaches, disputes, trials, offenses, misunderstandings, and losses. They're like juggernauts, steamrollers that wound and crush your spirit, poised to roll over you and sink you into the earth. But if, like Elisha, you could see woes as God's vehicles of victory, you'd rise above these cares in triumph.

EVENING - *Hope for Tomorrow*

"You saw how the LORD your God carried you, as a father carries his son, all the way you went until you reached this place."
DEUTERONOMY 1:31 NIV

God, some days I feel as if I'm still wandering around in the wilderness. But You've brought me so far, Lord, I never want to turn back. Thank You for carrying me through so many heartaches—big and little. And, although I'm not as far as I think I should be, I praise You for bringing me to where I am today and giving me hope for tomorrow.

DAY 337

MORNING - *The Insightful Woman*

Elisha, the man of God, would warn the king of Israel,
"Do not go near that place."
2 Kings 6:9 nlt

To better understand the concept of the chariots of God, read the story found in 2 Kings 6. There the king of Syria kept coming against Israel, but Elisha always knew via supernatural revelation exactly where the enemy was going to invade, allowing the king of Israel to avoid surprise attacks. *(Notice here that when you're tuned in to God, like Elisha, He gives you insight and revelations you need to avoid the enemy.)* To thwart Israel's military advantages gleaned from Elisha's revelations, the king of Syria decided to capture him and surrounded the town of Dothan, where Elisha was staying, with his horses and chariots. But Elisha did not fear because he walked by faith—not by sight!

EVENING - *Walking by Faith*

We walk by faith [we regulate our lives and conduct ourselves by our conviction or belief respecting man's relationship to God and divine things, with trust and holy fervor; thus we walk] not by sight or appearance.
2 Corinthians 5:7 ampc

I want to be like Elisha, Lord, living my life by faith, not by sight. For I know when I do I will not only have more peace and less fear, but You will grant me the insights and revelations I need to do Your will, to make wise decisions. May my divine union with You grant me such walking faith!

DAY 338

MORNING - *The Fearless Woman*

There were troops, horses, and chariots everywhere. "Oh, sir, what will we do now?" the young man cried to Elisha [his master]. "Don't be afraid!" Elisha told him. "For there are more on our side than on theirs!"
2 KINGS 6:15–16 NLT

❧

Elisha knew God would protect him, that when—not *if*—he prayed, God would send His forces (see Psalm 68:17)! Would that you would see your worldly woes with spiritual vision, that you would open your eyes to the invisible powers of God that come to your rescue! Such "eyesight" would allow you to sit calmly within your physical houses with no fear, knowing the intangible force of God would allow you to rise above your juggernauts in God's chariots, "in heavenly places in Christ Jesus" (Ephesians 2:6 KJV) where victory over everything below would be yours!

EVENING - *Open-Eyed*

Then Elisha prayed, "O LORD, open his eyes and let him see!" The LORD opened the young man's eyes, and when he looked up, he saw that the hillside around Elisha was filled with horses and chariots of fire.
2 KINGS 6:17 NLT

❧

Show me the true reality, Lord. Reveal Your chariot for me so that I can rise above this world. Remove the scales of worldly woes from my eyes. Make it clear to me that You will never leave me defenseless. Give me twenty-twenty spiritual vision to see that Your army of hosts is always here to lift me up into the heavens!

MORNING - *The Chariot-Riding Woman*

If you see your enemy hungry, go buy him lunch;
if he's thirsty, bring him a drink.
PROVERBS 25:21 MSG

The story continues. When the king of Israel saw the Syrian forces inside Samaria, he asked Elisha if he should kill them. But Elisha said, "You shall not kill them. . . . Set food and water before them, that they may eat and drink and go to their master" (2 Kings 6:22 NKJV). So a great meal was prepared, and after the soldiers had sated themselves, they were sent back home.

Elisha's faith and fearlessness allowed him not only to rise above his visible enemies but to do good to them after defeating them. The result? They stayed away!

Like Elisha, you have a choice. You can allow your juggernauts—big or little—to crush you, plunging you down into fear, defeat, and despair, or you can jump into the chariots of God and rise above them in triumph.

EVENING - *Charitable in Triumph*

Your generosity will surprise him with goodness, and GOD will look after you.
PROVERBS 25:22 MSG

Remind me, Lord, that You always have a better way. Show me how I can ride in Your chariot, in faithfulness and fearlessness. In so doing, may I not only triumph in You but be charitable by showing my enemy mercy and love!

DAY 340

MORNING - *The Heaven-Bound Woman*

God has brought us back to life together with Christ Jesus and has given us a position in heaven with him.
EPHESIANS 2:6 GW

All the losses, trials, minor irritations, worries, and woes that come to you become chariots the moment you treat them as such. Smith wrote:

> *Whenever we mount into God's chariots the same thing happens to us spiritually that happened to Elijah. We shall have a translation. Not into the heavens above us, as Elijah did, but into the heaven within us; and this, after all, is almost a grander translation than his. We shall be carried away from the low, earthly groveling plane of life, where everything hurts and everything is unhappy, up into the "heavenly places in Christ Jesus" [Ephesians 2:6 KJV], where we can ride in triumph over all below.*

EVENING - *Riding High in Faith*

Suddenly a chariot of fire appeared with horses of fire, and separated the two of them; and Elijah went up by a whirlwind into heaven.
2 KINGS 2:11 NKJV

Lord, what happened to Elijah was amazing. But by abiding in You, uniting myself with You in divine love, I can have an inner translation to the heaven within. And I enter into this whirlwind of Your loving presence right now! Carry me away, Lord, from the heartaches of this life and into the bliss of You where, by faith, I can ride high in victory over all!

DAY 341

MORNING - *The Chariot-Riding Woman: Step No. 1*

We know that in all things God works for the good of those who love him. He appointed them to be saved in keeping with his purpose. . . . Since God is on our side, who can be against us?

ROMANS 8:28, 31 NIrV

So what steps can you take when, like Elisha's servant, you cry out, "Alas, my master! What shall we do?" (2 Kings 6:15 NKJV) First, you need to quiet yourself by word. You need to find encouragement in God's Word. "Do not fear, for those who are with us are more than those who are with them" (2 Kings 6:16 NKJV). No matter what comes against you—to destroy, offend, or frighten you—God is infinitely more powerful. When you are magnifying the causes of your fear, you need to take hold of yourself with clear, direct, great, inspiring thoughts of God and His invisible, intangible world. Know that God will not only work all things out for your good, but that He's a place of safety and strength!

EVENING - *Quieted by Word*

God is our place of safety. He gives us strength.
He is always there to help us in times of trouble.

PSALM 46:1 NIrV

I'm coming to Your Word, Lord, to quiet my fears. May its encouragement roll over me, fill me, and warm me. You are more powerful than anything that may come against me. And you mean all things for my good! So, I'm coming to You, my heavenly Rock, Refuge, and Strength!

DAY 342

MORNING - *The Chariot-Riding Woman: Step No. 2*

The chariots of God are twenty thousand,
even thousands of thousands; the Lord is among them.
PSALM 68:17 NKJV

After quieting yourself by word, do so by vision. Elisha knew by faith that he was safe from the Syrian forces. But he knew his servant was very troubled. So he prayed for him. "LORD, I pray, open his eyes that he may see" (2 Kings 6:17 NKJV). And so the Lord did. The servant's eyes of faith were opened to God's multitude of chariots! This is the prayer you must pray, that God would open your spiritual eyes. Once He does, the dangers of earth and the fear that arises from them will vanish as the darkness before you, allowing you to be carried into the heavenly places in your chariot "paved with love" (Song of Solomon 3:10 KJV).

EVENING - *Quieted by Vision*

God is love.
1 JOHN 4:8 NKJV

In my temporal world, Lord, my chariots don't seem like they are paved with love. Slights from people I once considered friends. Betrayals by loved ones. The cruelties of neglect, greed, malice, and selfishness practiced in the world. Yet every chariot sent by You (whether of first or second cause) must be paved with love, for You, Lord, are love. So help me with my spiritual vision. Help me see Your love in all things. For I know once You open my eyes, I will be carried to that heavenly realm with You!

MORNING - *The God-Dependent Woman*

Sing to God. . . . Who rides upon the highest heavens.
PSALM 68:32–33 NASB

God is a heavenly rider (see Habakkuk 3:8)! Thus you must look to Him and His chariots to carry you over the trials and tribulations, torments and troubles of this tangible world. You won't prosper if you look to an earthly conveyance to help you through. For God says, "Woe to them that go down to Egypt for help; and stay on horses, and trust in chariots" (Isaiah 31:1 KJV). Your "Egypt" consists of tangible resources you can see. You find yourself tempted to rely on them because they look real and dependable, whereas God's chariots are intangible and invisible, not seen except by faith. Going "down to Egypt for help" may be depending on money alone to make you feel secure or possessions to make you happy. It may be the counsel of a friend whom you've come to lean on more than God. It may be the Sunday school class or a favorite preacher you believe you can't live without or you'll weaken, then die, for lack of spiritual strength. Look to the Windwalker!

EVENING - *With the Heavenly Rider!*

He makes the clouds His chariot; He walks upon the wings of the wind.
PSALM 104:3 NASB

You're the heavenly rider, the windwalker I vow to look to when I'm in trouble, Lord. Not the things that I can see—but the ultimate unseen power of which this world is merely a reflection. Only You can save!

DAY 344

MORNING · *The Courageous Chariot Rider*

*The LORD your God carried you, as a father carries his son,
all the way you went until you reached this place.*

DEUTERONOMY 1:31 NIV

Anything you rely on other than God will, at some point, be taken away. Smith wrote, "God is obliged often to destroy all our own earthly chariots before He can bring us to the point of mounting into His." God longs to have you depend on Him more than anything or anyone else. For He was, is, and will be the only One you can truly depend on. History proves it.

Joseph had a vision of his future victories and reign, but the chariots that took him there—betrayal, slavery, imprisonment—looked more like juggernauts of agony and failure. Yet because God and His chariots were with him, giving him strength and courage, he didn't get discouraged but rose above his earthly cares, even while in a dungeon. Joseph's earthly travails were a strange route to becoming a ruler of Egypt and saving himself and his family, but he couldn't have gotten there any other way. In the same regard, your road to the heavenly mansion awaiting you is often reached by similar chariots.

EVENING · *Rising above Earthly Cares*

*In thy majesty, ride prosperously because
of truth and meekness and righteousness.*

PSALM 45:4 KJV

I want to depend on You more than anything else, Lord God. I'm entering into Your chariot, gaining strength and courage while doing so. I rise above these earthly cares and glory in Your presence!

DAY 345

MORNING - *The Chariot Rider Mounting Up*

*I was sliding down into the pit of death, and he pulled
me out. He brought me up out of the mud and dirt.*
PSALM 40:2 NIrV

Do not allow the juggernauts of this world to roll over you and sink you into the pits of despair, desperation, and fear. Instead, mount up with God, taking each offense, bitter word, tragedy, loss, trial, and temptation as your chariot of God that will take you to the "heavenly places in Christ Jesus" (Ephesians 2:6 KJV). Take the inroad and forget every external obstacle, knowing that God has established your steps (see Psalm 40:2). In doing so, you cannot help but triumph. Become like Paul, whose "thorn in the flesh" and losses were nothing compared to the richness he found in gaining Christ (see Philippians 3:7–9). Instead of allowing worldly woes to cast him down, Paul "[ascribed] strength to God," whose "strength is in the clouds" (Psalm 68:34 NKJV).

EVENING - *Set on God's Strength*

*He set my feet on a rock.
He gave me a firm place to stand on.*
PSALM 40:2 NIrV

You are the only person that gives me firm footing, Lord. In You alone, do I triumph over my troubles. I'm mounting up in You whose strength is in the clouds!

DAY 346

MORNING · *The Woman Riding Prosperously with God*

Ascribe power and strength to God; His majesty is over Israel,
and His strength and might are in the skies.
PSALM 68:34 AMPC

Before you may have been blind, but now like Elisha's servant, you see the mighty chariots of God. Take each juggernaut event in your life—big or little—and gird yourself in the Word, open your spiritual eyes, and board the chariot for your soul. Allow your chariot to take you to the heavenly places where you can "ride prosperously" (Psalm 45:4 NKJV) with God on top of all, allowing you to triumph within and without! Hannah Whitall Smith wrote:

> There can be no trials in which God's will has not a
> place somewhere; and the soul has only to mount into
> His will as in a chariot, and it will find itself "riding upon the
> heavens" with God in a way it had never dreamed could be.

EVENING · *Over All!*

LORD, were you angry with the rivers? Were you angry with the streams? Were
you angry with the Red Sea? You rode your horses and chariots to overcome it.
HABAKKUK 3:8 NIrv

I know, Lord, that I can overcome all things of this earth by mounting up in Your heavenly chariot, where I can ride with You over all! My spiritual eyes are opened! In Your conveyance, I can live a life beyond my dreams! Thank You for this privilege!

DAY 347

MORNING · *The Joy-Filled Woman's Path Marker: Promise No. 19*

The chariots of God are twenty thousand, even thousands of thousands. . . .
Blessed be the Lord, who daily loads us with benefits, the God of
our salvation! . . . His strength is in the clouds. . . . The God of
Israel is He who gives strength and power to His people.
PSALM 68:17, 19, 34–35 NKJV

God's Word promises that when you live your life by keeping your eyes on Him, setting your sights on the heavenlies, and riding in His chariot, you will be blessed with benefits each day and given strength and power beyond your imagination! Imprint this promise on your entire being!

EVENING · *Whisked Away*

I cried to my God for help. He heard my voice from his temple, and my cry
for help reached his ears. . . . He spread apart the heavens and came down
with a dark cloud under his feet. He rode on one of the angels as he flew, and
he soared on the wings of the wind. . . . He reached down from high above
and took hold of me. He pulled me out of the raging water. He rescued me.
PSALM 18:6, 9–10, 16–17 GW

Lord, hear my cry! Reach down from above and pull me out of this sea of difficulties and into Your chariot. I long to rest in You, to feel Your touch. I have eyes of faith, Lord. Reveal Your chariot and whisk me away!

DAY 348

MORNING - *The Joy-Filled Woman's Path Marker: Proof No. 19*

We know that the one who brought the Lord Jesus back to life will also bring us back to life through Jesus. He will present us to God together with you. . . . That is why we are not discouraged. Though outwardly we are wearing out, inwardly we are renewed day by day. . . . We don't look for things that can be seen but for things that can't be seen. Things that can be seen are only temporary. But things that can't be seen last forever. . . . I know a follower of Christ who was snatched away. . .to paradise.

2 CORINTHIANS 4:14, 16, 18; 12:2, 4 GW

God's Word contains the proof that when you are in a new life with Jesus, keeping your spiritual eyes on Him and the intangible chariots, you, too, can be swept up to paradise!

EVENING - *Far above the Fray*

O LORD my God, You are very great. . . . He makes the clouds His chariot; he walks upon the wings of the wind.

PSALM 104:1, 3 NASB

You, God, are grander than I can imagine. All of nature heeds Your voice. You know my troubles, Lord. Today I lift them up to You. I feel hurt, discouraged, and anxious. But I know that those emotions are not what I should focus on. So, Lord, keep me from bowing under the weight of my woes. I raise my eyes to heaven. Mount me up in Your chariot, far above this fray.

DAY 349

MORNING - *The Joy-filled Woman's Path Marker: Provision No. 19*

All praise to God, the Father of our Lord Jesus Christ, who has blessed us with every spiritual blessing in the heavenly realms because we are united with Christ.
EPHESIANS 1:3 NLT

God's Word shows God the Father of Jesus has provided you with every spiritual blessing you could dream of. Those blessings reside in the heavenly realms, to which you are conveyed in the sky-high chariots you are riding in. And all because you are united with Christ! Mount up and believe this provision!

EVENING - *Eyes upon God*

O our God. . . .We have no might to stand against this great company that is coming against us. We do not know what to do, but our eyes are upon You.
2 CHRONICLES 20:12 AMPC

I don't understand this world, Lord. I feel like such a stranger here. I am so grateful that I have You to cling to. I am not strong enough to fight this latest battle, Lord. Even if I did, I'm not sure what to do. So I am looking to You, watching for You, waiting for You to pull me up into the heavens. You are my rock, my refuge, my rest. You are my heavenly conqueror!

DAY 350

MORNING - *The Joy-Filled Woman's Path Marker: Portrait No. 19*

Since you were brought back to life with Christ, focus on the things that are above—where Christ holds the highest position.
COLOSSIANS 3:1 GW

❧

God not only *promises* that by riding in His chariots you'll be daily loaded with benefits and strengthened (see Psalm 68:17, 19, 34–35) and *proven* that by living this way, with your eyes firmly fixed on Jesus, you'll be swept upward (see 2 Corinthians 4:14, 16, 18; 12:2, 4), but He also *provides* all these heavenly blessings because you are united with Christ (see Ephesians 1:3). Because of all God has promised, proven, and provided, claim this next part of your *portrait* (based on Colossians 3:1):

In Christ, I am raised to new life, setting my eyes on the realities of heaven.

EVENING - *Belief Clears the Path*

Believe in the Lord your God and you shall be established; believe and remain steadfast to His prophets and you shall prosper.
2 CHRONICLES 20:20 AMPC

❧

I believe! I believe, Lord! Because You are the great I AM, I know that You will always be with me. I am sticking to You for all my needs. Make my path clear, God. And when I am down, give me a lift in Your chariot. Resting in You, trusting You, I know nothing can harm me. All I need to do is believe.

DAY 351

MORNING · *The Heavenly Woman: Result No. 8 of the Higher Life*

The LORD is waiting to be kind to you. He rises to have compassion on you.
The LORD is a God of justice. Blessed are all those who wait for him.
ISAIAH 30:18 GW

God wants you to fix your soul's intellectual eye upon Him, seeking Him above all things. If fact, you will be blessed with joy and peace—even amid the storms—when you do so (see Jeremiah 17:7). And the way to keep your eyes on Him is to "wait upon the LORD" (Isaiah 40:31 KJV). The Hebrew word for "wait" is *qawa*, which means to bind together by twisting, to expect—look—patiently. Wait on the Lord with expectation and you will be amazed at the strength you are given as you mount up close to Him!

EVENING · *Wholehearted Flight Up*

You will seek Me, inquire for, and require Me [as a vital necessity]
and find Me when you search for Me with all your heart.
JEREMIAH 29:13 AMPC

I want to be riding high with You, Lord, needing You as I do my bread and water. I'm seeking You above all things, searching for Your presence, expecting You to work in my life as I hope in You with my whole being. Thank You for the strength this gives me. Beam me up to You, Lord!

DAY 352

MORNING · *The Eager Fledgling*

Through his glory and integrity he has given us his promises that are of the highest value. Through these promises you will share in the divine nature because you have escaped the corruption that sinful desires cause in the world.

2 PETER 1:4 GW

First Corinthians 6:17 says that "the person who is joined to the Lord is one spirit with him" (NLT). You are a partaker of His divine nature. With your soul's eye on Him and your spirit joined with His, you can mount up as an eagle to the highest heights, eternally secure and protected, with an open doorway to all of God's blessings (see John 10:28; Romans 8:31–39; Hebrews 7:25; 1 Peter 1:4).

Christ is your high place—in Him you have your foundation. In Him you make your nest, like an eagle in the highest tree or cliff face. As a new woman hidden in Christ, you are His fledgling.

EVENING · *Flying High*

We have been born into a new life which has an inheritance that can't be destroyed or corrupted and can't fade away. That inheritance is kept in heaven for you.

1 PETER 1:4 GW

I love this new life in You, Jesus. It is one that is eternal, indestructible! In You, I am protected. The doorway is open to all of our Father's blessings! Thank You, Jesus, for being my high place! I am Your fledgling, eager to fly to You every moment of every day!

DAY 353

MORNING · *The Female Eaglet*

Imitate me, just as I also imitate Christ.
1 Corinthians 11:1 nkjv

Yet how do you learn to fly spiritually? The same way an eaglet does. Eaglets are not born with instinctive knowledge about how to fly or hunt. Shortly after birth, an eaglet will become attached to the first moving object it sees! This is called *imprinting*. If a baby eagle receives food or care from any source other than an adult eagle during this time, it becomes emotionally attached to that provider. God is *your* Creator, source, and provider. When you're spiritually reborn, the first thing you "see" is Christ and His life. It is to Him you look and become attached. You don't instinctively know how to fly spiritually, but you can learn by imitating Christ.

EVENING · *Craving Strength and Peace*

Since you have been raised to new life with Christ, set your sights on the realities of heaven, where Christ sits in the place of honor at God's right hand.
Colossians 3:1 nlt

Lord, I thank You for bringing me new life in Christ. I am setting my sights on Your heavenly kingdom. These troubles here on earth will be but a dim memory someday. So instead of wallowing in self-pity or trying to fix situations on my own, I am going to journey inward to Your side, knowing that when I do, You will give me the strength and peace I crave.

DAY 354

MORNING - *The Eaglet of the Secret Place*

I will say of the LORD, "He is my refuge and my fortress;
My God, in Him I will trust."
PSALM 91:2 NKJV

You'll never get off the ground, however, until you first strengthen your body and wings by waiting on God as a baby eagle waits upon its parents to feed, protect, and teach it. As you wait upon the Lord, you're also abiding in Him, hidden in Christ. Resting in Him in that "secret place of the Most High" as Psalm 91:1 (AMPC) says, you "remain stable and fixed under the shadow of the Almighty [Whose power no foe can withstand]." And the promised benefits in that secret place found in Psalm 91 are realized only when you have determined to trust and surrender yourself to your loving God.

EVENING - *Surrendered in Promises!*

He will give His angels [especial] charge over you to accompany and
defend and preserve you in all your ways [of obedience and service].
PSALM 91:11 AMPC

In making You my refuge and fortress, I'm protected against anything and everything. As I learn to lean and rely upon You, Lord, my confidence and trust build! You are the first place to which I fly. Thank You for preserving, helping, and protecting me. Thank You for the renewed strength and courage, patience, hope, daily blessings that come from being under Your wing and totally surrendered to and trusting in You!

MORNING - *The Patient Eaglet*

Be still and rest in the Lord; wait for Him and patiently lean yourself
upon Him; fret not yourself because of him who prospers in his way.
PSALM 37:7 AMPC

As you wait upon God, do so prayerfully (see Psalm 25:4–5), seeking His pathway for you and hoping in Him. Wait with patience (see Psalm 37:7; 145:15), not getting overanxious. Learn how to sit still and not fret over every little thing, knowing that He will provide you with the food you need, when you need it. With single-mindedness of purpose, abide in Him (see Psalm 62:5), putting heart, mind, soul, and strength wholly into the endeavor, and do it expectantly (see Psalm 62:5–6; 123:2; Micah 7:7), longingly (see Psalm 130:5–6), quietly (see Lamentations 3:26), and continually (see Hosea 12:6). It's an ongoing process that leads not only to joy but to peace!

EVENING - *Silently Awaiting*

My soul, wait silently for God alone, for my expectation is from Him.
PSALM 62:5 NKJV

Help me to tap into the silence I find in waiting patiently for You, Lord, with all my heart, mind, body, soul, and strength. I refuse to fret, knowing You will give me what I need when I need it. I am abiding in You continually! You alone are my expectation!

MORNING - *The Transformed Eaglet*

Be transformed by the renewing of your mind.
ROMANS 12:2 NKJV

To increase your strength, stay deep in His Word and constantly renew your mind (see Romans 12:2). You do this by rejecting what the worldlings think and feel, renouncing their ignorance of God and hardness of heart (see Ephesians 4:17–18). Instead, you learn about and watch Christ (see Ephesians 4:20). As you constantly take hold of your fresh attitudes, you'll develop a new nature, the one God planned from the beginning of time. You'll attain new knowledge (see Colossians 3:10) and gifts from God (see 2 Timothy 1:6–7): a spirit of boldness (see Romans 8:15); a spirit of power (see Luke 24:49; Acts 1:8; 1 Corinthians 16:10; 1 Timothy 4:14) to soar upon the heavens, take new challenges, and serve Him; a spirit of love (see 1 Corinthians 13:4) for friends, enemies, and God Himself, prompting you to encourage and forgive others and to pant after Him; and a spirit of a sound mind, which gives you understanding, peace, and self-control (see Galatians 5:22–23).

EVENING - *Spirit Empowered!*

God has not given us a spirit of fear,
but of power and of love and of a sound mind.
2 TIMOTHY 1:6–7 NKJV

Change me up, Lord! I want to have Your mind only, not that of the worldlings! For when I've got Your attitude, I also gain a spirit of boldness, power, love, and good judgment! What more could an eaglet want?

DAY 357

MORNING - *The Fledgling Attempting Flight*

Because You have been my help, therefore in
the shadow of Your wings I will rejoice.
PSALM 63:7 NKJV

You've been well fed as God, your eagle parent, has brought you the food of His Word, giving you new insights each time you look to Him for answers. Now you've grown to the point of soon being able to really try out your wings—one of which is trust and the other surrender. For if you have only one wing—trust *or* surrender—you'll never rise above the nest. You need two wings—trust *and* surrender—to become airborne!

Your eyesight is as sharp as your papa eagle's. Still in your nest but far above the world, you have keener perception and view things more clearly, for you're looking from a God-perspective. Your problems no longer look interminable or insurmountable or significant.

EVENING - *Peace and Quiet*

The Holy One of Israel, says: You can be saved by returning to me.
You can have rest. You can be strong by being quiet and by trusting me.
ISAIAH 30:15 GW

Somehow, Lord, I feel as if I've fallen out of my nest, my foundation in Christ. My wings are tired, and I don't want to spiral down. So let me stay with You for a while, resting until I can soar again. In You, I'm saved from the calamities that rush at me. Build up the strength in my wings, Lord, as I linger here with You, in peace and quiet, in love and trust.

DAY 358

MORNING · *A Stirred-Up Eaglet*

"As an eagle stirs up its nest, hovers over its young, spreading out its wings, taking them up, carrying them on its wings, so the LORD alone led him."
DEUTERONOMY 32:11–12 NKJV

God is teaching you to be like Christ. So your parent eagle now stirs up your nest. God permits you to have troubles so that you don't get comfortable where you are but leave your nest—your comfort zone. Yet while you are in the midst of your ongoing transformations, as you become more and more like Christ, God continually cares for and protects you as you grow stronger and stronger. And when necessary, He will carry you until you are ready to soar where He wants you to soar. Tentatively at first, you follow your Master, rising above your nest in brief test flights. The more you allow your soul to fly up out of yourself, fueled with His courage and steeped in Christlikeness, you leave your comfort zone and take flight. You become a full-fledged eagle!

EVENING · *Riding High*

"He made him ride in the heights of the earth, that he might eat the produce of the fields."
DEUTERONOMY 32:13 NKJV

This is amazing, Lord! What heights I can see from as You make me more and more like Christ! Yet when I need You, You carry me upon Your wings. Thank You, Lord, for taking me up. For making me a full-fledged eagle—in Christ!

DAY 359

MORNING - *A Shaded Lady*

There shall be a. . .place of refuge and
a shelter from storm and from rain.
ISAIAH 4:6 AMPC

An eagle knows when a storm is coming long before it breaks. Able to rise above the earthly tempest and soar into the heavens, it seeks a high spot and waits for the winds to come. Like an eagle, you, too, can soar above the storms when you spread your wings and allow the Holy Spirit to lift up your spirit. As a full-fledged eagle, you can rise high above the storms of life, taking each and every opportunity to do as Jesus did. But if you find yourself weak—emotionally, spiritually, physically, mentally—you know that if you do not have the strength to fly, you can always look to God as your place of safety from the storm. Amid life's tumults and tempests, all you need to do is pray, and God will either cover you or give you the strength you need to soar.

EVENING - *Finding Shelter*

In the shadow of Your wings will I take refuge and be confident
until calamities and destructive storms are passed.
PSALM 57:1 AMPC

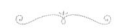

Holy Spirit, lift me up high above the storms of this life. Father God, be my place of refuge. Jesus, give me Your strength to rise above it all. Give me the power to soar—in You!

DAY 360

MORNING - *An Educated Eaglet*

Your Teacher will not hide Himself any more,
but your eyes will constantly behold your Teacher.
ISAIAH 30:20 AMPC

You can fly only when you do three things. First, *use* your wings, for why should you walk around or tunnel through your obstacles if you can fly above them? Second, don't look to your emotions, for often they're false indicators of your spiritual reality. Instead, rely solely on your wings of entire surrender to God and absolute trust in Him. Third, stop looking to earthly solutions to your problems. Don't "flee upon horses" (Isaiah 30:16 KJV), because if you do, you'll find your enemies have swifter ones and will quickly catch up to you. Your best assurance is to look to God, who wants your eyes constantly upon Him and longs to rescue you.

EVENING - *Lifted Eyes*

God has brought us back to life together with Christ Jesus
and has given us a position in heaven with him.
EPHESIANS 2:6 GW

Jesus, I come to You, my burdens falling off my back as I lift my eyes to the heavens. My spirit longs to feel Your presence, to see Your face, to touch the hem of Your robe. Because of Your love for me, I can rest here in You. You give me the power to live this life for You. Teach me Your way. Guide me. Whisper in my ear. Fly with me to the Father of lights.

DAY 361

MORNING - *An Eagle Arisen*

They that wait upon the L<small>ORD</small> shall renew their strength;
they shall mount up with wings as eagles.
I<small>SAIAH</small> 40:31 KJV

You'll be more than a conqueror (see Romans 8:37) as you seek things above because your life is hidden in Christ (see Colossians 3:1–3). You who wait on God *will* mount up with wings as eagles—not "perhaps mount up" but "will"! So lift up your soul and allow the power of the Holy Spirit to lift you up in flight, knowing the imprint of Christ is upon you as you pray, feast upon the Word, and wait upon the Lord. Sing a song to the Lord in the midst of your trials, and you'll be as Christ, "sorrowful, yet always rejoicing. . . poor, yet making many rich. . .having nothing, and yet possessing all things" (2 Corinthians 6:10 NKJV).

EVENING - *Lifted Spirit*

For He commands and raises the stormy wind, which lifts up the
waves of the sea. . . . He calms the storm, so that its waves are still.
P<small>SALM</small> 107:25, 29 NKJV

God, at Your call the earth shakes, the mountains rumble, the lightning strikes, the rains come, the sea rises, and the storm rages. Right now, Lord, I feel so out of control, so weak. But I know I am not to live according to my emotions. So please, Lord, calm the tempest within me and without. Give me peace in Your presence. Lift my spirit to bind with Yours.

DAY 362

MORNING - *The Joy-Filled Woman's Path Marker: Promise No. 20*

Those who wait for the Lord [who expect, look for, and hope in Him] shall change and renew their strength and power; they shall lift their wings and mount up [close to God] as eagles [mount up to the sun]; they shall run and not be weary, they shall walk and not faint or become tired.

ISAIAH 40:31 MSG

God's Word promises that when you wait on Him with great expectations of Him coming through for you, He will renew your strength and power so that you can mount up to Him! May this promise allow you to ride high in God!

EVENING - *In the Secret Place*

He who dwells in the secret place of the Most High shall abide under the shadow of the Almighty. I will say of the LORD, "He is my refuge and my fortress; my God, in Him I will trust."

PSALM 91:1–2 NKJV

Lord, my eyes are looking up to You. I long to live in Your presence, in the secret place, hidden in Christ. Here with You, I am no longer afraid. I know that when I am with You, nothing and no one can hurt me. You are an amazing fortress, impenetrable. Bless my soul, Lord. I trust in You to keep me safe within Your arms and to strengthen me in Your love and light.

DAY 363

MORNING · *The Joy-Filled Woman's Path Marker: Proof No. 20*

The LORD found Israel in a desert land. . . . He took care of them and kept them safe. He guarded them as he would guard his own eyes. He was like an eagle that stirs up its nest. It hovers over its little ones. It spreads out its wings to catch them. It carries them on its feathers. . . . The LORD made them ride on the highest places in the land.
DEUTERONOMY 32:10–13 NIrV

God's Word contains the proof that He's looking to take care of you and keep you safe. But when it's time for you to test your wings, He'll stir up your nest, getting you out of your comfort zone. But never fear! He'll remain hovering over you—while you learn to ride high!

EVENING · *A Winged Refuge*

Surely He shall deliver you from the snare of the fowler and from the perilous pestilence. He shall cover you with His feathers, and under His wings you shall take refuge. . . . You shall not be afraid.
PSALM 91:3–5 NKJV

I'm ducking for cover in You, Lord. Keep me safe from these worldly things that are begging for my attention. I rise up to You; hide me under Your wings. Keep my feet free from snares. Help me understand that You will never leave me nor forsake me, that I can abide with You not only when I am afraid but every moment of every day, looking to You for wisdom and strength.

DAY 364

MORNING - *The Joy-Filled Woman's Path Marker: Provision No. 20*

For He will give His angels charge concerning you, to guard you in all your ways. They will bear you up in their hands, that you do not strike your foot against a stone.

PSALM 91:11–12 NASB

God's Word says the Lord has provided angels to watch over you. In fact, He has *charged* them to guard you! So, when mountainous obstacles block your way, you won't have to go through them or under them. Instead, His angels will lift you up over whatever impedes the pathway He's already carved out for you! Remember angels are present, watching over you—whether you see them or not!

EVENING - *Forces to Be Reckoned With*

Praise the LORD, you angels, you mighty ones who carry out his plans, listening for each of his commands. Yes, praise the LORD, you armies of angels who serve him and do his will!

PSALM 103:20–21 NLT

God, thank You for sending reinforcements to watch over me. Although they are invisible, I know Your angels are forces to be reckoned with. So I will not be afraid, no matter what comes into my life. For with Your presence, the Holy Spirit's power, and Christ's love, I won't trip and fall headlong into trouble. You will keep me safe.

MORNING - *The Joy-Filled Woman's Path Marker: Portrait No. 20*

God has brought us back to life together with Christ Jesus and has given us a position in heaven with him.
EPHESIANS 2:6 GW

God not only *promises* that by waiting on Him, you'll be transformed, mounting up as an eagle (see Isaiah 40:31) and *proven* He'll keep you safe on your flight (see Deuteronomy 30:10–13), but He also *provides* angels to guard you on your way (see Psalm 91:11–12). Because of all God has promised, proven, and provided, claim this next part of your *portrait* (based on Ephesians 2:6):

In Christ, I am raised up and sitting in heaven.

EVENING - *Free Flying*

"Because he has set his love upon Me, therefore I will deliver him; I will set him on high, because he has known My name. He shall call upon Me, and I will answer him; I will be with him in trouble; I will deliver him and honor him. With long life I will satisfy him, and show him My salvation."
PSALM 91:14–16 NKJV

I love You, Lord, with all my heart, mind, body, and soul. Lift me up into Your presence. Let me see things from a higher perspective. Deliver me from the ties that bind me. I want my spirit to fly freely with You, up above this world and all its woes. For the true light, life, and love is all tied up in You, and it is there I want to be. In all this, I have absolute and perfect joy!

The Lord bless you and watch, guard, and keep you;
the Lord make His face to shine upon and enlighten you
and be gracious (kind, merciful, and giving favor) to you;
the Lord lift up His [approving] countenance upon you
and give you peace (tranquility of heart and life continually).
NUMBERS 6:24–26 AMPC

SCRIPTURE INDEX

IF YOU LIKED THIS BOOK,
YOU'LL WANT TO TAKE A LOOK AT. . .

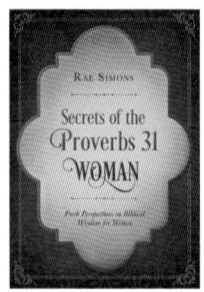

Secrets of the Proverbs 31 Woman

This devotional, offering equal parts inspiration and encouragement, will uncover the "secrets" of the Proverbs 31 woman. Each reading, tied to a theme from Proverbs 31:10–31, is rooted in biblical truth and spiritual wisdom. Women of all ages will be inspired to emulate the virtues extolled in this memorable passage of scripture.
Paperback / 978-1-63058-861-8 / $12.99

Everyday Moments with God

This lovely prayer collection is designed for those "everyday moments" in a woman's life—the tired moments, the stressed-out moments, the joyful moments, the tearful moments, the peaceful and chaotic moments. . . Dozens of practical and encouraging prayers, complemented by related scripture selections, will inspire women of all ages to strengthen their heart-connection to the heavenly Father.
Paperback / 978-1-63409-132-9 / $4.99